THOMAS G. HIGGINS, C P A
An Autobiography

THOMAS G. HIGGINS, CPA
An Autobiography

New York   1965

Copyright © 1965 by Thomas G. Higgins

All rights reserved
Designed by David R. Starwood
Manufactured in the United States of America
by The Comet Press, New York City
Library of Congress Catalog Card No. 65-25763

Photograph at frontispiece by George Cserna

To Madge,
 my companion of almost forty years,
 whose wisdom, gaiety, and complete
 devotion to family have made our home
 a grand place to live in

CONTENTS

Foreword *by Ralph E. Kent* / ix

Author's Preface / xiii

CHAPTER ONE
Family Background / 3

CHAPTER TWO
Omagh in County Tyrone / 17

CHAPTER THREE
The Fabulous City of New York / 43

CHAPTER FOUR
The Firm of Arthur Young & Company in 1921 / 57

CHAPTER FIVE
My First Year with Arthur Young & Company / 69

CHAPTER SIX
Getting Established in America / 91

CHAPTER SEVEN
Engagement and Marriage / 103

CHAPTER EIGHT
Accounting in the 1920s / 113

CHAPTER NINE
Life on the Audit Staff / 125

CHAPTER TEN
    The Great Depression / *137*

CHAPTER ELEVEN
    The Years 1933 to 1940 / *155*

CHAPTER TWELVE
    The War Years: 1941 to 1945 / *179*

CHAPTER THIRTEEN
    The Postwar Years / *205*

CHAPTER FOURTEEN
    Religion / *229*

CHAPTER FIFTEEN
    A New Look at Life / *243*

CHAPTER SIXTEEN
    Long-Range Planning / *261*

CHAPTER SEVENTEEN
    Professional Activities / *271*

CHAPTER EIGHTEEN
    The Firm Today / *299*

CHAPTER NINETEEN
    Time to Be Old / *309*

Some Photographs / *325*

Partners of Arthur Young & Company, 1921-1965 / *333*

Index / *339*

FOREWORD

Thomas G. Higgins, CPA IS THE STORY OF A MAN who began his life in the year 1900 in a small village in the North of Ireland; emigrated to the United States at the age of 21; commenced, within a month of his arrival in New York, a business career which was to last forty-four years with one firm; and rose from a low position in the cashier's department to be senior partner of his firm and one of the leaders in his chosen profession.

It was the great good luck of Arthur Young & Company that the job which Tom Higgins began on July 1, 1921, through a happy "connection" of his brother Hugh, was with our firm. In telling of his own personal fortunes and misfortunes in the years that followed, Tom Higgins also tells much of the history of the firm and, to some extent, of the accounting profession itself. Neither the firm nor the profession, I think, could wish a better teller of its story.

Indeed, if there is any portion of the author's life which receives short shrift in these pages—perhaps because he did not think it would be of interest to others—it is his life at home, with his wife Madge and their two daughters. Those of us who have known something of Tom Higgins's personal life are aware of the great source of strength and encouragement, of ready humor and light-heartedness, that Madge Higgins has been to her husband over the years.

Tom Higgins was 37 years of age, and ready for admission to the partnership, when I started work as a junior accountant with Arthur Young & Company. Hence, the men in the firm who are named in these pages are also true-life characters for me. The kindness and gentleness of Arthur Young, the quick thinking and sound judgment of Jim Burton, the gruff exterior which protected W. D. McGregor by concealing his soft heart, the drive and professionalism of Warren Nissley—these qualities are known to many of us.

But this is the story of Tom Higgins. His many contributions to the firm and to the accounting profession are understated in these pages. This in itself is typical of the man. His humility is boundless, his integrity unassailable, and his fairness in relations with others a natural way of life for him. Never one to bang tables, or to show anger, or to seek the limelight, he has gone his way through life quietly and with great effectiveness. His careful and thorough preparation for any assignment, combined with his inherently sound judgment and an ability to ease strained relations with ready wit and good humor, have made him one of the real builders of the firm of Arthur Young & Company.

Many men cease to grow as they become older. Certainly

this has not been true of Tom Higgins, whose greatest accomplishments have come in his fifties and sixties. He played an increasingly important part in all aspects of the firm's operations from his early forties, and as senior partner, beginning in 1954, he provided the leadership during the firm's greatest period of growth, both in the United States and abroad.

His active participation in professional society activities did not begin until age 47. This participation increased rapidly to the point where, in recent years, well over half of his working time has been devoted to the profession. In 1960 he served simultaneously as president of the New York State Society of CPAs, as a member of the Accounting Principles Board of the American Institute of CPAs, and as chairman of the Institute's Committee on Professional Ethics. Each of these activities demanded considerable time and effort, and the combination of all three at the same time resulted in a particularly heavy professional workload.

Within months of his election as senior partner of the firm, Tom Higgins encountered serious illness for the first time in his life. One of the most moving chapters in this autobiography is that which tells the story, beginning in 1955, of his battle with cancer. Surely no one can know better than the patient himself the stark fear that a diagnosis of cancer can bring. As I think back to those days of ten years ago, I am still amazed by the complete absence of any expression of concern on Tom's part. And yet that concern must have been very great indeed in the months immediately after the operation which disclosed the malignancy. I think that very few of us, in a similar situation, could go about our daily routines and exhibit the personal courage he did during this critical period of his life. The seriousness of his illness was a well-kept secret;

only a very few of his partners were made aware of it until the worrisome first five-year recovery period was over. Most of his partners learned of it in May 1960, at the time his portrait, painted by Paul Trebilcock, was presented to him by his partners.

In May 1964 Tom Higgins was honored by the New York State Society of CPAs with an award "for his unexcelled record of service to his chosen profession at the national as well as the state level." In May 1965 he was selected by the American Institute of CPAs to receive that organization's highest award, its Gold Medal for distinguished service to the accounting profession. This award will be presented at the September 1965 annual meeting of the Institute. How appropriate it is that our national professional society will make this well-deserved presentation to Tom Higgins just a few days before his retirement, after more than forty-eight years in the practice of accounting.

Those of us in the firm and elsewhere who have had the good fortune to know Tom Higgins and to be associated with him have had our lives thereby made brighter and more enjoyable than they otherwise would have been. We, as well as the many who will be a part of Arthur Young & Company in the years to come, are very much indebted to him for writing his story.

RALPH E. KENT

AUTHOR'S PREFACE

I HAVE ALWAYS THOUGHT IT CURIOUS THAT certified public accountants, who spend so much of their time putting things into writing, have written very little about their own lives. They have produced whole libraries full of books and articles on accounting principles and auditing procedures and all sorts of technical matters, but very few of them have written at any length about themselves and their times.

When the clock struck sixty for me, I began to think seriously of writing some kind of accountant's memoir. I had in mind an informal story that would describe my own life and the life of Arthur Young & Company, where I have spent so many years, letting the two lives intertwine as they evolved. So, at odd moments, mostly over weekends and on vacations, I began making notes and jotting down certain experiences. Before I realized it, writing this story had become my chief recreational pursuit. Now, finally, the job is finished.

Life has been good to me. For anyone destined to be a public accountant, I was born at the right moment in time. Professional accounting is essentially a product of the twentieth century; the century was just three months old when I was born. There were only about 250 CPAs in the United States in 1900; today there are about 90,000.

I was also fortunate in starting with Arthur Young & Company at a very young age, and in moving up in the firm at interesting points in its history. It has been an exciting experience to see how the demands for accounting services have grown and changed over the years, and it has been even more exciting to be a part of a firm which developed an organization to meet these increasing demands.

The accounting world of 1917, when I began my accounting apprenticeship in Ireland, was vastly different from the accounting world of today. Then it was a world of manual bookkeeping and the preparation of relatively simple financial statements and tax returns. Now we are in a world of computers and automation, a world from which simplicity seems to have gone forever.

During all the years I have been with Arthur Young & Company, the partners of the firm have naturally played a very important part in my life. A few of these partners are mentioned by name in the text, simply because they happened to fit into my story. But many whose names are not mentioned were equally important to me. Because this is so, I have included, as an appendix to the text, a complete list of all partners of Arthur Young & Company from 1921, when the first national partnership was formed, to date. I knew all of these individuals. Many of them, in addition to being my business associates, were my close personal friends.

To the extent that this story represents an informal history of Arthur Young & Company, it ought really to have been written by my predecessor in the firm, James Campbell Burton. Not only was Jim the connecting link between Arthur Young and my generation in the firm, but it was his great administrative and organizational ability that laid the solid foundation which supports the firm today.

This story could not have been written without relying on the memory of others. I should like to express my appreciation here to all those who answered my many questions concerning the early days of Arthur Young & Company, and particularly to J. C. Burton, W. D. McGregor, and A. V. McPhee, all of whom were very active partners in former days. A. V. McPhee put in writing a great deal of information about his early years in the Chicago office, and this information has been invaluable to me.

I should also like to express my appreciation to the following individuals in Arthur Young & Company who reviewed the manuscript and made many helpful suggestions: Paul J. Adam, George V. Carracio, John J. Deering, Thomas D. Flynn, Charles G. Gillette, Ernest L. Hicks, Ralph E. Kent, Ralph F. Lewis, Robert McDevitt, René A. Miller, Harold A. Mock, T. T. Shaw, J. Harold Stewart, and Herman E. Ward.

I am heavily indebted to John L. Lawler, managing director of the American Institute of Certified Public Accountants, who read the manuscript and was kind enough to put his comments and criticisms in writing. His suggestions were especially helpful because his viewpoint was that not only of a professional writer but also of one who has no close familiarity with the firm of Arthur Young & Company.

Then I am thankful to my secretary, Mrs. Doreen Connor, who typed the entire manuscript not once but many times, as countless revisions were made. She never once complained about my poor handwriting, nor about my incurable habit of forever trying to improve what I have written.

Finally, I wish to thank Albert Newgarden, the editor of *The Arthur Young Journal*, and his assistant, Mrs. Patricia Quinn. Al edited the manuscript and brought so much enthusiasm and energy to the task that it was a sheer delight to work with him. His collaboration and his creative ideas made this a far better book than it would otherwise have been.

THOMAS G. HIGGINS

New York City
June 30, 1965

THOMAS G. HIGGINS, CPA
An Autobiography

Despite the very English appearance of the surname Higgins, as it is usually anglicized, it is in fact a purely native Irish Gaelic name which should normally have been O'Higgin in English, the Irish form being Ó hUigin, pronounced O'Higgeen. The name, according to modern scholarship, is derived from the old Gaelic word "uiging," akin to the Norse Viking, not from the word "uige." Originating as a branch of the O'Neills of the midlands of Ireland (not the Ulster O'Neills) this sept spread westwards as far as Co. Sligo where they held large estates. They were still extensive landowners in 1878, having estates in nearly all the western counties. The really remarkable fact about them is the number of distinguished poets they produced during three centuries, from Tadhg Mór Ó hUigin who died in 1315 to Tadhg Dall (d. 1617).

EDWARD MAC LYSAGHT: *Irish Families*

CHAPTER ONE

FAMILY BACKGROUND

I AM DESCENDED FROM AN OLD IRISH FAMILY named Higgins, and from various Scottish and English people who settled in the North of Ireland during the past three hundred and fifty years.

My Higgins ancestors were originally of the Roman Catholic faith, but sometime around 1800 they became Presbyterians. In the 1840s they changed their faith again, this time joining the Anglican Church, known in Ireland as the Church of Ireland. The Anglican Church is the same, for all practical purposes, as the Episcopal Church in America.

It is not entirely clear why my Higgins ancestors left the Catholic Church. There is some evidence, however, that the change occurred when one of my ancestors married a Scottish girl who would not give up the Presbyterian faith of her fathers.

We have more definite information on why my great-grandfather left the Presbyterian Church. It was during the time of the potato famine, and my great-grandfather had a bitter quarrel with the local Presbyterian minister, whom he accused of selling him a quantity of bad potatoes. This may sound like a trivial matter today, but potatoes were life itself during the famine.

My family's mixture of blood is typical of the people who have lived in the North of Ireland for centuries. It is for this reason that the province of Ulster is sometimes compared to a three-legged stool: one leg Irish, one leg Scottish, and one leg English.

My father's house

I WAS BORN on March 20, 1900 in the tiny village of Aughnacloy in County Tyrone. My father, Robert McQuiston Higgins, was 31 years old at the time, my mother a few years older. My brother, Hugh, was also born in Aughnacloy, some six years before me.

Since March 1892, my father had been working for a man named Hamilton, a solicitor. (In Great Britain, a "solicitor" is a lawyer who advises clients and prepares their cases but is permitted to plead in only a few of the minor courts.) Father was to continue working for Hamilton until 1917.

My father had come from Dervock, in County Antrim, to take the position with Mr. Hamilton. My mother, on the other hand, had grown up in Aughnacloy, and my father first met her when he joined the choir of the local Episcopal church, in which she was a contralto.

When I was two years old Mr. Hamilton moved his office to Omagh, the county seat of Tyrone, some twenty miles away, and our family moved with him. A year later my sister Elizabeth was born. Beth, as we call her, was the third and last child in our family.

When I was baptized in Aughnacloy I was given three Christian names: Thomas for my paternal grandfather; Gilbert for *his* grandfather, Gilbert Logan; and McQuiston for a friend of my paternal grandparents named William John McQuiston.

The name of McQuiston

The nature of our relationship with the McQuistons is not clear. I know that they had no children, and that they were fond of my father as a child. In any event, the relationship was close enough that my father was named Robert McQuiston and the name McQuiston carried over to me.

William McQuiston was reputedly well off, and possibly it occurred to Grandfather Higgins that, if he named my father for him, some part of the McQuiston wealth might eventually be left to my father. It did not work out that way, however. When McQuiston died in 1893, his will provided that, after certain legacies, the balance of his estate was to be applied to the erection of a Presbyterian church, the site and design of which were to be approved by his trustees and executors. In 1897 the McQuiston Memorial Presbyterian Church was opened in Belfast, and today it is a well-known church in those parts.

MY FATHER'S ROOTS were deep in County Antrim. He was born in Ahoghill, where his father and grandfather and great-grandfather had lived before him.

My grandfather, Thomas Higgins, was born in 1844. His father's family had owned a farm in Ahoghill but lost it during the potato famine. In those days people in the North who had financial reverses frequently turned to linen weaving, and so it was

Grandfather Thomas Higgins

with my grandfather's father and his brother, who apparently had owned the family farm jointly.

Grandfather Thomas Higgins had little formal education. After serving fourteen years in the Army, he was selected for the permanent Depot Staff but then was disqualified for reasons of health. He returned to Ahoghill and started work as a linen weaver. In June 1876, Grandfather obtained an appointment as sub-agent on the estate of George Travers Macartney, in Dervock, and soon afterwards he moved his family there.

Some time after the Macartney appointment, Grandfather received a similar appointment on the estate of Ralph Smyth. He kept both appointments until his death in 1931 at the age of 86. Grandfather knew every inch of the land on these two estates.

Grandfather Higgins had married Elizabeth Herdman, whose father was successful in the linen trade. The Herdmans were Presbyterians, but the marriage took place in the Episcopal Church. Nine children were born of the marriage, my father being the eldest.

The house in Dervock, where three of my father's sisters still live, and which was built about 1800, has been occupied by the Higgins family since April 1880. The previous tenants were tanners, and the remains of the tanneries can still be seen in the area back of the house. The tanning of hides used to be an important industry in the North of Ireland, and in the eighteenth and nineteenth centuries a number of small tanneries were established in towns close to birchwoods—the bark of the birch tree being used in the tanning process.

I knew my grandfather, Thomas Higgins, about as well, I suppose, as anyone can know his grandfather; he was my senior by fifty-five years. When I visited Dervock as a child I was scared to death of him and avoided him as much as possible. As I grew older, however, I got to like him and we conversed a good deal.

I am not sure what Grandfather's responsibilities were, but I suppose he supervised workers on the land, collected rents, and kept whatever records were necessary. I often saw him examining large maps and making entries in what seemed to me then to be enormous books.

Grandfather read a great deal. Considering that he had virtually no formal education, it is amazing the sort of literature that interested him. He had read most of Shakespeare's plays and a great many historical works, including Gibbon's *Decline and Fall of the Roman Empire*, Hooker's *Roman History from the Building of Rome to the Ruin of the Commonwealth* (six volumes), lengthy histories of France and the Indian Empire, and books about the conquest of Peru and Mexico.

Grandfather loved the poetry of Lord Byron. I remember two verses in particular that he quoted frequently. They are to be found in the fourth canto of *Childe Harold's Pilgrimage* (CLXXVIII and CLXXIX):

> There is a pleasure in the pathless woods,
>   There is a rapture on the lonely shore,
>   There is society, where none intrudes,
>   By the deep Sea, and Music in its roar:
>   I love not Man the less, but Nature more,
>   From these our interviews, in which I steal
>   From all I may be, or have been before,
>   To mingle with the Universe, and feel
> What I can ne'er express—yet can not all conceal.

> Roll on, thou deep and dark blue Ocean—roll!
> Ten thousand fleets sweep over thee in vain;
> Man marks the earth with ruin—his control
> Stops with the shore;—upon the watery plain
> The wrecks are all thy deed, nor doth remain
> A shadow of man's ravage, save his own,
> When, for a moment, like a drop of rain,
> He sinks into thy depths with bubbling groan—
> Without a grave—unknelled, uncoffined, and unknown.

The name Byron was so well known in Grandfather's house that one might have thought Byron was a member of the family. Practically every dog the family acquired—and there were many—was automatically named Byron.

Grandfather was the strong character in our family. He was tall, erect, and quite heavy. Extraordinarily opinionated and positive, he prided himself in being a nonconformist. He was inclined to be hotheaded, and I somehow think he was feared by certain of the villagers. Obedience and punctuality meant a great deal to him. In Dervock the main meal was served in the middle of the day. At whatever time the meal was supposed to be served, Grandfather would seat himself at the head of the dining-room table, exactly on the minute. At no time, to my knowledge, did he ever inquire whether something might have delayed the meal.

My parents

MY MOTHER'S NAME was Martha Jane Henderson, and her background was essentially Scotch-English. At the age of nine, when her father died, she was adopted by her mother's sister and brother, Mary and John Cave—both unmarried, and both schoolteachers—and she lived with them until her marriage. By that time my mother also had become a teacher.

The schools in which the Caves taught were Episcopal, and as such were under the close supervision of the local rector. For a long number of years the rector was John Whitley Stokes who, in addition to being rector, was Archdeacon of Armagh Cathedral.

In those days the Church of Ireland was the established church, and because of this the Archdeacon was an important and influential figure in the Aughnacloy area. John Stokes was well off. He had two curates to assist him in the local church and more than a dozen servants at home.

I did not know my mother's family as well as my father's. This was partly because the members of my mother's family were older and not as long-lived. It was also because the house in Dervock had been a gathering place for the Higgins family since before I was born, whereas there was no similar meeting place in my mother's family.

My parents lived frugally, and they both led simple lives. Father, I suspect, must have been bored many times with the routine nature of his existence. As a solicitor's clerk he did not have to work hard. His office hours were 9:30 a.m. to 6 p.m., five days a week, with the closing hour 1 p.m. on Thursdays.

Father read a good deal, walked a good deal, and usually spent some part of every evening chatting with his cronies in the town. He would run into them when he went to buy the evening paper. He was interested in politics and was a loyal supporter of the Conservative Party.

Mother was well adjusted to life, and I do not believe she was ever bored. She was kind and thoughtful and had a marvelous disposition. I can recall no time when I heard her say an unkind word about anyone. She was completely devoted to her family.

Father was different. He was impetuous, abrupt, and capable of quick anger. Yet, like my mother, he had a keen sense of humor, and both of my parents seemed to derive great pleasure from the simple fact of being alive.

Father and Mother were deeply religious. They each knew thoroughly the Bible and the Book of Common Prayer, and they were both devoted to their Church. They had good memories and could recite long passages from the Bible and the Prayer Book, and they also knew by heart a great deal of poetry. Longfellow, Wordsworth, and Tennyson in particular meant a great deal to them. I recall my father telling me how, if he had difficulty going to sleep, he recited in his mind the service of Morning Prayer. He told me that he had no difficulty remembering the entire service but usually fell asleep before he reached the end of it.

Both of my parents were fond of music, and they hummed and sang a good deal as they went about their chores. Their favorites were Church of Ireland hymns and Gospel hymns and old Irish melodies. I can still hear Mother sing that grand Irish lyric, "The Bells of Shandon":

> With deep affection
> And recollection
> I often think of
> > Those Shandon bells,
> Whose sounds so wild would,
> In the days of childhood,
> Fling round my cradle
> > Their magic spells.

> On this I ponder
> Where'er I wander,
> And thus grow fonder,
> > Sweet Cork, of thee,
> With thy bells of Shandon,
> That sound so grand on
> The pleasant waters
> > Of the river Lee.

Mother's health, like her father's before her, was never good. She had trouble with her eyes both when she was young and as she got older. As a child she had rheumatic fever, which left its mark. In middle life she had an operation which was unsuccessful, and from then on she seemed to age very rapidly.

I HAVE ALWAYS had a special curiosity about the Stokes family and the Macartney family, because of the important roles they played in my parents' lives. Archdeacon Stokes was an important influence in the Cave home, where my mother was reared, and for sixty years the Macartney family were part and parcel of the Higgins household in Dervock.

I have mentioned that my mother was adopted, at an early age, by her mother's sister and brother, the Caves. In a sense, John and Mary Cave grew up as wards of the Church of Ireland. This came about when their parents, who died within six weeks of each other, requested on their deathbeds that their rector, Archdeacon Stokes, become the guardian of their young children. The Archdeacon agreed to do so, and took his responsibilities as guardian quite

Archdeacon Stokes

seriously, doing all he could to ensure that the Cave children were carefully brought up and well educated. In addition to being the guardian of John and Mary Cave, and their rector, Archdeacon Stokes was, as I have mentioned, the superintendent of the Episcopal schools in which they taught. It was only natural that he had a great influence on their lives, and on my mother's life as well.

John Whitley Stokes came from a fine family of clergy and scholars. Both his father and his grandfather were in the Church, and his son succeeded him as rector of Aughnacloy. (With the disestablishment of the Church in 1869, the union of Aughnacloy with the Archdeaconry was dissolved.)

Born in 1800, Archdeacon Stokes was apparently a brilliant man. He obtained honors in mathematics in each of his years at Trinity College in Dublin, and throughout his life he was keenly interested in education. Although he was 63 when my mother was born, he was active in the Church until the age of 80, and thus was an important force in my mother's early life.

Those who knew him say that the Archdeacon was strong-willed but kind. To my mother and to the Cave family, he was the Law and the Prophets and the Power and the Glory all rolled into one. For many years he was their boss, but he was a benevolent boss. Though they feared him, they also loved him. Apparently this attitude was shared by the Archdeacon's parishioners, for at his funeral in 1883 they ignored the waiting hearse and insisted on carrying his coffin to the graveyard on their shoulders.

LIKE THE STOKES FAMILY, the Macartneys were typical members of the Protestant ascendancy in Ireland—what would be called "the Establishment" today. This aristocratic class had close ties of education and interests. Its members were to be found predominantly in the Army, in the Church of Ireland, and in Government service. As a class, they owned most of the land in Ireland, although this condition was changed considerably by the passage of the Land Acts, which enabled tenants to buy their property, over a period of years, with Government assistance.

When the revolutionary spirit made itself felt in Ireland during the First World War, things went badly for landowning families like the Macartneys—especially in the South of Ireland. They had always been looked on by Irish Catholics as an alien and privileged class. Grievances were remembered. Many a peasant farmer who could not pay his rent had been forcibly evicted from his small farm by the local agent of some absentee landlord who seldom visited his property.

For a while the Macartneys were afraid that their house might go up in flames one night, and I recall their storing some of their prized possessions in the attic of my grandfather's house in Dervock. One night my aunt let me look at the collection. Some of these treasures were large portraits of past generations of Macartneys while others were miniatures.

Who were the Macartneys? Well, I suppose the accountant in me made me curious enough to find out.

The Macartneys came to Ireland in the person of George Macartney in 1649. George was born in Kirkcudbright, Scotland, and he was 23 years old when he settled in Belfast. He was successful as a merchant and also became well known as a public official.

One of George Macartney's sons, also named George, made two substantial purchases of property, some of which eventually was to become closely identified with the life of my grandfather. These purchases included the lands of Dervock and the castle of Lissanoure.

Shortly after this, George Macartney made Lissanoure his home. The castle was occupied by succeeding generations of Macartneys until 1847, when it was almost completely ruined by a gunpowder explosion. Ellen, the wife of George Macartney, who was then the owner, lost her life in the explosion. In those days houses were fortified in case of uprisings, and gunpowder and ammunition were usually stored in cellars. On the day of the explosion the gunpowder was to be removed from the dwelling house, and some of the casks were in a room where Mrs. Macartney was writing. By some means or other a spark set off the explosion.

The castle was never rebuilt, and for many years Lissanoure was empty. During my days in Ireland the Macartney family lived in the Lodge, which was within a stone's throw of the remains of the castle.

I remember visiting Lissanoure in the early years of the First World War. Captain Carthanach George Macartney, then about 47, and his son Travers, then about 20, were both away at the war as British officers, and Mrs. Macartney had asked one or two of my aunts to stay with her for a while. I was 14 or 15, and I can still remember how thrilled I was to have an opportunity to roam around Lissanoure. The property was extensive, with terraced lawns around the house and a large tennis court on the grounds. I suppose any boy would love a castle, and I can recall as though it were yesterday standing on the terrace in front of the ruins of the castle, looking across the lough on a hazy summer's evening.

That night I wandered through the Lodge itself, and I thought it immense. For years I used to wonder how big the Lodge really was. Fully thirty-five years later I saw the application for probate of the will of Captain Macartney, who died in 1936. I then found that the Lodge consisted of: Dining Room, Drawing Room, Hall, Study, Landing, eight Bedrooms, Back Landing, Maid's Bedrooms, Laundry, Larder, two Store Rooms, Pantry, Kitchen, Scullery, Cloak Room, Lavatory, Bathroom, and Wine Cellar.

The last of the Macartneys was Travers, who did not marry and who died in July 1943 at the age of 48. His mother lived a few years after him. When they died all the property, which had seen eight generations of Macartneys, passed to charity.

The capital of the County Tyrone is Omagh, but it
has only been the capital since the end of the
eighteenth century, and the exact date seems to be in
question. Until that time the old capital of the
O'Neills, Dungannon, was the County Town, and
it is not at all clear why the change took place. . . .
There is also much uncertainty about the derivation
of the name of Omagh. Some would have it Eo Magh, the
Plain of the Yew Tree, and others Oig Magh, the
Plain of the Chiefs, but the oldest authorities spell the
name Oghmagh, and later it is spelt Omy and
Omey, which is what the pronunciation of Oghmagh
in Irish might sound like to English ears.

RICHARD HAYWARD: *In Praise of Ulster*

CHAPTER TWO

OMAGH IN COUNTY TYRONE

The omagh i grew up in was a typical country town in Ireland, with a population of about five thousand. I always thought the surrounding countryside perfectly beautiful, but the town itself, like most old towns, was a haphazard sort of place. With the exception of Main Street and High Street, most of the streets in my day were narrow and winding, and many of them quite hilly.

The most imposing building in the town was the Court House, which was situated at the very top of High Street. In front of the Court House, just a little way down the hill, was a monument, and the first thing I can remember about Omagh was the unveiling of that monument. It was erected in memory of the men of the Royal Inniskilling Fusiliers who had fallen in the Boer War, and it consisted of three bronze figures on a large granite pedestal. It was a big day in the town when the monument was unveiled, and, as so often happens on big days, the rain pelted down on us as we stood there shivering in the crowd.

When we gathered on the hill that day (it was November 25, 1904), the monument was covered with a large black canvas. After several speeches, which cannot possibly have been as long as, in my memory, they seem, and some stirring music by the Inniskillings' regimental band, the Duchess of Abercorn "unveiled" the monument by pulling a long cord which removed the canvas.

"All boys love soldiers"

ALL BOYS, it seems, love soldiers, and I loved the Royal Inniskilling Fusiliers. A great part of the life of Omagh was identified with the Inniskillings. Soldiers were a familiar sight in the town, and every day was punctuated by bugle calls, which began very early in the morning. Omagh had been the regiment's home for generations, and many Omagh families, Catholic and Protestant, had proud associations with it. It was in Omagh that the recruits had their training.

The Royal Inniskilling Fusiliers came into existence in 1688 and in the years to follow fought in many campaigns. These campaigns were listed on the flags of the regiment, and on the drums as well. As a boy I knew the name of every campaign in which the regiment had fought.

It was grand to see the Inniskillings when they were attired in scarlet full dress with busbies. These occasions included the parade to the Church of Ireland every Sunday and the opening day of the County Assizes in March and July, when they acted as a guard of honor. It was also grand to see them when they went off attired in khaki on one of their periodic route marches into the country. Always they were led by the Depot band.

The most impressive sight of all was when there was a military

18

funeral. It would parade very slowly through the town with the gun-carriage draped in the Union Jack. Usually the band played Chopin's "Funeral March," but when it was the pipe band it always played "The Flowers of the Forest." I used to follow the funeral to the graveside and watch until the coffin was lowered into the grave and the workmen started heaping earth on top of it. It always came to me as a shock to see how quickly after the burial the poor unfortunate was forgotten. On the way to the graveyard and at the graveside everything was dignified and solemn. On the way back to the barracks, however, the slow march became a quick march as the funeral music gave way to something like "Under the Double Eagle."

In those early days all the glitter and the music connected with the Inniskillings seemed grand to me, but within a matter of years I was to realize that there was another side to the coin. When war was declared in August 1914 all the reserves and the militia of the Inniskilling Fusiliers were immediately called up. I remember them all marching off to the railway station on a summer's evening, with crowds lining the streets, led not only by the Depot band but also by local Catholic and Protestant bands. Most of the soldiers in the reserves and the militia were well known in Omagh, and naturally enough their trooping off created a highly emotional scene. It was just a short time afterwards that the names of many of them appeared on casualty lists.

I remember the first wounded soldier I saw. It was just a month or two after war broke out, and I was about 14 at the time. He was on crutches, and we all looked at him in great wonder. All the time he was with us the townsfolk questioned him about his experiences, and he did not seem to mind telling the story over and over again.

In a month or two he was better, and off he went to France again. His name was on the next list of deaths.

Then I remember seeing a deserter. It was in the summer of 1915, and I had gone into town early on an errand. The whole town was astir. Someone said that a soldier had deserted, and that the military police were searching for him in the area back of the Post Office. I and a couple of other boys went along the narrow alley that skirted the left side of the Post Office, and just as we got to the back of the Post Office we saw two big, broad-shouldered military policemen with a sorry-looking wretch, who was obviously the deserter, in tow. One of the military policemen had his left arm wrapped tightly around the deserter's neck and was punching his face with his right fist. By this time a crowd was gathering, so the two military policemen grabbed the deserter by either arm and started marching him off to the barracks. The deserter was deathly pale, and trembling.

Someone said that the deserter would be shot when they got him to the barracks, so a number of us followed to see what would happen. The trio marched up High Street past the Court House, continued down Castle Street, and then turned right into the barrack lane. Inside the entrance to the barracks was a small building which we used to call the guard house, outside which a sentry continually marched up and down, very stiff and formal, with a tremendous clicking of the heels each time he did an about-face. The deserter was bundled inside the guard house, and he was no sooner inside than we heard a terrible cry, and then there was silence, and the guard kept marching up and down, seemingly unperturbed. We hung around the barrack gate for about an hour, but nothing happened; and so I went back to town to finish my errand.

IN MY DAY, Omagh was an important railway junction, and I became fascinated by trains at a very early age. Our house was perched on a hill overlooking the main line of the Great Northern Railway Company, and as a boy I used to sit on the hill and record the numbers of the carriages and the engines. Father was very conscious of this "hobby" of mine and went out of his way to encourage it. He got me enormous timetables, which I pored over, and he also bought me a large book in which to record all the railway facts that interested me. When the Seventeenth of March or the Twelfth of July celebrations were held in or around Omagh and there were special excursion trains, Father always got me a choice spot from which I could watch the carriages that were drawn for the occasion from other places throughout the North.

A watcher of trains

Some days, when I was especially fortunate, I got a ride in a locomotive. I remember one day in particular when I was loafing around the engine shed and a big locomotive driver called to me to hop up beside him and the fireman. I do not remember how long I was with them on the ride, but I recall seeing them both prepare and eat their midday meal. They had steak that day which they cooked on a large shovel. It was the fireman's job to clean the shovel, and this took a good while. When the engine driver was satisfied with the condition of the shovel, he put the steak on it and shoved it in on top of the tremendous fire that powered the locomotive. I don't know whether the steak was good or bad, but my heroes polished it off in very short order.

At about the age of 12 my preoccupation with trains began to lessen, and very gradually it was replaced by a preoccupation with music. My interest in music really began with the outbreak of the First World War, when there was a great deal of military activity

I discover music

in and around Omagh and military bands were always very much in evidence. Around this time an uncle of mine gave me a guitar zither with an instruction book, and I learned to play just about all of the marches that the Inniskillings' band played.

Shortly after the war began, a retired British bandmaster, who got an appointment in the Depot, came to live near us. My family got to know him, and when he learned of my interest in music he gave me two books on the theory of music and spent some time coaching me. I studied the books carefully and enjoyed learning about music. Father thought I should learn some instrument other than the guitar zither, which was very limited in scope, so he bought me a violin and arranged for lessons. But I never succeeded in mastering the violin.

My next venture at a musical instrument was with the piccolo. I was then 19. One of my friends asked me if I would like to join the local flute band to which he belonged. The band was looking for a piccolo player, and someone had suggested that I would be ideal for the part, so I joined the band and immediately became the possessor of a brand-new piccolo. The piccolo is a marvelous little instrument, and I got a great deal of pleasure out of it. Perhaps even more than the music itself, I enjoyed the opportunity to associate with the people in the band, most of whom were a good deal older than I was, and I also liked the instructors, who were retired Army people.

SO MUCH FOR SOLDIERS and trains and music. Now let me say something about religion and education, and about my beginnings in public accounting.

Few people, I suspect, realize the great emphasis that was placed on religion in Ireland in my day, both by Catholics and by Protestants. There were five main churches in Omagh: one Catholic (the largest of the churches), two Presbyterian, one Church of Ireland, and one Methodist. On a Sunday morning the town was always astir with people hurrying to their churches. I can still hear the patter of their feet.

Religion in Omagh

Everybody in Omagh had some church affiliation, and everyone knew what that affiliation was. In some cases the individual might not be a regular attendant at church, but there was no doubt in anyone's mind what his or her official affiliation was. As might be expected in such an atmosphere, religion was a frequent topic of conversation.

For Protestants generally, Sunday was a day given over almost completely to religion. We, as children, had Sunday School at 9:30 a.m., Morning Service at 11:30, Children's Service at 3:30, and Evening Service at 7 p.m. I no longer recall how many services I missed for one reason or another, but I have the impression that my father was more strict about attendance with my brother, Hugh, who was six years older, than he was with my sister Beth or myself.

As I think back to my early days in Omagh I continue to marvel at how completely Protestants and Catholics were separated from each other in almost every area of life. I suppose it would not have been so noticeable if either sect had been just a small minority of the population, but the fact is that Protestants and Catholics were almost equal in numbers, not only in Omagh but throughout County Tyrone, although in Northern Ireland generally Protestants have long comprised about two-thirds of the total population.

Despite the passing of more than forty years, there is still a division of Protestants and Catholics today, although it may be much less emphatic than it was in my time.

A recent book has this to say about the tension between Protestants and Catholics in the North of Ireland:

> In politics, in education, in business, in social life, and in recreation, strong forces tend to place a man according to the church with which he worships—in the Ulster phrase, according to which foot he digs with. There is no assurance that the divisions are becoming less with the passage of time; on the contrary, a divided education and a divided social and political life tend to deepen and confirm the fundamental cleavage. That cleavage is, of course, much more than a difference of theology, for the differences of religion run alongside differences of race and of historical origin. The Catholic community gathers to itself the memories of an oppressed nation, the pride of a remote Celtic past before the Norman invaders came, the bitterness of a people leaderless and dispossessed at the time of the Plantations. The Protestant community has its own proud memories of the struggle for freedom of conscience at Derry and the Boyne, of high principles successfully maintained, of ordered and productive agriculture and industry brought to an undeveloped land, of an ascendancy held by constant vigilance, enterprise, and hard work.*

The main reason for this deep division of Catholics and Protestants goes back to the Ulster Plantation of 1608-1610, when Scottish and English people were "planted" on forfeited lands in Ulster to introduce a population that would be loyal to England. The important thing about this plantation, from the viewpoint of England, was that within a short time one of the four provinces of

---

*Denis P. Barritt and Charles F. Carter, *The Northern Ireland Problem*, London: Oxford University Press, 1962.

Ireland for the first time had a Protestant majority. But from then on there existed side by side two communities that were enormously antagonistic to each other.

It should be remembered that in 1608, when the Ulster Plantation got under way, almost 450 years had elapsed since the Normans had invaded Ireland. The struggle with Ireland, however, which commenced with that invasion, was never completely successful from England's viewpoint. Ireland was conquered and reconquered many times over, but she was never permanently subdued nor was she assimilated. England's trouble further increased when Henry VIII made himself the head of the English Church. Despite everything that he and his successors attempted, most of the Irish remained Catholics. This was an age of religious wars, and England felt unsafe in her proximity to a continent whose population was largely Catholic. She continued to be preoccupied with the thought that Ireland would be used as a center for intrigue by England's enemies on the Continent. In the sixteenth century two or three plantations were attempted, but none of them had more than limited success.

One of the end results of all of this was that there was precious little mingling of Catholics and Protestants in the schools in Omagh. Catholic girls attended the Loretto Convent, and Catholic boys attended one or both of the Christian Brothers' schools. Protestants went to the Omagh Model School, which was the national school, and then, if they could afford a secondary education and had good marks, the Omagh Academy.

The schools in Omagh

In addition to these schools there was a so-called Technical School which gave courses in a variety of subjects in evening classes, and where at the end of each school year certificates were issued by the Royal Society for the Encouragement of Arts, Manufactures and Commerce in London. It was really only in the Technical School that Protestants and Catholics sat side by side and were instructed by both Catholic and Protestant teachers.

In the Ireland of my day most boys and girls finished their education at national school level. The law required attendance until age 14, but attendance until about 15 was necessary to finish all the grades at the national school.

I attended the Model School and did well there. Between the ages of 10 and 12 I was at the top of my class. I liked the school work and the teachers, and I was extremely conscientious about homework.

On my twelfth birthday Father talked about the possibility of my going to the Academy and shortly afterwards began making inquiries. Mother favored the idea.

The Academy at that time had been in existence for nine years. The principal was Henry A. Perdue, and the teaching staff, which was small, included his wife. The Perdues had no children and apparently had no interest in anything but the Academy, to whose welfare they were devoted. The school, which was financed essentially by fees from the pupils, was under the supervision of the Intermediate Education Board for Ireland. There were five grades —Preparatory, Junior I, Junior II, Middle, and Senior—and certificates were issued at the end of each year by the Board. Most of the pupils at the Academy were from the general neighborhood of Omagh, but in addition there were usually ten to twenty boarders from some distance away.

Father boasted to Mr. Perdue about my record at the Model School and later on took me to be interviewed. He was sufficiently persuasive that Mr. Perdue agreed to enroll me in the fall of 1912 at a fraction of the regular school fee, which my father felt was entirely too stiff for a law clerk.

I did not like the Academy and soon began wishing I could devise some means of getting away from it. This feeling increased with the years, and it came to a climax as I approached my sixteenth birthday. I then quit the school. Neither my parents nor the Perdues nor anyone else could dissuade me.

At the Academy

I started at the Academy at a disadvantage. Rightly or wrongly, I was sure that Father had overstated my ability in his conversations with Mr. Perdue. I knew that Father was sincere in what he had said, but I had a strong feeling that it was impossible for me to live up to the expectations he had generated. I became even more convinced of this as time wore on, because it became crystal-clear to me that a number of the pupils who were paying full fees were better students than I was. I also had the definite feeling that Mr. Perdue's sole interest in me was as a potential prize-winner. As I look back on it now I am inclined to doubt that this was really so, but such were my feelings at the time.

It is true, of course, that at least in my day intermediate schools like the Academy were keenly competitive in Northern Ireland. Every principal wanted to boast more prizes and exhibitions for his school than any other school of comparable size. The principals drove themselves hard, and they drove their pupils hard—particularly those who, like myself, were thought to have "potential."

Some idea of the way we worked can be gleaned from the school schedule: Our normal workday in the Academy ran from 9 a.m. until about 4 p.m., and from 5:30 p.m. to 7 p.m. On Saturdays it ran from 9 a.m. until 1 p.m., and from 7 p.m. to 9 p.m. Day sessions from Monday to Friday ended officially at 3 p.m., but corrections of papers usually took about an hour. Most of the corrections had to do with translations from Latin to English or English to Latin. It was a leisurely process. We all took turns in seeing Mr. Perdue. As he discussed each paper with the pupil at some length he drank tea and munched biscuits. Mr. Perdue was a perfectionist; no translation ever seemed exactly as he wanted it.

The worst session for me was the Saturday evening session. The idea of going to school on Saturday night, when the town was full of all kinds of excitement, was something that gnawed at me all the time. I don't recall now whether the Saturday evening session was for everybody or just for the potential prize-winners.

In addition to classwork there was, of course, a good deal of homework. This kept me up late many a night, and also claimed many precious weekend hours.

Both Mr. and Mrs. Perdue were always very serious and withdrawn. Mr. Perdue had a violent temper, and many of the pupils, myself included, were afraid of him. There was physical punishment frequently, and the threat of physical punishment seemed always to lurk in the background.

If Mr. Perdue failed to get some point over to his class he would clench his fists, look up at the ceiling, and lament in a loud voice, "My heavens, what a class!" Sometimes when he had given out an assignment he would walk around the classroom, row after row, peering over each pupil's shoulder. When he spotted something in a pupil's paper that was clearly wrong he usually grabbed the pupil's hair immediately above one of his ears and tugged at it as hard as he could, calling out, almost in a shriek, "*Will* you, for heaven's sake, *think!*" Today, more than fifty years later, I can still feel that disturbing sensation above my ear, and whenever I come across one of those "THINK" signs that IBM made famous I invariably sense Mr. Perdue at my back.

These were the negative aspects of life at the Academy. It would be unfair, however, not to mention the positive aspects. I suspect I learned more during my years at the Academy than in any similar period before or since. Mr. Perdue lived and thought mathematics, and we spent more time on mathematics than on any other subject. We seemed to have Euclid morning, noon, and night. In his leisure moments, or when he was waiting for the class to finish an assignment, Mr. Perdue sought diversion by dreaming up mathematical problems and working on them till he solved them. Next to mathematics his chief interest was Latin. He was almost as painstaking in teaching Latin as he was in mathematics.

As I look back on it now I am sure the tremendous emphasis on mathematics and Latin was good for me. In those years at the Academy I seem to have developed an understanding of mathematics and language that has never left me. The one glaring weakness in the setup was the almost complete lack of recreation. I loved soccer, but there was practically no time for it, since the only free day was Sunday and it was considered a sin to indulge in sports or other amusement on the Sabbath. Compounding this lack of recreation was the fact that I was probably far more conscientious about my school assignments than I should have been.

WHILE I WAS ATTENDING the Academy I had frequent fits of depression. I don't know why this was so. Possibly it had to do with

A time of tension

the school atmosphere or the religious atmosphere or the political atmosphere; perhaps it was a combination of all three.

Certainly the political situation was acute. I don't suppose anyone who did not live through the events of 1912-1914 can realize how tense things really were in the North of Ireland.

I can remember as though it were yesterday Mr. Perdue addressing our class of 14-year-olds in May 1914. He told us with a heavy face that the Home Rule bill had just passed the Commons for the third time, and that nothing could now prevent the bill from becoming law. We sat there quivering as we heard this disturbing news. The impact was just about the same as if a schoolmaster in the United States today were to tell his young class that the Communists had just won a sweeping victory in the national elections, and that the country would now have a Communist President, a Communist Cabinet, and a large Communist majority in both the Senate and the House.

The Protestant leaders and the Protestant newspapers for years had made it all too clear that "Home Rule was Rome Rule" and that "Ulster would fight and Ulster would be right." They said that under Home Rule there would be no more freedom of religion or speech, and that education would pass over into the hands of the Catholic Church.

The Protestant leaders had also made it clear that there would be civil war and that this civil war would involve England and the Army, for the Conservative Party in England and the officers in the British Army, they said, would never let their Protestant brothers down. There was some justification for saying this, for in March 1914 General Gough and fifty-seven other cavalry officers stationed with the British forces at the Curragh, a large military camp near Dublin, had refused to obey Government orders to move against Ulster. This event was widely publicized, and even today people in Ulster still talk about "the Curragh mutiny."

Nobody in Ulster, Protestant or Catholic, doubted that there would be civil war. Large bodies of Protestants and Catholics were drilling practically every night. At first they drilled with dummy rifles, but after the gun-runnings they had regular rifles. There was nothing very secret about the drilling. The two "armies" usually went in opposite directions from the town and conducted their drills several fields away from the road. Sometimes I would come upon them, or at least hear the sounds of their voices, when wandering at night along one of the country roads near Omagh. I was scared to death of the whole thing.

Guns at night

The Ulster gun-running took place in April 1914. I remember it well. Father came home to tea one evening just as usual, but I noticed that he seemed preoccupied all through the meal. Later on I heard him whisper to Mother that "something really big" was afoot. I did not understand the import of what he said, but a day or two afterwards our schoolmaster told us all about it. He said there had been a great gun-running exploit at Larne in County Antrim, where a ship from Hamburg, Germany, had landed thousands of rifles and millions of rounds of ammunition, and that this shipment was sufficient to arm a large part of the 100,000 or so Ulster Volunteers. He told us that virtually every loyal Ulsterman had played some part, direct or indirect, in the great adventure, some of them engaging in battalion exercises far from Larne for the sole purpose of hoodwinking the police.

In the spring of 1914 it became clear to all of us that things were coming to a head. British regiments moved into Ulster, and

31

boats from the British Navy were ordered to the waters off Belfast. There was, I remember, a great stir in Omagh when a company of the Bedfordshire Regiment arrived in town.

Although in the early summer of 1914 it seemed that nothing could prevent civil war in the North of Ireland and elsewhere, civil war did not break out, because with the beginning of the war with Germany the effective date of Home Rule was postponed.

BY ORDINARY STANDARDS I suppose I did quite well in the Academy. But while I did much better than average, it was entirely clear to me that I did not do as well in Junior II as Mr. Perdue had expected. He had obviously hoped that I would get a prize or an exhibition, but I failed to get either. It required honors in three subjects for an exhibition, but I received honors in only two. I felt that I had let the Perdues down, and this caused me a good deal of anxiety.

Looking for a career

When I left the Academy I had no definite course of action in mind. I had a vague idea that I wanted a civil service appointment, but I didn't know what chance I had of getting one. I don't recall now where I got guidance, but in any event I started studying to take one of the civil service examinations. After some months and a number of inquiries, however, it became clear that no male applications would be acted upon until the war was over. At that time the general feeling was that the war would go on for many years more.

At this point Father started inquiring around town, and he came up with what he considered some good leads, the most promising of which appeared to be an apprenticeship with H. B. Brandon & Co., a firm of chartered accountants. I had no idea what a chartered accountant did, but Father explained to me that every business had to keep books by certain rules and that it was the job of the accountant to check the books and make sure they did not violate the rules. Father thought I should be good at this kind of work, since I had demonstrated some ability at mathematics and since the records of trains I had kept as a child seemed to suggest a predisposition toward orderliness and correctness. He talked with Robert L. Reid, who was in charge of Brandon's office in Omagh, and Reid seemed favorably disposed to hiring me. I again thought that Father had overstated my ability, but at that time I would have settled for work of any kind and under any conditions. So after the necessary interviews it was mutually agreed that I would set out to become an accountant. I then enrolled at the Technical School for bookkeeping and other business courses.

I WAS A MONTH short of 17 when I started my apprenticeship with H. B. Brandon & Co. on February 26, 1917. As I learned later, Brandon's was one of the better-known firms of chartered accountants in the North of Ireland. The head office of the firm was in Belfast, and there were branch offices in Portadown, Ballymena, Londonderry, Waterford, and Omagh. I don't know what the total headcount of the firm was in those days, but as I recall there were about thirty people in the head office, with small staffs in the branches.

H. B. Brandon & Co., Chartered Accountants

Although I met Mr. H. B. Brandon only once, and then very casually, it was quite clear to me from everything I saw and heard that he was the strong character in the firm and its guiding spirit. It also became clear to me later on that there was considerable doubt about what would happen to the firm when Mr. Brandon died. He was then about 70.

As I have said, Robert Reid, an incorporated accountant, was in charge of the Omagh branch when I started work. Reid was then 27, and I grew to respect him. He gave the impression of being cold and aloof, but I found he wore well, and he and I seemed suited to each other. He was energetic and a fast worker. He seemed to have a great deal of self-confidence, and he was capable of long periods of concentration. Sometimes when he was in particularly good form he would sing to himself snatches from Percy French's song, "Come Back, Paddy Reilly, to Ballyjamesduff."

Reid was under the supervision of Fred Allen, also an incorporated accountant, who was in charge of the Portadown branch. Allen had formerly been in charge of the Omagh office, and I suppose it was only natural that when he moved to Portadown, a much larger town, he continued to keep a fatherly eye on Omagh. He visited Omagh every ten days or so, Omagh being about an hour and a half from Portadown by train. Allen would arrive in Omagh about 10:30 a.m. and leave shortly after 4 p.m.

Allen was stern, blustery, and aggressive; sometimes he was disdainful. When I first met him, shortly after starting with Brandon's, he was about 33 years old.

Fred Allen was married to Robert Reid's sister, and it was evident that Allen and Reid were friendly to each other. But I, for one, was always glad to see Allen pick up his briefcase and start off for the railway station after a day in Omagh. Reid would always walk him to the train.

H. B. Brandon & Co. was the only firm of accountants in Omagh, and, as might be expected, the firm was kept quite busy. Practically all the businesses in Omagh were audited and then, as now, taxes were an important part of the work. The Brandon audits in Omagh were typical of the audits one would expect to find in any small town. These included the gas company, the two local newspapers, the local printers, the local bakery, most of the important stores, and many of the creameries in the general Omagh area. In addition to regular audit and tax work, the firm would frequently be called on for special services of various kinds, including work in connection with bankruptcies and receiverships. I remember once being asked to act as an auctioneer's clerk almost when the auction was about to begin. Another time I was dispatched in quite a hurry to take charge of a department store which had become bankrupt. I was then 20 and had no idea how to "take charge" of anything. My boss, however, said there was nothing to it. He said to let things follow their normal routine but control every penny of cash, incoming and outgoing. This was somewhat of an oversimplification, but things worked out all right.

The work in Brandon's

All the firm's audits were detailed audits. We checked every entry, beginning with the books of original entry, and we checked all footings. Every entry and every footing that was checked bore the initial of whoever did the checking. The identifying initial given me when I started to work was "T" (for Tom), so that "T," in red ink, appeared opposite every item I checked. Postings were usually checked by pairs of accountants, one calling to the other. If, for example, the postings to be checked were those to the

35

customers ledger, the junior would take the book of original entry and the senior would take the customers ledger. The junior would call "Page 251," pause; "John Jones," pause; "January 3rd," pause; "Three pounds four and two." The senior would call, "Right," and simultaneously the junior and the senior would place their initials on the entries in the two books.

Most of the private ledgers of clients were kept the year 'round in a safe in our office. Each ledger had a lock and key. Frequently a key would be lost, but oddly enough it would usually show up eventually. If it did not, we would have a substitute made.

The controlling accounts were frequently out of balance, and we would spend day after day running down the differences. Sometimes we would have to recheck both the postings and the footings. As might be expected, this matter of checking footings and postings was terribly boring. Our office was poorly ventilated and we often had quite a time trying to keep awake.

As in most auditing firms in those days, our work in Brandon's was highly seasonal. We were the auditors of a great many creameries, all of which were on a calendar-year basis. Beginning early in January the books would start arriving in our office. Some would be delivered personally by the manager of the creamery. Others would come by mail. Still others would come by messenger, the messenger usually being some neighbor who for one reason or another had to make a trip to Omagh. By the end of January our office would be bulging with books, and we would all be working morning, noon, and night trying to get on top of the backlog.

Most of the managers of the small creameries in the outlying districts were farmers who knew nothing about bookkeeping and cared even less. Some of the books were in horrible shape, with all kinds of clerical errors. What a blessed relief it used to be to see a confused mass of transactions finally reduced to a nicely typed balance sheet and profit and loss account, and then to get the books and papers on their way to some lonely spot in the country where they would remain for another year. Those creamery managers were an interesting breed, and I always liked to see them. They varied all the way from a gentle, pleasant-mannered fellow who was deeply religious to a big broad-shouldered, blue-eyed Irishman who, always with liquor on him, would shout his instructions to us in excited and often blasphemous terms. Sometimes his eyes looked so wild I thought he would kill us all off.

We had few engagements that required absences from home. Most clients brought their books to our office and, apart from getting answers to questions, all our work could be done there. Although we did little interim work in those days, I do recall three engagements in which we did a good deal of interim work on the clients' premises. These were all relatively large engagements: the Omagh Gas Company, the Omagh Cooperative Agricultural and Dairy Society (or, as we called it, "the Creamery"), and the Catholic newspaper, *The Ulster Herald*. We probably also did interim work on the Protestant newspaper, *The Tyrone Constitution*, although I don't recall it now.

I liked to get away from the office on assignments. The staff of the three clients mentioned were very friendly, particularly those in the *Ulster Herald* office, who were full of fun and merriment.

I think I spent more time on the Omagh Gas Company than on any other account. The manager of the company liked his accounts checked currently, so whenever there was a lull in the office

I went to the Gas Company. Sometimes I helped out with odds and ends in the office there, particularly when the manager or his assistant stepped away from the office. The Gas Company sold coke, and frequently a man with a horse and cart would appear outside the office window to buy some. If no one else was around I would take care of him. There was a weighbridge at the window, and the charge for the coke was determined by taking the weight of the empty cart on its way to the pile of coke and of the full cart on its way past the window again. Thereafter a "coke ticket" was made out and the sale was completed. I don't recall now whether these were cash or credit transactions. I spent so much time at the Gas Company that most of the people who came to buy coke thought I worked for the company.

Years ago people used to tell jokes about the Irishman who kept a pig in his parlor. Only once did I see a pig in a parlor. It was in a public house about ten miles from town. I had been sent there to prepare a balance sheet and income account to be used in a tax return. It involved just a few hours' work.

A pig in a parlor

I got there about ten in the morning and was greeted by the proprietor, who was behind the bar and who asked me what I would like to drink. I said I did not drink, but he insisted that I needed something "to warm my belly," so he poured me a large glass of port wine. I asked him if it would make me drunk and he gave a laugh. So I drank the port and then he showed me into a parlor off the bar. There was a table in the middle of the room with about five or six chairs lined up against the wall. I was amazed to see an enormous sow stretched out on the floor with its litter all noisily sucking their nourishment.

The proprietor paid no attention whatever to the activity on the floor. He spread the books and records out on the table, explained a few things to me, and then said he would be back about one o'clock with my dinner. The port was beginning to have its effect, and I tackled my work with a grand feeling of warmth and optimism.

It seemed no time at all before the proprietor was back with a plate piled high with beef, cabbage, and potatoes. The bar at that time was getting active, but the proprietor kept popping in and out to see how I was getting on with my dinner and to keep up a running conversation with me. He was in ripping good form.

I finished my assignment at three. As I left the parlor I glanced at the sow and her litter. They were in exactly the same position as when I arrived, and seemed contented.

One day when I had been with Brandon's a year or two, Robert Reid surprised us all by announcing that he had decided to leave the firm. He said that he had accepted a position with one of the well-known accounting firms in Dublin, that he was satisfied he would have a real future there, and that he had already discussed the matter with Mr. Brandon. I was naturally sorry to hear of his leaving, but it was clear to me that he had already begun to look forward to his new career.

Reid was succeeded by the number two man in the Omagh office, J. P. Jamison. Jamison was a hard-working, deliberate individual who had transferred to Omagh from the Ballymena office about a year or so after I joined the firm. He did not seem to be unusually smart, but he was extraordinarily shrewd and had a keen trading sense. He seemed to have no interests other than his work and his investments, and I believe he made a good deal of money out of both. When H. B. Brandon died in 1923, the firm divided into two parts. Jamison stayed with Brandon's son to form Brandon, Jamison & Company, while the other part of the Omagh branch became Fred J. Allen & Company.

The roots begin to loosen

SOMETIME IN 1917 Father started talking about joining the Army. His brother John, my brother Hugh, and my three male cousins all were in the service. Hugh had emigrated to New York in 1913, and when the United States entered the war in 1917 he tried to enlist in the U. S. Army but was turned down because he was not yet an American citizen. He then crossed the border to Canada and enlisted in the Royal Flying Corps.

Father passed the medical examination and joined the Inniskillings in October 1917. He was then 49 years old. I did not realize it at the time, but this was the beginning of a chain of events that resulted in my joining Arthur Young & Company in New York on July 1, 1921.

Shortly after enlisting, Father was transferred to the Army Pay Corps. After a period in Dublin he was transferred to General Headquarters in Wimereaux, France. He was not demobilized until May 1920.

When Father returned to Omagh he had no interest whatever in staying there. He took a position with the Ministry of Pensions but soon started talking about emigrating to the States. My brother Hugh encouraged the idea, so after exchanging a number of letters Father took off for New York in December 1920.

It was generally understood that Mother and Beth would follow Father later on, but I myself was quite undecided. I thought

I was doing quite well in Brandon's, and I had the feeling that the transition from a small country town in the mountains to a city like New York would be difficult. I was also fond of Omagh and felt very much a part of it. There was the band in which I was active, and there was soccer. Not only was I an avid follower of the local football team, but I also followed, through the newspapers, the fortunes of the professional teams in England and Scotland as well as Ireland.

So I decided not to rush into emigrating. Instead, I would wait and see how things turned out in the next year or two.

In this soft, this somewhat languid air, the ship glowed like an immense and brilliant jewel. All of her lights were on, they burned row by row straight across her 900 feet of length, with the small, hard twinkle of cut gems: it was as if the vast, black cliff of her hull, which strangely suggested the glittering night-time cliff of the fabulous city that was her destination, had been sown with diamonds.

THOMAS WOLFE: *Of Time and the River*

CHAPTER THREE

THE FABULOUS CITY OF NEW YORK

O<small>N SAINT PATRICK'S DAY 1921 MY BROTHER</small> Hugh called at the Cunard office in New York and, with money borrowed from his father-in-law, bought an open ticket from Liverpool to New York and then sent me the following cable: "Obtain passport. Mailing steamship ticket. Hugh."

Although the cable was addressed to my home the messenger, who knew me, delivered it at Brandon's. Hugh's message came as a complete surprise to me, and not an altogether happy one, for it meant that I now had to make a major decision which I would have preferred to put off for a while.

I showed the cable to Madge Corker, who was the only other person in the office that day. Madge, whom I had known since I was a child and who had attended the Academy with me, had been a staff assistant at Brandon's for about two years. I asked Madge not to mention the cable to anyone until I had made up my mind what to do about it.

When I got home that evening, I talked to Mother about the cable. She was never one to exert pressure, but it was quite obvious that she hoped I would emigrate. She herself had no desire to leave Omagh, but she wanted very much to have the family together. I was noncommittal.

Ten days after I got the cable I received a letter from Hugh enclosing the ticket and also a certified check for $25 (then about £5), the amount that all immigrants required for admittance to the United States. Hugh's letter was optimistic. He told about how well he had done in America with much less education than I had, and he also said his inquiries about accountants indicated that there was an increasing demand for them. He said the fact that New York was bigger than Omagh was no particular disadvantage for, as he put it, "arithmetic is the same the world over."

I decide to emigrate

I had by now gradually convinced myself that I should emigrate, so when I got Hugh's letter I called on the local Cunard agent and asked him to set the wheels in motion. In a few weeks the agent told me he had worked out the details and that I could sail in the middle of May.

When this much was definite I talked to J. P. Jamison. Jamison did not say much at the time, but in a few days he talked at great length to me. He said it would be a mistake for me to leave, that I was the sort of person who should make rapid progress in the firm, and that in fact he was already planning to give me more responsibility. He also said that I could never expect to get the same sort of satisfaction from accounting in America as I had gotten at Brandon's. The real satisfaction, he said, was in preparing final figures, and the businesses in America were so large that I could never expect to get near the final results. He offered me more money, but I told him I had gone too far to turn back.

A week after this conversation, the minister from the First Omagh Presbyterian Church talked to me at the Technical School, where I was still taking some evening courses. (The local clergy used to drop in, from time to time, on classes.) The minister was highly critical of my decision to emigrate and prefaced his remarks with "I hear you are now another of the foolish young men who are leaving this country of ours, where the future holds such great opportunities."

At that time most of the clergy were quite disturbed by the large number of young people who were leaving the country. They felt that if this tide of emigration was not stemmed only the very old and the very young would eventually be left, and Ireland's prospects would be even bleaker than they were.

Jamison's right-hand man, Coulter, then talked to me, presumably at Jamison's urging. I am not sure that Coulter's heart was in the conversation, but in any event what he said was much the same as what Jamison had said. He emphasized the satisfaction to be derived from having complete responsibility for an audit, and warned that I would never get to see the "whole picture" of any of the big companies in America.

During the several weeks after I received the cable from Hugh, I kept Madge Corker posted on developments. I told her about the conversations I had had with Jamison, Coulter, and the Presbyterian minister, and she said she thought I had made the right decision. Brandon's, she said, had no future for me or her or anyone else.

I SAILED FROM LIVERPOOL on the *Caronia* on Wednesday, May 18, 1921. The *Caronia*, then sixteen years old, was considered one of the good Cunard liners. She was approximately 20,000 gross tons and was equipped to carry some 1,700 passengers. During the First World War the ship had seen active service as an armed merchant cruiser.

There were 973 passengers on the May 18th sailing: 39 first class, 394 second class, and 540 third class.

I thought I would be in New York City in eight days. Actually it was two weeks before I walked down the gangway at the Battery in New York. Not only did we have scheduled stops in Queenstown (now Cobh) and Halifax, plus an unscheduled stop of some twenty-four hours near Newfoundland because of icebergs, but the majority of the passengers spent five days on the *Caronia* in New York, awaiting health examinations.

Arrival in New York

When I arose early on Friday, May 27th, the *Caronia* was anchored off Quarantine. I watched with great interest as later on we moved slowly past the tip of Staten Island, past the Statue of Liberty, and up the North River, where the *Caronia* docked at Pier 54.

The first thing that impressed me about New York was the climate. The sun that shone down on the *Caronia* seemed extraordinarily strong, and the sky was cloudless. I had never seen a sky like that in Ireland.

The second thing that impressed me was the immenseness of everything. I had heard about skyscrapers, but I was amazed to see how many there were and how close they seemed to be to one another. I thought, what a fabulous city New York is, and what a contrast to Omagh!

In those days all third-class (steerage) immigrants had to pass a medical examination at Ellis Island before they could be admitted to the States. I had come third class, and as the day of our arrival wore on it became quite apparent to all of us that there was no hope of our being cleared that day. In fact, it was rumored, it might be Tuesday or Wednesday or perhaps even Thursday of the following week before we would be cleared. The *Caronia*, it seemed, was only one of a number of liners which had arrived at Quarantine at more or less the same time. Also, this particular weekend was a big holiday weekend in America, Monday being Decoration Day.

The three largest ships which docked on May 27th were the *Adriatic* and the *Celtic* of the White Star Line and the *Caronia* of Cunard. In all, they had some 1,400 third-class passengers to be cleared through Ellis Island.

When the *Caronia* was made fast to the pier most of the third-class passengers gathered around the rail to see what was going on. First of all, the first- and second-class passengers trooped down the gangways. Most of these passengers were greeted by friends and relatives, and small groups of them started milling about the pier. It was some time before the last of the first- and second-class passengers were gone. Then, almost immediately, the stevedores began to unload the cargo. This was a long, leisurely process which lasted all day Friday and part of Saturday. Next came the loading of the cargo for the return trip, and this too was a leisurely process. The stevedores sweated freely and shouted a great deal to one another. I did not understand what they said. Someone told me they were Italians.

There were mixed reactions among the third-class passengers

when we learned we were to spend a long weekend on the *Caronia*. Some were quite disturbed, particularly those whose relatives had come a long way to meet them. Others, like myself, did not seem to mind very much. For my part, the days on the *Caronia* after I got my sea legs had been a new and thrilling experience. In Omagh the vast majority of the inhabitants had grown up in the North of Ireland, most of them close to Omagh. But the third-class passengers on the *Caronia* comprised a wide variety of nationalities which I found enormously interesting. Many of them were from Central Europe and from the South and West of Ireland. There were some from England but practically none from Scotland, and as far as I could determine there was no one from the North of Ireland except myself. Those who were from the Continent spoke very little English, so inevitably the passengers tended to divide themselves into two groups: an English-speaking group and a non-English-speaking group. These were both large groups, however, and as the days wore on the passengers within each group got to know one another extremely well. The people from the South and West of Ireland became acquainted with one another almost immediately. This was easy, because many of them came from the same towns or townlands. Mostly they were from the land, and they were sincere, simple, warmhearted people. Almost every one of them had a delightful sense of humor, and I got to know many of them quite well.

My brother Hugh

WHEN THE *CARONIA* DOCKED in New York I had a letter from Hugh saying that either he or his wife Maudie (whom I had never met) would be at the pier to meet me. At that time I did not know

Hugh very well. He had left school to take a position as an apprentice in a department store in Belfast at the age of 14, when I was 8. During the five succeeding years he had a position in Lurgan and one in Fintona, but he never worked in Omagh. He emigrated at the age of 19 (when I was 13), and during the eight years since we had not seen him nor had we heard much from him.

Hugh loved people; he was our family's great extrovert. Just as I had had a passion for trains and music as a child, Hugh had always had a passion for entertainment—vaudeville, the theater, particularly circuses and clowns. He had always said that someday he would buy a circus. But Father had an unshakable belief that all entertainment, and particularly anything connected with a circus, was the work of the Devil.

Hugh had a fairly good voice and knew the words of all the popular songs. He delighted in joining a group around the piano. He was always full of wisecracks and good humor, and he had a remarkable memory for faces and names.

Hugh had married Margaret Hansmann in 1918, and they had one child, Robert, who was about 18 months old when I arrived in America. Mr. Hansmann had a store in Staten Island, and it was while working for him that Hugh had met his daughter Maudie, as she was called.

Shortly after lunch on Sunday, while I was sitting in the lounge of the *Caronia* reading, one of the passengers came running up to me to say that there was someone in a small boat in the river calling my name. I was certain it was a mistake or some sort of practical joke, but sure enough there was Hugh in a very small boat manned by three swarthy, rough-looking individuals.

After we shouted generalities to each other Hugh asked if I

"Someone in a small boat"

needed anything. I shouted down that I needed nothing but cigarettes. After a few more words the boat disappeared around the corner of Pier 54.

Half an hour later the boat was back, with Hugh clutching a large brown paper bag. He shouted up that he had pastry and cigarettes for me. He then proceeded to throw things up to me one at a time, first the pastry and then the cigarettes. His aim was poor with the first three pastries, all of which splashed against the side of the *Caronia*. There was near panic on the small boat, because not only did Hugh almost fall into the water as he fired the pastry upwards but the boat almost turned completely over. Hugh's aim improved with each succeeding throw, however, and four or five of the pastries and three packages of Lucky Strikes all made the deck, although two of the pastries were smashed beyond recognition.

By this time what had started out to be a dull afternoon on the *Caronia* had become an exciting one, and quite a number of passengers were gathered around the rail of the ship. Hugh, who loved the dramatic, was in his element. With a look of satisfaction on his face and a look of relief on the faces of his companions, the boat finally disappeared again around the corner of Pier 54.

I was not particularly impressed with the American pastry, but I was tremendously impressed with the Lucky Strike cigarettes. I lighted one of them and inhaled deeply, and it seemed to me to be by far the best cigarette I had ever smoked. The looseness of the tobacco, as compared with the hard English cigarettes I had been used to smoking, appealed to me particularly. I was also fascinated by the burnt, smoky flavor. I passed some of the cigarettes around and everybody was equally impressed.

I WAS CLEARED by the immigration officials on Wednesday, June 1, and walked down the gangway at the Battery about 2 p.m. Maudie met me and we walked a short distance to the Staten Island ferry terminal. After about a half-hour ride on the ferry, we arrived at St. George, in Staten Island, where we took a Tottenville train to New Dorp and then a taxi to New Dorp Beach, where Hugh and Maudie and their baby were spending the summer in a bungalow that Maudie's parents owned. Mrs. Hansmann was at home to greet me. Later on Mr. Hansmann arrived, and still later Hugh. All of them made me welcome.

In Staten Island

The Hansmanns were German, and in the weeks to follow I was to meet a great many of their German relatives who came to visit New Dorp, usually during the weekend. Some of them lived in Brooklyn, others in Manhattan.

Mr. Hansmann was 48. He was small, wiry, and quiet. Mrs. Hansmann was 43. She was large, broad-shouldered, aggressive, and good-looking.

It was agreed that I would spend the summer in New Dorp, and everyone was of one mind that I should not think of looking for work for a couple of weeks. I found New Dorp very pleasant, and I thoroughly enjoyed myself loafing around the beach.

Hugh loved Manhattan, particularly the Times Square area, and shortly after I got to New Dorp he and I made a couple of trips there to shop. More than anything else I needed suitable clothing.

Toward the end of my second week in New Dorp I got an indication that I might have difficulty in getting an accounting position. A relative of the Hansmanns who dropped down to the beach one day turned out to be a "seasonal" man on the staff of

Price Waterhouse & Co., and he talked to me at some length about public accounting as practiced in America. I had never heard of a seasonal staff, but he explained to me that all the major accounting firms doubled their staffs in the winter months and dismissed their seasonal people in the early spring. He said that it worked fine for him—he worked like a demon for six months of the year, most of the time on an expense account away from New York, and usually loafed for the remainder of the year. He said that as far as I was concerned it would be quite unlikely that any accounting firm would be interested in hiring me in June or July, these usually being the least active months of the entire year. He also pointed out that my experience in Ireland would be of no practical value in a city like New York.

Hugh at this time was working as an insurance agent for the Metropolitan Life Insurance Company on Staten Island. He had started there just a few months before I arrived and already was showing signs of doing well. Hugh was a natural for that kind of job. He was lively and energetic and had an excellent personality. He had unbelievable nerve and always got a thrill out of doing what others thought impossible. He was impulsive and quite erratic at times. Always he was talking about some great "lead" or other. If there is such a thing as a born salesman, Hugh was it.

Exploring in Manhattan

NOT LONG AFTER my conversation with the "seasonal accountant," Hugh suggested that we go exploring in Manhattan. First of all we went to the head office of Metropolitan, where Hugh had a letter of introduction to one of the officials. This was a very leisurely procedure and took most of the forenoon. I filled out an application for "an accounting or clerical position," sat around a good while, saw a couple of people, and ended up in the Medical Department. After a brief examination the doctor said he would have to turn me down, at least temporarily, because I had something wrong with my throat. He was not specific but simply said it appeared to be some kind of infection.

I was discouraged by this, but not Hugh. He said that our going to the head office of Metropolitan was a "trial balloon" and that, as far as he was concerned, being turned down was a blessing in disguise. He said the real future in Metropolitan was not in the head office but in the field.

We had a quick lunch in the Automat and then Hugh suggested we try our hand at one or two accounting firms. He got a classified telephone directory and picked a couple of names which for some reason or other appealed to him. So we went first to one and then to the other. I don't recall the names of the firms. Our experience was exactly the same at each: The telephone operator, who was also the receptionist, told us that the firm was not hiring anyone and suggested that I come back in September and file an application then. At this point it was about 3:30 so we, or rather Hugh, decided to call it a day and head for Staten Island.

Two days later Hugh came home to say he had a marvelous lead to a good job for me—one that was just hand-made. He said one of his calls that day had been with a Mrs. Waldschlagel, whose husband had a life insurance policy with Metropolitan. Hugh said that in chatting with her it had developed that her husband was an auditor with Sinclair Oil Corporation, that he was presently on an assignment in Mexico, and that Mrs. Waldschlagel had promised on his return to ask him to get me an accounting job.

It sounded fantastic to me that any woman could commit her husband to get a job for me, but if there was any doubt in Hugh's mind he certainly failed to show it.

Some days after this Hugh announced at dinner time that he had had a telephone call from Mrs. Waldschlagel to say that her husband had agreed to see Hugh and me at his office at 45 Nassau Street at ten o'clock the next day. So off we went the next morning to Manhattan again. It was pouring from the heavens, but nothing could dampen Hugh's spirits.

A. G. Waldschlagel turned out to be a pleasant individual. He wasted no time. He said he knew all about me from what his wife had told him, and that he had decided to give me an introduction to the only hundred percent CPA he knew—Frederick George Colley of Arthur Young & Company. I had no idea what a "hundred percent CPA" might be except that it conveyed to me an image of perfection. Waldschlagel thereupon picked up the telephone and talked to Mr. Colley. He described me and said it seemed to him I had the makings of a good junior accountant. He exchanged some pleasantries over the phone and ended by asking Colley to do him the favor of seeing me. Colley suggested that I come right over to see Fred Riedell, the firm's office manager, at Room 1413 in 71 Broadway. He said that Riedell would give me an application form to fill out.

So over we went to Broadway, still in a driving rain. I filled out the application form and was immediately ushered in to see Mr. Colley. I handed him the letter of reference I had received from H. B. Brandon & Co. and the letter of introduction from A. G. Waldschlagel. Mr. Colley was gracious. Although he seemed unimpressed with the Brandon letter, which he handed back to me

I meet a "hundred percent CPA"

(presumably because he thought the file would be better without it), he apparently was impressed with Waldschlagel's letter, which he kept. After glancing at my application he asked me to return to the reception room, saying he would call me back in a little while.

In the meantime, Hugh, who had remained in the reception room, had been looking things over. He had inspected the furniture and felt the rug and taken special note of the individuals who were passing in and out of the reception area. He expressed the opinion that Arthur Young & Company was a "high-quality outfit," and he also said he was confident that I would get a job on the strength of Mr. Waldschlagel's letter.

When I returned to Mr. Colley's room a tall, very severe-looking individual was standing at the side of his desk. Mr. Colley introduced him as "my partner, Mr. McGregor" and said they had decided to give me a trial at a salary of $65 a month. Mr. Colley pointed out that this was about £13 a month, and also noted that it was more than I had been earning in H. B. Brandon & Co. Mr. Colley also said that he and Mr. McGregor had decided I could start work the next day. I presume Mr. McGregor agreed with what Mr. Colley said, although he himself said nothing. He just stood there, terribly erect and with a determined look on his face.

I am hired by Arthur Young & Company

AND SO THE FIRST PERIOD in my life came to a close. Omagh and County Tyrone and H. B. Brandon & Co. had now faded far away into the distance. I was about to start on a new and vastly different career. It was June 30, 1921. I was 21 years old.

Prior to 1921 the offices of Arthur Young in various cities, including New York, were local partnerships, conducted more or less independently. In that year they were united into a single partnership under the firm name and style of Arthur Young & Company.

J. C. BURTON: *Arthur Young and the Business He Founded*

CHAPTER FOUR

THE FIRM OF ARTHUR YOUNG & COMPANY IN 1921

At this point in my story I want to make a brief digression, to explain the background of the firm that had just employed me and to give some general idea of what the men who were its partners were like.

I don't really know how Arthur Young & Company compared, in size or reputation, with other public accounting firms in 1921. In those days accountants were not nearly so free to exchange information with one another as they are today. In New York, Arthur Young & Company was undoubtedly one of the top eight or ten accounting firms in the city. In Chicago it probably ranked much higher because of Arthur Young's close association with so many important members of Chicago's business and financial community.

In 1921 the organization had been in existence for twenty-

The beginnings of the firm

seven years. The firm had started in the Monadnock Building in Chicago in 1894 under the name of Stuart & Young, its two partners being Charles Urquardt Stuart and Arthur Young. The beginnings were modest: one office, one stenographer, and capital of $500, of which each partner had put up half. The following year an office was opened in Kansas City, and early in 1896 Arthur Young's brother Stanley, a Glasgow University graduate, came over from Scotland to take charge of this new office. Stanley remained in charge of the Kansas City office, except for about a year in Chicago, until his death in 1915.

During the twelve years to 1906 the firm's work increased slowly but steadily, but Arthur Young did not find Stuart a compatible partner. At Arthur Young's initiative the firm was dissolved in 1906, and the two partners went their separate ways. With his brother Stanley as a partner, Arthur Young then began the firm of Arthur Young & Company, which took over the business of Stuart & Young.

In its initial stages the business of Stuart & Young seems to have been a combination of accounting services, investment services, and the work of general agents. In those days there was a great deal of British money in America. Many British investments were in the form of new ventures—some of them highly speculative—and these gave rise to a good deal of accounting work.

It was a blow to the firm as well as to Arthur Young personally when his brother Stanley died of a brain tumor at the age of 44, just nine years after the new partnership had begun. The first of two operations was performed in December 1914, and Stanley passed away in the following March at the German Hospital in Kansas City.

Despite the separation of Arthur Young and Charles Stuart in 1906 and the death of Stanley Young in 1915, the firm continued to grow. An office was opened in New York in 1907, in Milwaukee in 1908, in Los Angeles in 1920, and in Pittsburgh in 1921. With the rapid growth of the New York office, Arthur Young moved his residence from Chicago to New York in 1917.

I don't know how many people the firm had in its various offices in 1921, but I would guess that the total permanent accounting organization, plus office staff, numbered about a hundred and fifty. This is not a very useful figure for purposes of comparison, however, since in those days most of the junior work was done by temporary staff. For this work, men with bookkeeping experience, regardless of education, were usually preferred to college graduates without experience.

While temporary men were usually hired in the fall and released in the spring, some of them might be rehired for part of the summer if a rush of unexpected work developed. Most of the men with public accounting ambitions could be almost certain of being discharged at the end of their first season. Some went through this experience again at the end of their second season and did not become members of the permanent staff until after their third winter season. Many of the older men worked in public accounting only during the winter and had other employment during the rest of the year.

Although I did not realize it at the time, the year 1921 was an important milestone in the firm's progress. In that year the first national partnership was formed, with eight partners signing the partnership agreement. All these men were British, seven of them having been born in Scotland and one (F. G. Colley) in England.

The first national partnership

Two of them—Arthur Young and Harry Boyack—were bachelors and were to remain so.

Over the years I was to get to know all of these eight men. Some of them I knew better than others, but I knew all of them well enough to have a point of view about them.

Viewed in the context of their time, this group of men made a good team. Like any cross-section of professional people they comprised a wide range of human qualities, but they had certain traits in common. All of them had disciplined themselves to work long hours, often under great pressure; all of them served their clients to the very best of their ability; and all of them had as their prime interest the perpetuation of the firm.

The following brief biographical sketches of these "founding fathers" will, I trust, provide some general idea of what these men were like.

Arthur Young (New York)

ARTHUR YOUNG was 57 in 1921, and it was fifteen years later before I really got to know him. But during the last twelve years of his life—and he was mentally alert almost to the end—I saw a good deal of him. When he was in New York, he used to drop into my office frequently, and he would occasionally write me a letter when he was away. I also spent a couple of weekends with him at his home in Aiken, South Carolina.

Arthur Young was a tall, distinguished, good-looking Britisher who was always casually attired in tweeds and whose gray or white tie always flowed through a silver ring just beneath his collar.

I would say that Arthur Young's outstanding qualities were his business judgment and intelligence, his kindness, his integrity, but above all his energy and enthusiasm for life—this despite the fact that he was completely deaf from his late sixties on and had lost the sight of one eye at about 52. His deafness was hereditary; the loss of sight came as the result of a riding accident, when a horse in front kicked up a small pebble which struck him in the eye.

Born in Glasgow, Scotland, on December 17, 1863, Arthur Young was educated for the Scottish bar, but after a few years with a firm of lawyers he was forced to give up any further thought of a career in law because of his increasing deafness. He emigrated to New York in 1890, at the age of 27, and through letters of introduction became associated with the then well-known international banking firm of Kennedy, Tod & Company. He was with this firm only a few years when the partners, who were quite wealthy, decided to withdraw from business.

Arthur got his start in accounting through the Kennedy, Tod partners, who asked him to go to Chicago to supervise the liquidation of a number of their investments there. He joined forces with Charles Urquardt Stuart, then controller of a large Boston-owned copper company, and together they opened an office in Chicago under the firm name of Stuart & Young.

The following description of Arthur Young in his early manhood was written by James A. McCallum, a prominent Glasgow lawyer, whose early friendship with Arthur continued all through life:

> I did not meet Arthur Young in his school days. I met him when he came up to Glasgow University, and my real contact with him began when he entered the same law office that I had entered about a year before.

He was educated at Glasgow Academy, which was one of the two leading schools in Glasgow, the other being the Glasgow High School, which dated back to mediaeval times and was under the jurisdiction of the Town Council and afterwards of the Education Authority. The Glasgow Academy was a West-end school started by a number of the West-end people who wished to give their sons an education more on public-school lines. Arthur Young in his time was Dux of the school.

I remember perfectly the first occasion on which I set eyes on him. It was in the senior mathematics class in Glasgow University in November 1881, when Arthur Young was called up by the professor at the oral examination to answer a question. Looking around and upwards from one of the front benches where I sat, I saw a huge fair-haired figure, with the most remarkable pair of blue eyes I had ever seen, rise and answer the question.

I was much impressed; but I saw very little of him, as I was finishing my arts course and he was beginning his.

He had a distinguished career at the university, where he took both his arts and his law courses. He was a prizeman in several of the arts classes and took his M.A. Degree in 1883; but he did still better in the Law School, where he took the first prize in the Scots law class and in 1887 took the LL.B. Degree, which was a very good degree, really on an honors standard.

He also was distinguished in athletics. He played in the football (rugby) fifteen and was also chosen to play in the inter-city match between Glasgow and Edinburgh rugby clubs. He was a powerfully built and agile young man, and these qualities, accompanied by his mental alertness and "go," made him an excellent football player. But work was his first consideration, else he might have aspired to international honors.

I had entered A. J. & A. Graham's office (one of the leading solicitor firms in Glasgow) in January 1883, as an apprentice at the end of my arts course. Great was my delight when, rather more than a year later, Mr. Coats of that firm marched into the front room and introduced the new apprentice, Arthur Young, a huge, jolly, good-natured young fellow, full of life and energy, keen at work, and full of fun.

* * *

We became close friends and notwithstanding immense distances have remained so. I was from the far North, a country boy, educated at a country school. Arthur Young was Glasgow born, and his father, Robert Young, was one of the leading shipbrokers and a well-known citizen in Glasgow.

* * *

The Youngs lived in a good house in the West end of Glasgow: 11 Great Western Terrace, which at that time was the furthest west, and its gable windows had a clear outlook to the west.

Arthur Young was destined for the bar and would have been a triumphant success in the legal profession; but unfortunately partial deafness asserted itself before he had gone to the bar, and for a considerable period his career was determined by efforts to find a climate that would be more favorable to checking the progress of the complaint than the west of Scotland, with its liberal allowance of rain. He went to the continent of Europe and spent some time in the Pyrenees. Then he went to Algiers and spent some time in superintending French Estates there. I am sorry that I cannot lay my hands on the letters he wrote me from there. Arthur Young was very observant and had a keen sense of humor.

WILLIAM SUTHERLAND was 43 in 1921, and at that time had been with the firm for eighteen years. He was Arthur Young's right-hand man. Not only was he the firm's administrative partner, but the partnership agreement provided that in the event of Arthur Young's death Sutherland would succeed him as the senior partner of the firm. Sutherland must have carried a very heavy load of

William Sutherland (Chicago)

responsibility, particularly in the early days of the firm. He was severe. He drove himself hard and he expected a great deal from others in the organization. Obviously Arthur Young had great confidence in him and relied heavily on his judgment.

William Sutherland was born near Glasgow, Scotland, and became apprenticed to a Glasgow firm of chartered accountants before he was quite 16. His name came to Arthur Young's attention when Arthur was inquiring about accounting help in Glasgow. After an exchange of letters, Sutherland set out for Chicago in 1903 at the age of 25.

James P. McGregor
(Chicago)

JIM MC GREGOR was 44 in 1921. He was a small, quiet, dignified man who gave the appearance of being quite withdrawn. At the same time, he always gave the impression of being sound and sensible in his judgments.

McGregor was born near Aberdeen, Scotland, and got his training with a firm of chartered accountants in that city. He came to the United States at the age of 26 and after practicing for a few years in New York and Chicago became resident manager of the Chicago office of Deloitte, Plender, Griffiths & Co. He joined forces with Arthur Young & Company in Chicago in 1918.

Frederick G. Colley
(New York)

FRED COLLEY was 49 in 1921 and had been with the firm for over two years. He was a brilliant accountant, but emotional and somewhat erratic. He had tremendous energy and was capable of working long hours without letup. No one could have been more attentive to the needs of his clients. He was particularly interested in systems work, and it was he who designed the forms and procedures for internal use in New York.

Colley did not sit for the CPA examination until he was 40 years old. When he did sit for it in New York he was given a 100 percent rating in each of the four parts of the examination. On two different occasions he showed me his certificate, which was quite distinctive. It had attached to it a blue seal inscribed "100%," and the legend "With Honor" appeared beside the seal. Colley was (and still is) the only New York CPA ever to receive a grade of 100 percent in all four parts of the CPA examination, which he took at one sitting. (This, of course, was why Mr. Waldschlagel had referred to him as a "hundred percent CPA.")

Fred Colley was born in England and emigrated to the United States in 1892, at the age of 20. He had held a variety of positions before he joined Arthur Young & Company in 1918.

HARRY BOYACK was 42 in 1921, and at that time he had been with the firm for fifteen years. He was a sound technician and always one of the most popular of the partners. He had a warm personality and a melodious Scotch voice, and he seemed to go out of his way to be friendly to everyone in the office.

Harry Boyack (Chicago)

A bachelor, Harry Boyack lived simply. He kept to himself from Monday to Friday but spent a good deal of time at his golf club over the weekends.

Harry Boyack was born near Dundee, Scotland, and got his training with a chartered accountant in that city. He emigrated at the age of 27 to join the Chicago staff of Arthur Young & Company.

William D. McGregor
(New York)

WILLIAM D. MCGREGOR was 34 years old in 1921 and had been with the firm for about six years. He was a likable, boisterous, competent Scot with an impressive appearance and a violent temper. McGregor was well thought of by Arthur Young. Not only was Mac an extraordinarily able accountant, but he worked with terrific intensity, always at top speed. No one else in the firm could equal the speed with which he reviewed working papers.

William McGregor was born on the outskirts of Glasgow and received his accounting training with the Glasgow firm of Moores, Carson & Watson. After eight years with this firm he emigrated in 1912 to join the New York staff of Marwick, Mitchell & Co. (now Peat, Marwick, Mitchell & Co.), where he remained until he joined Arthur Young & Company in the fall of 1915.

Thomas H. Clarke
(New York)

TOM CLARKE was 46 in 1921 and had been with the firm for more than two years.

He was an uncomplicated sort of person—sound, sensible, dignified, and restrained. William McGregor told me once that in the early days of the partnership Clarke had been the "balance wheel." He was well liked by his partners and seemed to be temperate in all things.

Tom Clarke was born in Edinburgh, Scotland, and received his training with a firm of chartered accountants in that city. He emigrated in 1910 to join the staff of Marwick, Mitchell & Co. in New York. From 1916 to 1918 Tom was the Clarke in Judson, Higson & Clarke, a small New York accounting firm. After certain negotiations which McGregor promoted, Clarke and Judson joined forces with Arthur Young & Company in November 1918.

JIM BURTON was 35 in 1921, and it was through the efforts of W. D. McGregor that he joined the partnership in April of that year. Mac had described Jim Burton to Arthur Young as the most brilliant accountant he had ever met, and he urged Arthur Young to persuade Jim to join the partnership. McGregor did a great deal for Arthur Young & Company throughout his long years of service, but it is doubtful that anything he did compared in importance with his introducing Jim Burton to Arthur Young.

James Campbell Burton (New York)

Jim's great qualities were his concentration, his quick perception, his sense of organization, his broad-mindedness, and his enormous energy. This combination of qualities made him stand out not only among his partners but also among most of his contemporaries in the accounting profession. Next to Arthur Young, Jim probably contributed more to the firm than any other person.

Jim had a good educational background. In addition to M.A. and LL.B. degrees from Glasgow University, he passed the Scottish chartered accountants' final examination "with distinction." His accounting and business experience prior to joining Arthur Young & Company consisted of five years with Moores, Carson & Watson of Glasgow, three years in the New York office of Marwick, Mitchell & Co., and eight years with Kaufmann's Department Store in Pittsburgh, where he was successively auditor, secretary, and general manager.

*A journey of a thousand miles
begins with one step.*

CONFUCIUS

CHAPTER FIVE

MY FIRST YEAR WITH ARTHUR YOUNG & COMPANY

I STEPPED OFF THE ELEVATOR ON THE fourteenth floor of 71 Broadway at 8:40 a.m. on Friday, July 1, 1921 and took the scene in carefully. The only person in evidence was an office boy. He was leaning over the reception desk with his eyes glued to something that was written on a pad of paper. I told him I was a new employee and asked where I was supposed to go. Without lifting his eyes, he pointed in the direction of what he said was the staff room and then headed off in the opposite direction—still with his eyes fixed on the pad.

My first day at work

The staff room which I went into was a large room with a long table in the center and chairs scattered more or less haphazardly around the floor. The windows at the end of the room looked toward the North River. The walls were completely bare except for one prominent sign which read "NO SMOKING BEFORE 1:30

p.m." The "no" in the sign was in red; the other letters were in black.

At nine o'clock three or four individuals joined me in the room, and by 9:15 a.m. the number had grown to about fifteen. None of the men appeared to have any work to do. They read the morning newspapers and strolled up and down. Some conversed, but I gathered that most of the men were unknown to one another. From time to time the phone rang; always it seemed to be an inquiry for someone who was not there. Once the door opened, and when I looked up I saw the familiar figure of Mr. McGregor framed in the doorway. He glared at everyone for a moment or two and then closed the door with a bang.

The morning went by slowly. At twelve o'clock the man sitting next to me, who had introduced himself as Wilkins, suggested we go to lunch. I welcomed the idea. I was hungry and I wanted to smoke. He said he had eaten at Childs the day before and suggested we go there. So we went to Childs, which was about half a block south of 71 Broadway. We ate the same lunch—a ham sandwich, apple pie, and one cup of coffee—25 cents.

I soon discovered that Wilkins was as ignorant about Arthur Young & Company as I was. He was from London, and he, too, had just started work that morning. He was neatly dressed and had a pronounced English accent.

After lunch we strolled leisurely around the Battery and got back to 71 Broadway shortly after one. Half an hour later everyone was back in the staff room, all looking much more relaxed than they were in the morning. Some of the men started talking to one another. Most of them were now smoking. One man said he had heard that the office would be closed the next day (Saturday), since Monday was the Fourth of July. Nobody else, however, had heard this rumor. Another man said he was going to stay home unless someone specifically asked him to come in.

A few minutes before five o'clock everyone started getting ready to leave, and I followed suit. On the way out I again addressed myself to the office boy and asked him whether the office would be open on Saturday. He said none of the unassigned men would be needed and that I could consider myself free until Tuesday.

THE FOLKS IN NEW DORP were naturally curious about how I had made out on my first day at work in America and plied me with all kinds of questions. When Mr. Hansmann learned how inactive everyone had been he expressed grave doubt about the future of the firm. He even suggested that I might not get paid for Friday, since I had not really reported to anyone. Hugh, however, had concluded that Arthur Young & Company was a high-quality outfit, and so far as he was concerned the matter was closed. Besides, Hugh had a much more important thing to think about that evening. His great preoccupation was the big fight that was to take place at Boyle's Thirty Acres in Jersey City the following afternoon, between Jack Dempsey and Georges Carpentier. The papers had played Carpentier up a great deal but Hugh, who was a staunch Dempsey fan, predicted that Dempsey would demolish the Frenchman in the first round. Hugh had wanted very much to get a ticket for the fight but had not succeeded in doing so. Dempsey, as it turned out, won by a knockout in the fourth round.

The long weekend went by very pleasantly. A large number

A long weekend

of the Hansmanns' relatives came to visit them. The beach was swarming with people, and almost every bungalow had a Victrola which poured out popular music through the screen doors and windows and gave an air of gaiety to the whole beach area.

ON TUESDAY MORNING I was back in the same room at 71 Broadway. Additional men had joined the group and the room was full. Around 9:30 a.m. the telephone started ringing, and soon after this the men began to leave the room very gradually in ones and twos. Wilkins was one of the first to disappear. By 11:30 a.m. there were only four people left, and by 3 p.m. I was the sole occupant of the staff room.

My first assignment

At about four o'clock a man whom I hadn't seen before came into the room, looked around it casually, and then walked slowly over to me. He asked me if my name was Higgins, and when I said it was he introduced himself as Smith. He said that I was to assist him on an audit and that he would meet me at nine o'clock the next morning in our office. He said he would get together some stationery and the previous working papers, and that he and I would walk to the client's office, which was not far away.

When I met Smith the following morning he told me the name of the audit. It was R. E. Dietz Company, manufacturers of lanterns and automotive lighting equipment, at 60 Laight Street.

Smith was pleasant and seemingly good-natured. We walked out the front entrance of 71 Broadway, turned left on Rector Street, and then turned right on Greenwich Street, which we followed for twenty-odd blocks until we came to Laight Street. As we walked Smith gave me a running commentary on New York, its streets and its people. He, too, seemed to know practically nothing about Arthur Young & Company.

The first person we met at R. E. Dietz Company was a Miss Lewis, perhaps about thirty, who seemed to be a combination chief accountant and office manager. Smith, after some pleasantries with her, suggested that I count the petty cash and asked if she would be good enough to introduce me to the custodian.

The contents of the petty cash box seemed to me a complicated maze. It was bulging with coins and bills and letters and IOUs and papers that looked like invoices. I started with the coins. This was a very laborious process because, not being familiar with American money, I had to examine each of the denominations carefully. The custodian, who was elderly, saw my predicament and suggested that I compare my count with the written count he had just made and ask him any questions that occurred to me. This did the trick. With a great feeling of relief I found the petty cash fund O.K. and so reported to Mr. Smith. After this I was in more familiar waters; I reconciled the bank accounts, checked the trial balances of the accounts receivable ledgers, and then tested some of the sales and purchases and other transactions in the profit and loss account. I found the detailed records very interesting. It was exciting to see all the strange places in the world to which Dietz lanterns found their way.

Miss Lewis chatted with me from time to time. One day she talked about the Dietz business. She said the business had been founded by the original Mr. Dietz in 1840 and that it was still controlled by the Dietz family. She also talked to me about Mr. Colley and about the great respect that everyone in Dietz had for him. Miss Lewis said he thought as much of the Dietz business as if it were his own.

On Friday afternoon (July 15th) Smith got a telephone request to come down to 71 Broadway to see Mr. Colley. He told me he would be back at Dietz early the following morning. When we met the next morning Smith said the office was never busier and that there were no staff men in sight anywhere. He said that we had to finish Dietz that day so that he could start another job in Jersey City on Monday and so that I could report to a finance company which was to be audited, under Smith's supervision, by another staff man. Smith said that Mr. Colley had agreed to write the Dietz report himself so as not to delay matters. So Smith and I set to work and cleaned up all the odds and ends and left the Dietz office on that Saturday afternoon about 5:30. I was hot and tired when I reached New Dorp.

The finance company was just a few blocks from 71 Broadway. I met the senior there and I found him a delightful, cheerful fellow. We ate lunch together daily. He had been on the audit of The Texas Company and he talked a good deal about Houston.

One afternoon, after the lapse of about a week, I got a hurried call from the office to come over to see Mr. Colley. I packed up and left immediately. I had not seen him since the day he hired me, some three weeks before. He was in the same gracious, pleasant mood. He asked me if I knew where 42nd Street was. When I said I didn't he told me to cross the street, go down the subway steps opposite 71 Broadway, take any train, and get off at the fourth stop. This, he said, would be 42nd Street or, as most people called the stop, Grand Central. Before I left him he took one of his personal cards from his desk and addressed it to "Mr. Blomqvist,

Uptown to Union Oil

74

Union Oil Co., 17 East 42nd Street, 11th Floor," with the simple message "Introducing Mr. Higgins."

I gave the card to the receptionist at Union Oil Company, and within a matter of minutes Erik Blomqvist appeared. He seemed to be in a great hurry. I thought him impressive. He was tall and clean-cut. His dark hair was parted and well brushed back, although a few unruly hairs came down close to one eye. He was clutching the remaining half of a cigar between his fingers, and on one side of his mouth there was a slight trace of tobacco saliva.

Erik Blomqvist greeted me in a slightly foreign accent. (He was, as I later learned, born in Holland.) He said quickly that the special investigation now in progress was an important one, that I would have a great deal of overtime until it was finished, and that I would, for the most part, be working for a Mr. Corcoran. He thereupon took me along a corridor to a large room where a number of men, including Corcoran, were working. During the next two weeks or so I was to see a great deal of Corcoran. He was a friendly fellow, and through him I began to learn about the preparation of working papers and how to run down information in them.

There were three groups of people working on the Union Oil investigation: representatives of Arthur Young & Company, representatives of another accounting firm which seemed to be working jointly with us, and representatives of the company itself. Since I knew nobody I had difficulty in remembering which people belonged to which group. I never did get them completely straight.

It was a great thrill to be working practically on the corner of 42nd Street and Fifth Avenue, two streets I had heard so much about, and I loved every minute of it. Corcoran and I ate our lunch and dinner together, frequently at the Automat, and I began to feel very much at home. We got on well together.

I am not sure how long I was at 17 East 42nd Street, but one day we suddenly got orders to move our headquarters to 71 Broadway. So downtown we all went—quite a crowd of us—with a terrific pile of working papers. The titles on the working papers impressed me: Union Oil Company of Delaware, Union Oil Company of California, Shell Company of California, Roxana Petroleum Corporation, Ozark Pipe Line Corporation, Matador Petroleum Company, Manhattan Oil Company, and Indian & Central Refining Company.

The work was staffed by three offices—New York, Chicago, and Los Angeles—and was under the supervision of Mr. Colley and J. Gordon Steele, a burly, boisterous Scot who smoked cigarettes constantly and who always referred to Colley (though not in his presence) as "Old Hundred Percent."

One day Corcoran told me that the reason for the Union Oil investigation was that important oil properties were about to change hands. He also said that Colley and a man named Cushny (a supervisor) were to go to London to participate in the final negotiations.

I learned nothing further about the nature of the investigation at that time, but later on someone showed me a clipping from the Tulsa *Tribune* of October 16, 1921, which read as follows:

ST. LOUIS—Negotiations which will make the Royal Dutch interests a powerful factor in the oil industry in this country have been partly concluded, it was learned here yesterday. All doubts about these English, Dutch and French interests being unable to secure sufficient properties in the United States to give them a strong foothold have been dispelled in well-informed circles which were apprised that the deal pending for several months and involving properties of the Union Oil Co. of Delaware had been closed in the last few days.

    The Union Oil Co. is a holding and an operating company controlling complete producing, transportation, refining, marketing and distributing units. . . . The largest operating company of which it holds stock is the Union Oil Co. of California.

    I remember so well the Sunday before Colley and Cushny sailed for England. The work was finished and the working papers were packed in trunks and ready to be sent to the ship. I had little to do that day. Sunday in downtown New York is always a dull day, but that Sunday seemed particularly dull. I listened to the Trinity Church clock toll off each quarter of an hour, and I thought the day would never pass.

A quiet Sunday

    I took a long lunch period and strolled leisurely around the old graveyard of Trinity Church. The graveyard is a lively place in good weather, and sometimes people eat their lunch there. But on that Sunday the graveyard was deserted except for flocks of pigeons which circled round and round the towers of the church.

    The only thing that enlivened that Sunday was an interesting encounter between Colley and Erik Blomqvist. Around three o'clock Blomqvist, in a tremendous hurry, came into the room where three of us were working. He said he was going to make just one more change in one of the working papers. Then he started taking binder after binder out of one of the trunks.

    Just when most of the contents of the trunk were on the floor the door opened and Mr. Colley came in at a sort of half trot. I can still see the expression on his face as he caught sight of the papers on the floor. He stopped dead in his tracks and shouted, at the top of his voice, "Blomqvist, what *are* you doing?" When Blomqvist said he was merely going to make one slight change in a statement Colley virtually shrieked that the curtain was down on all changes, small or large; that under no circumstances would he countenance any further changes; and that he wanted every paper back in the trunk immediately. Colley also added, with biting sarcasm, that the ship could be halfway to England and Blomqvist would still be making changes. With this parting shot Colley left the room, slamming the door behind him.

Blomqvist turned around and looked at the rest of us sheepishly. He said wryly, "Well, boys, it was a good try." Then he began to put the binders back in the trunk, one by one.

So the day came when Colley and Cushny, with all the papers on "Union Oil Company—Special," set sail for England. What a feeling of calm prevailed when this came to pass. No more noise and confusion and agitation. A number of men, including myself, became unassigned. Erik Blomqvist took off for a two-week vacation in the Adirondacks.

I become unassigned

Thus, between July 1st and the middle of August I had worked on three different engagements. On August 15th my salary was increased from $65 per month to $85 per month. I began to feel I was getting established.

THINGS WERE QUITE DULL for some weeks, and the number of unassigned men increased. One morning the office manager, Fred Riedell, told me that the firm was moving over the Labor Day weekend from 71 Broadway to 82 Beaver Street and asked that I help out another staffman, named Maloy, in rearranging certain working papers in contemplation of the move. So in I went to the file room. Maloy was perched on top of a stepladder reviewing the contents of working-paper binders, and another staffman was holding the ladder and taking binders as Maloy handed them down to him. Maloy seemed to be enjoying his task thoroughly. He called down that if he found anything really interesting in a report he would read it to us. So from time to time he read interesting pieces to us with great deliberation. One morning, with a great whoop of delight, he found a $100 error in a footing in a typed report. He asked the other staffman if he thought Mr. Colley would give him a salary increase for finding the error. The staffman said his chances of an increase would be improved if he could find a much bigger error, say a million dollars.

So in a very leisurely, casual manner Maloy, with our assistance, "rearranged" the files. I'm not sure what the "rearranging" really consisted of, but Maloy was firm in his conviction that the three of us were performing a useful service.

On the Thursday before Labor Day Riedell requested all unassigned men to be present on Saturday to help in the move. Wilkins, who was sitting next to me in the staff room, whispered to me that he had come to America to learn something about public accounting and not about how to move from one building to another. He told me he'd be damned if he would have anything to do with the move. I did not feel nearly so independent, so I decided to report, as usual, on the Saturday before Labor Day.

On Saturday I went directly to 71 Broadway, but finding everything in a state of great confusion I strolled over leisurely to 82 Beaver Street. There, things were even more confused. Riedell, who was the captain of the entire operation, had his coat off, and

The move to Beaver Street

with a cigarette clutched between two fingers was running up and down shouting instructions to the movers and everyone else who came anywhere close to him. I decided that the further I kept from Riedell the better it would be for me. So I avoided Riedell and everyone else and at four o'clock took off for Staten Island and what was left of the Labor Day weekend.

I thought that was the end of the move so far as I was concerned, but it was not quite. Fully five weeks later Riedell came after me one day with fire in his eye. In a loud voice he told me that through my carelessness an entire shelf of working papers had not been moved from 71 Broadway. He said that Mr. Colley was ripping mad and would certainly have plenty to say to me. I told Riedell that nobody had said that it was my job to see that all the working papers were moved, but he brushed that reply aside as "nonsense." Happily, Colley never talked to me about the matter.

After Labor Day I and a great many others continued unassigned. There were several salary cuts at this time and a number of people were dropped.

Years later I talked to Jim Burton about this situation. He explained that in the years after the war the salaries of many staffmen had got completely out of line, and that it was decided in the fall of 1921 to face up to the matter and make reductions. Jim also told me that, as things had turned out, he personally felt it had been a mistake to make so many cuts. As might be expected, a number of men left shortly after their salaries were cut.

SOMETIME IN THE FALL OF 1921 Riedell assigned me to work in the report department. Fitzroy D. Maclean, now a partner in

Haskins & Sells, was in charge of the checkers. Mac was young and energetic, and he and I got on well together. That association started a friendship which has continued to this day.

In the report department

The boys and girls in the report department were an interesting group, two of them in particular. Both of these boys were of Irish extraction, although temperamentally they were about as far apart as any two human beings could be. They were about twenty years old.

Johnny, as I'll call him, had been an office boy in the cashier's department, and he was popular with everyone. He was small and dark-haired, with the bluest of blue eyes. He dressed carefully, and his hair, which was parted in the middle, was always brushed back with a plentiful supply of hair oil. Mr. Colley liked Johnny and apparently decided to promote him to the report department. Johnny, however, hated the report department and everything connected with it, and wished he were an office boy again. He was a ladies' man and almost every night took off for a dance in some part of the city. In the morning he was always full of stories about the previous night's experiences and romances. He used to sing "When Frances dances with me, holy gee!" accompanying himself with a kind of tap dance.

In those days the report department consisted of three rooms. Ernest Ovens, who was in charge of the department, occupied the first room, which was very small. It had two doors, one leading into another small room where two stenographers sat, the other leading into the room where the checkers worked. Another door in the checkers' room opened into the statistical typists' room. When the door to Ovens's room was closed, Johnny entertained us with songs and with detailed descriptions of the girls who brightened his nights. Finally the day came when Johnny went in to tell Ovens that he disliked the report department and wanted to be an office boy again. Ovens tried to dissuade him, but he made no impression whatever on Johnny. The upshot of the discussion was that Johnny quit.

Peter, as I'll call him, was entirely different. He was not good looking. In addition to having an unhealthy complexion he had a nervous habit of blinking his eyes. He was always very serious, and sometimes when you caught him unawares he seemed to be completely in a trance. Ovens and some of the people in the report department said he had a brilliant mind, but Johnny thought he was what he called a "goof."

Peter had a phobia about time reports. He was always the last one in the department to submit his report, and the report would get done only if someone sat beside him as he prepared it. Time after time Ovens would open the door and call out, "Peter, will you for God's sake get your time report in." Peter would say, "Right away, Mr. Ovens," and immediately dash over to a drawer to get a time report blank. He would write down his name and the period covered by the report, but this done, his pen would rest on the blank. If nobody bothered Peter the pen would rest there for hours. Periodically he would make a pretense of looking up information for the report, rushing back to his desk with great gusto and grabbing his pen; but then the pen would simply sit there, unmoving, on the paper. Finally Ovens would come in and sit beside Peter and volunteer to help him. But Peter did not really need help, for as soon as Ovens sat beside him he completed the report with no apparent difficulty.

One day Ovens asked Peter if he was worried about something, and Peter admitted that he was. He said he had passed a major "bull" in an important report and could not get the matter out of his mind. Peter could remember nothing about the report except that he thought it was a report on a client of Mr. McGregor's. This intrigued Ovens, so he and Peter started going over all the recent reports on McGregor's clients. After three days' search Ovens decided that the "bull" was simply a figment of Peter's imagination, and Peter was dropped.

I ran into Peter about a year later. He was coming along Broad Street near J. P. Morgan's. I chatted with him and he inquired about all the people at 82 Beaver Street. When I asked him what he was doing, he said he was teaching in a high school in Brooklyn. It was the last time I saw Peter.

I HAD A FRIGHTENING EXPERIENCE in the report department one day. We had a rush job for Mr. Colley. It consisted essentially of a set of detailed consolidated financial statements, the balance sheet containing about twelve columns in all. In addition to an elimination column there was also a column for "proposed refinancing adjustments." It was about 9:30 a.m. when Ovens opened his door to say impatiently that Mr. Colley could not wait much longer for his statements, that he had his hat and overcoat on and wanted to take the statements personally to his client—who, Ovens emphasized, was a very important one. At this point the statements had been compared and referenced, and I was to check the footings. Every few minutes the door opened and Ovens would say the same thing: "For God's sake, Higgins, how much longer will you be?" Finally I checked the last "down" column, so the

A million-dollar error

statements were bound up and Ovens rushed off with all copies except the office copy. Under the pressure I had decided not to check the "cross" footings, so when Ovens disappeared I took the office copy and started to check these. Everything went fine on the assets side, but much to my dismay one cross footing on the liability side was off by $1,000,000. There was no doubt about it. I checked the footing from right to left and from left to right. I was petrified.

Just at that point Ovens opened his door to say that Mr. Colley also wanted the office copy of the statements, and he grabbed it from me. I didn't know what to do at this point, so I decided to smoke a cigarette and appraise the situation. There was a large men's room on one of the lower floors of 82 Beaver Street, and it was there that most of our forenoon smoking was done. It was a friendly place, and there were always a number of staffmen there between 9:30 and 10 a.m. On this particular morning I lingered there a good while.

Although I thought and thought about my problem, I could not think of anything constructive to do about it. I wondered how long it would be before the $1,000,000 error was discovered. I also wondered where the offsetting error was. I decided to say nothing to anyone and await the storm. Every time Ovens's door opened, particularly if it opened suddenly, I thought the crisis had come. But nothing happened and the day passed quietly. The next day came and I arrived in the office fully convinced that all hell would break loose. Every time Ovens's door opened I jumped, but nothing whatever happened. I wondered why at least the office copy of the report did not come back. But again the day passed without incident.

When I arrived at work the next morning it was evident that something had happened. All copies of the report were on the table in front of Johnny, who was already tearing up all but one copy. I tried to be casual about the matter and tentatively asked Johnny what he thought he was doing. Johnny said that the entire refinancing plan had been changed and that a lot of reclassifications also were made in the individual companies. He said that the whole thing had to be retyped and that it was a great pain in the neck to him.

I don't know whether anyone ever noticed the $1,000,000 error that gave me so much concern. I never heard a peep about it, nor did I ever mention it to anyone. The report was retyped within the day and delivered without incident. What a feeling of relief I had when my problem disappeared. That experience was good for me. I decided there and then that, regardless of pressures, I would never again release anything with which I was not completely satisfied.

THE RULE prohibiting smoking before 1:30 p.m. made every morning in the report department drag. Saturday mornings, however, always seemed worse than other mornings. This was so mainly because we usually worked right through to one or one-thirty, so that we could quit for the day if no rush jobs were under way.

The "no smoking" rule

I don't know how long the "no smoking" rule was in effect in New York office. I think it died out gradually, by default, a year or two after I started with the firm.

This is the rule as it appeared in the little New York Staff Manual then in use:

> Members of the staff are not allowed to smoke in the offices of clients where the clients' own employees are not allowed to smoke. Smoking in our own office is not permitted until after luncheon. It is in all cases expected that employees will not smoke to excess during business hours, either in their own office or in the office of a client.

In the cashier's department

ONE DAY IN JANUARY 1922, Ovens said that Mr. Colley wanted me to help out in the cashier's department (in effect, the bookkeeping department) for a few months. He did not go into details so I cleaned up what I was working on and went around to the cashier's department to report to Riedell. Riedell in turn introduced me to a Miss O'Grady, who was in charge of the department.

There were three people in the department: Isabelle O'Grady, about 27; James Winchester, about 22; and Nathan Dimond, about 19. Fred Riedell had his desk in the cashier's department but really had nothing to do with the details except to convey requests from the partners from time to time for various information. In the days I'm speaking of Fred Colley was very close to the department and had a keen interest in all the details of its operations.

Winchester's main responsibility was keeping the time ledgers and preparing bills for clients. Dimond's main responsibility was the preparation of the payroll and the various details connected with that work.

Colley had hired Winchester in 1918, and I think he liked him. He had promised Jimmy a position on the audit staff after a few years' experience, and the reason for my transfer, I soon learned, was so that Jimmy could be released for the audit staff.

Jimmy Winchester and I worked together for about a week

before he left the department. He was a grand fellow and we got on well together. Jimmy had been born in Scotland and came to America as a child. He lived with his parents in Mineola, Long Island, and I recall spending a weekend with his family early in 1922. Mrs. Winchester had arranged a house party for the Saturday night of my visit, and I suppose there must have been somewhere between ten and twenty boys and girls at the party. It was my first such party in America, and I had a grand time.

When I started in the cashier's department Nathan Dimond had already been there about a year and a half. As it turned out, he was not to be there much longer. His departure came about with dramatic suddenness just a few weeks after my transfer. The crisis came on a Saturday.

About eleven o'clock I overheard Riedell say to Dimond that Mr. Colley had asked him to make sure that Dimond completed the payroll statement he had requested by nine o'clock Monday morning. I don't know exactly what the statement was, but I gathered it was some special statistical information that Mr. Colley wanted. Dimond said he could not complete the statement on that Saturday because he had a dentist's appointment at two-thirty near his home in Brooklyn, which meant that he had to leave the office not later than one o'clock. Riedell glared at Dimond and said couldn't he cancel the appointment, but Dimond said he could not, since it was hard to get an appointment and one of his teeth was bothering him. Riedell said heatedly that Mr. Colley would take no excuses and that Dimond must know this as well as he did. Riedell also added that if Mr. Colley did not get his statement on Monday morning Dimond could assume that he had been fired. Despite Riedell's threat Dimond kept his dentist's appointment.

I had assumed that Riedell's threat was passing emotion, but I was wrong. Although I did not know it, Riedell apparently talked to Colley on Saturday afternoon, and Colley presumably agreed that Dimond should be dropped.

When I got into the office on Monday morning Riedell and Dimond were already there, both working at their desks. Around 9:15 Mr. Colley came into the cashier's department. He raised his eyebrows in amazement as he caught sight of Dimond, and looking at Riedell he spluttered out, "Riedell, what is Mr. Dimond doing here? You know he resigned from our organization on Saturday." Riedell, clearly embarrassed, stuttered a good bit and then said that Dimond was waiting for his salary check. Colley's rejoinder was that the delay was inexcusable and that Mr. Dimond's check should be prepared immediately. With this exchange Colley stalked out of the room.

Riedell asked Isabelle O'Grady hurriedly to prepare Dimond's check, and when he got it he rushed out of the room to get Colley's signature on it. Dimond started to put on his hat and overcoat. When he got his check he said goodbye to Isabelle and me, and away he went. I never saw him again.

When Dimond had gone, Isabelle O'Grady opened fire on Riedell. She said it was ridiculous to fire anyone on such short notice at the busiest time of the year and that Dimond was a first-class worker and would be missed very much. She also told Riedell that he need not ask her to finish the payroll statement for Mr. Colley for she would have no part of it and, furthermore, if he wanted to fire her that would be just fine with her.

Riedell did not argue. He said he understood her feelings and that he personally would prepare the information for Mr. Colley with Jimmy Winchester's help. So Jimmy spent a few evenings in the cashier's department, and Mr. Colley finally got his statement.

ABOUT APRIL 1922 Isabelle O'Grady told me she was leaving the firm at the beginning of the summer to get married, and that she was going to ask Mr. Colley to let me have her position. I said I had no interest in working directly for Mr. Colley but she said that Colley, apart from his occasional nervous outbursts, was perfectly all right and well-intentioned. Isabelle said the job would be a good one for me, and she also said she would see to it that I understood everything about the job before she left.

Nothing more was said about the matter then, and things followed their normal course from day to day. In the meantime, things slowed up on the staff and more and more men were laid off. Jimmy Winchester lasted till May and then he too was dropped.

The uncertainty of staff life impressed me, and as the date of Isabelle O'Grady's departure drew near I began to develop an interest in the position of cashier. Finally one day Mr. Colley talked to me. He told me that Miss O'Grady was keen on my getting her position, that he thought it would be excellent experience for me, and that he personally would help me in any way he could. For the first time I realized that Colley had a streak of kindness in him. I told him that I appreciated his confidence in me, and thanked him.

I become cashier

So the day came when Isabelle O'Grady, in a very happy frame of mind, left to be married. She wrote me a letter a week after she left and sent me a copy of *If Winter Comes*, a popular novel of the day, and that is the last I ever heard of Isabelle.

*This famous Island great and grand
Where Thoreau wandered on its strand,
Where dwelt Ralph Waldo Emerson,
And Curtis's greatest work was done;
Where Garibaldi spent some years,
And Jenny Lind felt hopes and fears;* . . .

*Behold this Isle beside the sea,
It also shelters you and me.*

VERNON B. HAMPTON: From "Staten Island" (1925)

CHAPTER SIX

GETTING ESTABLISHED IN AMERICA

At the end of my first year with Arthur Young & Company our family was well on its way to being established in America. Father, Hugh, Beth, and I all had positions which, as things turned out, we were to hold for the rest of our working days.

Father, considering that he was 53, was more than fortunate. He had become active in a church on Staten Island and through one of its members got a position in Sailors Snug Harbor, a well-known home for old seamen. This position, which followed two or three unsatisfactory ones of short duration, suited Father to a T. The environment was congenial and leisurely, and he had plenty of time to read and move around and listen to the never-ending tales of the old men of the sea.

New roots for the Higgins family

Snug Harbor is a grand institution. It has a large estate on Staten Island with fifty-odd buildings. It was founded in 1801 through the will of Captain Robert Richard Randall, who left his 21-acre Manhattan farm to establish it, with the stipulation that the farm was never to be sold. The income from the property enables the Harbor to make old mariners very comfortable in their declining years.

Beth and Mother had arrived from Ireland in May 1922. Soon afterward, Hugh succeeded in getting Beth a position in the head office of Metropolitan Life Insurance Company. Hugh himself was doing well with Metropolitan. His energy, personality, and eternal optimism were standing him in good stead as an insurance salesman.

As for myself, I seemed to be getting a fairly firm footing in Arthur Young & Company. By July 1, 1922 I knew most of the people in the New York office. My salary at this time was $100 per month.

AS ONE MIGHT EXPECT, Hugh met a variety of people day after day in his business of selling insurance. At dinner every night, we had a blow-by-blow description of his triumphs and failures. Regardless of the fortunes of the day, however, Hugh was never discouraged.

One day in the late fall of 1921 Hugh ran into a Belfast man who owned a large home on Todt Hill Road in Staten Island but usually took his family into Manhattan for the winter. Hugh went to see the house, and he described it to us in rapturous terms at dinner that night. Within a matter of days Hugh had rented the Belfast man's house for the winter.

The Hansmanns came to see the house, and so did a couple by the name of Pierce who owned a bungalow at New Dorp Beach near the Hansmann's bungalow and who spent the winter months in an apartment in Jersey City. All of them liked the house. The Pierces suggested that they spend the winter with Hugh and Maudie instead of going to Jersey City.

So the outcome was that Hugh, Maudie, their two-year-old son, the Pierces, and I all spent the winter of 1921-1922 in the house on Todt Hill Road. The arrangement worked out well, at least for me, and I have pleasant memories of that winter. The Todt Hill Road area at that time was one of the loveliest parts of Staten Island.

A winter on Todt Hill Road

The Pierces had no children, and I imagine they were both close to 50 years old at that time. Mrs. Pierce had had tuberculosis in her younger days and was very health-conscious. She drank milk and ate cheese and rested a lot. She was a little roly-poly woman with a splendid appetite.

Mr. Pierce was a Vermonter and an altogether wonderful person. Everybody liked him. He was strongly built and erect, with firm features. He kept his gray hair carefully brushed back and he had a pleasant drawl. He loved cigars.

I thought Mr. Pierce one of the best-adjusted persons I had ever met. He was with a shoe concern in Manhattan and I think had spent most of his working days there. He had read a good deal, and he talked about American history and about his New England background. He was an excellent conversationalist, and I always enjoyed listening to him.

Pierce was a thoughtful fellow. One day he bought me a ticket to hear John Philip Sousa's band at the old Hippodrome. In Omagh, the band of the Royal Inniskilling Fusiliers used to play a great many Sousa marches, so naturally Sousa was one of my very special heroes. I never thought I would have an opportunity to see him.

The Hippodrome was crowded on the night of the concert. The band struck up "The Stars and Stripes Forever" and everyone in the house stood up and cheered, and for fully five minutes the music was lost in the cheering.

We had a grand time that Christmas season. In addition to the Pierces and the Hansmanns and myself, Maudie's brother Joe also joined us on Todt Hill Road. Hugh had managed to get some Scotch whisky for the occasion. He said it wasn't the regular bootleg stuff but the real thing, right off the boat. He said it had cost him plenty, "but better safe than sorry."

So Maudie played the piano and Hugh clowned and everyone sang to his heart's content. Joe had been badly gassed in the war and always showed the effects. He had spent a long time in hospitals and always breathed in short, quick gasps. He was a big, broad-shouldered fellow but he was only a shell, and he died while he was still relatively young.

But despite his disability, Joe thoroughly enjoyed himself that night. He agreed that the Scotch was certainly high-quality stuff and better than he had had in a long, long time.

SO THINGS WERE GOING WELL at home, and things were also going well at Arthur Young & Company. I was getting familiar with New

York, and I was getting to like the city. My favorite eating places, all modest in price, were Childs, the Automat, and the Exchange Buffet.

Some of the present generation may never have heard of the Exchange Buffet. It used to operate a chain of cafeterias on the "honor system" and was quite popular in my younger days. Patrons selected their food from counters, ate it at tables or at stand-up counters, and on the way out told the cashier what they had eaten. Some of our more cynical staffmen used to say that the initials of the Exchange Buffet stood for "Eat 'em and Beat 'em." Undoubtedly some of them treated the honor system pretty casually.

I was in charge of the cashier's department of Arthur Young & Company's New York office for some three years. Mr. Colley had said that this kind of work would be good experience for me. I doubted it at the time, but as I look back on it now I think he was right. Certainly I needed some kind of seasoning to change my small-town outlook and to give me some measure of motivation. I am sure I had practically no motivation when I started in the cashier's department early in 1922, but I am equally sure that I had a great deal of motivation three years later. By some means or other I became inspired by everything I saw and heard around the office.

My work as cashier

My job as cashier was an interesting one. I had contacts with everyone in the office, from the office boys to the partners, and I had a fairly good sense of what was going on from day to day in the New York office. As my first duty of the day I opened the incoming mail and read both it and the previous day's outgoing mail. This done, I assembled the mail and placed it on the large conference table in Arthur Young's room, where the partners perused it before tackling the problems of the day.

Fred Riedell left the firm at the end of 1922 and was not replaced. Strangely enough, I recall none of the circumstances of his leaving. Part of his work was taken over by Ernest Ovens and part by myself, but probably most of the load was assumed by Jim Burton. At this time Jim had been with the firm some twenty-one months and was already making himself very much felt in most of the things around the office. Fred Colley still continued to supervise the cashier's department, but Jim had taken charge of assignments and of the hiring and firing of staff.

The firing of staff was a fairly routine matter, particularly with temporary men. Jim Burton would prepare a list of the men to be dropped and give it to Ovens, who in turn would give it to a stenographer who typed the customary letter for each man. This letter was to the effect that the firm regretted it could use the man's services no longer and that a check for a certain amount was enclosed to pay the man to a specified date. While the letters were being typed I prepared the checks and had them signed by one of the partners. As soon as I got the letters I started looking for the men to deliver the bad news. When they saw me coming they usually knew the score. Many of them had been through that same experience at least once before.

FOR MOST OF THE YEARS I knew him, Fred Colley was active in the Episcopal Church. In the early 1920s he lived on the upper West Side in a house close to the church of which he was a parishioner. He and the rector of his church saw a great deal of each other.

Colley became interested in the restoration of Lincoln Cathedral in England, which was very old and in poor physical condition. An American committee was formed to raise funds for repairs, and if I remember rightly Fred Colley was a member of the committee. I recall our unassigned staff mailing all kinds of fund-raising literature about the Cathedral to potential contributors. The staff for the most part did not like this chore and used to say to one another, "Why should we give a hoot if Lincoln Cathedral crumbles to ruins?"

I recall the Dean of the Cathedral, Dr. Fry, coming into our office with his wife one day to see Fred Colley. They were a splendid old couple. The Dean had a white beard, which I thought gave him a fine patriarchal look. I met them because Colley had asked me to take them over to J. P. Morgan & Company to open a bank account.

I am not sure how successful the American drive for the restoration of Lincoln Cathedral was. The Dean raised $30,000 on his first visit, but I never heard how he made out when he returned to America the following year.

One day Colley went with the Dean to visit Bishop Manning at the Cathedral of St. John the Divine, but he found the visit disappointing. Colley told me later that the Bishop was not as enthusiastic about the restoration of Lincoln Cathedral as they had hoped he would be. The Bishop pointed out that he had ambitions for his own great cathedral in New York and felt it had to be uppermost in his thoughts.

Around this time Colley became friendly with the Reverend

Fred Colley, the Dean, and the "Bishop"

William Wilkinson, then a well-known figure in the downtown area. Wilkinson was popularly known as "the Bishop of Wall Street" because of the outdoor sermons which he delivered at noon each day, usually from the steps of the Sub-Treasury Building. The "Bishop" had been holding forth to the financial community at this time for about thirty years. I don't know how Fred Colley got to know him, but he used to drop into our office on Beaver Street from time to time to see Colley, frequently unannounced. The "'Bishop" was in his seventies and quite diffuse, and Colley was not always in the mood to see him. I recall one visit in particular when, quite by accident, I happened to see Colley fleeing in panic through the connecting doors of the partners' offices to avoid the "Bishop."

Tom Clarke becomes administrative partner in New York

IN THE FALL OF 1923 I became aware of two important organizational moves: (1) Tom Clarke became administrative partner of the New York office, and (2) the firm entered into a joint partnership agreement with Broads, Paterson & Co., chartered accountants of London, England.

The need for an administrative partner in New York had been clear for about three years. Alexander J. Baxter was in effect the administrative partner in New York until he left the firm at the end of 1920. When, a few months previously, he made known his desire to retire, Arthur Young's idea was that W. D. McGregor should succeed to Baxter's position. Mac, however, advised against this on the grounds that it would not be acceptable to either Colley or Clarke, each of whom was older than McGregor. That was the time when McGregor first talked to Arthur Young about approaching Jim Burton to join the partnership.

I don't imagine Colley was too happy about Clarke's being named administrative partner—if for no other reason than the fact that, as part of the change, Colley and Clarke were to switch offices. I happened to be in Colley's office when the move was being made, and I know that Colley was in anything but an amiable mood.

As I look back on it now, it was probably unfair to Tom Clarke to ask him to take the top spot in New York under Arthur Young. Clarke's health was not good (he had suffered from allergies for years, and in the 1920s he became troubled with ulcers), and he had a group of unusually strong-willed and opinionated partners to contend with in the New York office. The situation, however, was made a good deal easier for Clarke because Jim Burton was already emerging as a strong individual in the firm, and he and Clarke had been close personal friends for years. They had worked together in Marwick, Mitchell & Co., where they became managers on the same day (in the spring of 1912) and shared the same office.

So far as the arrangement with Broads, Paterson was concerned, this was announced officially on November 20, 1923. The announcement stated that the firms of Arthur Young & Company and Broads, Paterson & Co., 1 Walbrook, London, had formed a partnership to practice accounting in Continental Europe under the firm name of Arthur Young, Broads, Paterson & Co.; that an office had been opened at Dorland House, 13 and 15 Rue Taitbout, Paris; and that the Paris office would be managed by Charles Judson.

A partnership on the Continent

Charles Judson was an English chartered accountant who in 1923 was a local partner in the New York office. He had come to America in 1908 to join Marwick, Mitchell & Co. In 1915 he started a practice in New York in partnership with another Englishman named Higson, and some time later Tom Clarke joined them to make the firm Judson, Higson & Clarke. As mentioned earlier, Clarke and Judson joined forces with Arthur Young & Company in 1918.

Charles Judson looked older than his years. He was corpulent, stooped, and studious. He looked more like a professor than a practicing accountant, and in fact several of his clients were colleges. He was withdrawn and quiet, and had a great interest in mathematics.

Shortly after the formation of the national partnership in 1921 Judson, who was a bachelor, began to talk of retiring. When he learned about the joint international firm he volunteered to open an office in Paris and stay for a year or two. It was understood that London would take over supervision of the Paris office when Judson left. This happened a year or so afterward.

When the international partnership was formed there were seven Arthur Young & Company offices in the United States: New York, Chicago, Kansas City, Milwaukee, Los Angeles, Pittsburgh, and Dallas.

IN THOSE DAYS, tax practice was not a very important part of the New York office's work. There were only two or three people in the New York tax department. Apparently there was little expectation that the tax practice would grow, for the decision was reached that "a high-grade man" would be assigned to the New York tax department so that Charles Trobridge, who was then in charge of the department, "could get more into general accounting work."

There is a Lady sweet and kind,
Was never face so pleased my mind;
I did but see her passing by,
And yet I love her till I die.

From an English song
attributed to Robert Herrick

CHAPTER SEVEN

ENGAGEMENT AND MARRIAGE

I**N THE SUMMER OF 1924 I HAD ROUNDED** out three years in America, so I decided to pay a visit to Ireland. There was incentive for doing so, for I had been corresponding regularly with Madge Corker, and I wanted to see her.

It was a simple thing to make an overseas trip in those days. There was no trouble getting passage on any ship, and there was no trouble getting leave from the firm because most summers were very slack periods.

A trip to Ireland

The Anchor Line ships were convenient for anyone going to County Tyrone. All ships sailing to Glasgow usually made a call at Moville on the northwest tip of Ireland.

So on August 21, 1924, I boarded the S.S. *California* to begin what was to prove a very pleasant trip. Most of the other passengers were of Scottish birth, and practically all of them were returning to Scotland for a visit after many years' absence. They were all in grand spirits. I don't suppose there is anything that quite compares with a ship full of people returning for a holiday in their native land.

The trip was leisurely, and we anchored off the Donegal coast a little over a week later, at one o'clock in the night. A tender came out to pick up the Irish passengers, and I still remember how cold it was on that small boat as it pitched back and forth in the darkness. It was two or three hours before the tender got under way. As it finally moved away, the passengers leaning over the rail on the *California* sang "Will ye no come back again?"

I spent almost three weeks in Omagh that summer of 1924. Although it was just three years since I had emigrated, there were already quite a few changes in the town. One of the most noticeable, to me at any rate, was that H. B. Brandon & Co. had split in two after H. B. Brandon's death in 1923. Madge had continued with H. B. Brandon & Co. after I left, and in 1924 she was with the part of the firm that had retained the Brandon name. She had arranged to take her vacation while I was in Omagh, so we saw a good deal of each other.

Madge Corker and I become engaged

A week or so after I arrived in Omagh Madge and I became engaged. Although we had not discussed marriage during our three-year correspondence, this development was hardly unexpected. I suppose it may seem strange that a three-year correspondence could lead to marriage plans, but it must be remembered that Madge and I had known each other since childhood.

THE CORKER HOUSE in 1924 was a busy place. The household included Mr. and Mrs. Corker, their four children—Madge (the eldest), Gertrude (or "Bobbie," as she preferred to be called),

Winifred, and Fred—and a dark-haired, ruddy-faced, vigorous maid. Mrs. Corker's sister, who was a nurse, was also in and out of the house a good deal.

In those days, before the advent of radio and television, the piano was the great source of enjoyment. Madge and Bobbie both played well, and evening after evening we all sang with great gusto. Tea was the popular beverage, and all of us (except Madge's father, who preferred stout) drank it continuously and in great quantities.

I got on well with Madge's family. We had, of course, a great deal in common; we knew just about everybody in Omagh, and we never tired of talking about them, and about the old days.

The Corker family

The Corker family was officially Methodist, but only the children attended Methodist services regularly. Mrs. Corker had been brought up in the Episcopal faith, and she frequently went to the evening service in the Church of Ireland, accompanied by one or two of her daughters.

Mr. Corker had a loyalty to the Methodist Church but very seldom attended the services. He liked nothing at all about the Church of Ireland and tended to be critical of the people who went there.

Mr. Corker was Omagh's Town Clerk, and as such he was just about the best-known person in the town. Omagh to him was the world. He knew the town in a way that few people did—its interesting nooks and corners and its odd characters. He never seemed to have the slightest desire to leave the town, not even on vacations. About the only concession he ever made to the need for a holiday was to go occasionally with some of his companions to the races at the Curragh, near Dublin.

Madge's father was a big man physically, and he had tremendous strength in his hands. He was proud of the fact that his hat, which he wore on the back of his head, was the largest-sized hat in Omagh.

At the time Madge and I became engaged Mr. Corker was around 50 years old and in excellent health. Mrs. Corker also was in good health.

Practically everybody in Omagh went for long walks. There was really very little else to do. In those days there were very few automobiles, and of course everything was shut up tight on Sundays.

Often on Sundays Mr. Corker and his good friend P. J. O'Callaghan, the manager of the Omagh Gas Company, would take off for a long walk over the hills and up to the mountains. I went with them a few times and thoroughly enjoyed their companionship and the country. O'Callaghan, a great big long-legged man who came from County Cork, loved dogs and as a hobby reared Irish setters. When he came back from Mass on Sunday morning, he and Mr. Corker and three or four of the Irish setters would usually start out on their jaunt. As they walked through the town the church bells clanged in confusion and the dogs yelped with delight.

It's grand to get out into the country in Ireland early in the morning. Rain is never very far off, and there is a greenness and a freshness about everything. Things have changed very little since the days when I was a boy. There is still the familiar tang of turf smoke from the cottages, and the bluish tint of the mountains in the distance.

This visit of mine to Ireland, when I was 24 years old, was in a sense a sentimental journey. I visited all the people I used to know and all the places I used to frequent. The Brandon office and the offices of the old clients all looked exactly the same.

A sentimental journey

One day I visited the grave of Reggie Parkinson in Omagh Cemetery. Reggie had been our bandmaster. A year or so before I emigrated, he had died unexpectedly of influenza at a relatively young age. His grave was on a slope of ground behind the mortuary chapel. I looked at the wreaths and saw the one that we—the members of the band—had given. The writing was faded and blurred but still legible. I remembered the day of the funeral service, when the band had stood in a circle around the grave and played "Abide with Me."

During my visit I spent a weekend in Dervock, primarily to see something of Grandfather Thomas Higgins, and I also spent a day in Aughnacloy where I visited my mother's uncle and guardian, John Cave, in a rest home. Grandfather at that time was 79; John Cave was 82.

One of the clients I called on was P. J. O'Callaghan. This call turned out to be unfortunate because I agreed, at O'Callaghan's urging, to keep a watchful eye on an Irish setter which he was shipping on the *Cameronia*, the boat on which I was returning to America. It sounded simple as he explained it, but I had a good deal of trouble getting the dog through customs in New York and then shipping it to its destination in Arkansas.

MY ENGAGEMENT changed my outlook on life. The future now was a matter of much more immediate concern to me, and I realized that I had to get on the audit staff as soon as possible.

Madge and I had not set a date for our wedding, but it was understood that it would take place in Omagh Methodist Church in about two years.

I talked to Jim Burton and Fred Colley, and they agreed to my going on the staff as soon as a suitable successor could be found for the job of cashier. This took time; in fact, it was more than a year before I got on the permanent staff. In the meantime I enrolled in a correspondence course in accounting with the Walton School of Commerce in Chicago.

On the audit staff

My first assignment was in the summer of 1925. This was a proposed merger of a number of ice cream companies throughout New York State. I don't recall how many companies there were, but I remember that we had men in Elmira, Amsterdam, Rochester, Albany, Niagara Falls, Buffalo, Malone, Syracuse, and Schenectady.

I was assigned with a senior to the company in Niagara Falls. It was a pleasant engagement, even though we put in a considerable amount of overtime.

I recall one Sunday morning in Niagara Falls being aroused by a number of staff men who had called to invite us all to go with them on a trip into Canada, where, they said enthusiastically, there was plenty of beer available. These were Prohibition days, and Canada had a great fascination for everyone with a thirst. I had no great relish for beer, but I went with them to Canada and had a pleasant breakfast there instead.

After the ice cream investigation there was a lull, so I went back to the cashier's department for a month or so. I handled a variety of small matters on the staff in the fall of 1925. Then an investigation came up of a number of utility companies in Macon,

Georgia, and about eight of us were sent there. We finished the work about three days before Christmas.

I recall with amusement the trip home. One of the men had bought a grandfather clock, and I can still see him hugging it tightly as he lumbered along the corridor of the train. He would let nobody touch it.

It was snowing, and the train from Macon was three hours late. We had arranged to stay overnight in Atlanta, but did not arrive there until 1 a.m., and then it took us a long time to get cabs. My cab driver put some of the suitcases on the roof of the cab, and when we got to the hotel I discovered, to my dismay, that mine had apparently fallen off someplace. It eventually turned up, but by then it was almost morning.

In New York again, I did a number of odds and ends, and then I was assigned to the annual audit of the Midvale Company in Nicetown, Pennsylvania. Since W. D. McGregor was the partner in charge, and since everybody was scared to death of him, I took the assignment seriously. I pored over the previous year's working papers, reading carefully every comment in them, and I also boned up on iron and steel in the encyclopedia.

After that I had a succession of assignments, month after month, and before I realized it two years had gone by, and in July 1926 I sailed again for Ireland.

MADGE AND I WERE MARRIED on Wednesday, August 25th, in Omagh Methodist Church. The small church was crowded with relatives and with a great many people we had both known from childhood.

Madge and I are married

Our honeymoon

We had a leisurely three-week honeymoon. We went to Portrush, a well-known seaside resort, and from there to Dervock, Ballycastle, and Dublin. We particularly enjoyed Dublin. This was our first opportunity to see for ourselves some of the places that had been household words to us since childhood: Phoenix Park, O'Connell Street, Nelson's Pillar, Trinity College, the Four Courts, and countless others. We found Dublin, with its eighteenth-century architecture, a beautiful city, and it seemed very much at peace in that summer of 1926. People still talked about the Easter Rebellion of 1916, and about the civil war that broke out a few years later, but these events were now receding into the background. The Irish Free State was almost five years old, and already there was a growing feeling of optimism about the future.

We sailed for New York on September 25th. The seas were rough for most of the voyage, and Madge had a miserable time of it.

But when we got to New York the sun was shining. It was Sunday, and Hugh and Father and Beth were on the pier to welcome us. As it turned out, we were to welcome Hugh ashore instead of his welcoming us. Hugh always wanted to do the impossible, so he set out to get aboard the ship as soon as it docked. It is not easy to get on an incoming ship, but Hugh managed it through a liberal tip to a seaman on an inconspicuous gangway. This was fine, but when Hugh was ready to get off the boat the gangway and the seaman were both gone. Without a landing card or passport, it took Hugh fully an hour after Madge and I were clear of the ship to convince the immigration officials to let him go ashore.

I had rented an apartment on Victory Boulevard in Staten Island, so it was there that Madge and I started our married life together. Our apartment was next door to the one where Father, Mother, and Beth lived. This turned out to be a most fortunate arrangement, for I was to have a great deal of out-of-town work in the months ahead.

The status and responsibilities of an auditor who certifies or reports upon the annual accounts of a corporation are at present vague and indefinite; some accountants, I believe, would be glad to have them remain so. Why, they would ask, should we add to our responsibilities? The answer is, of course, simple. We cannot expect, for any length of time, to get something for nothing; and if we wish to see the prestige and authority of the profession, or for that matter its financial rewards, continue to increase, we must be prepared to assume correspondingly greater responsibilities.

GEORGE O. MAY: "A Proper Courage in the Assumption of Responsibility by the Accountant" (1926)

CHAPTER EIGHT

ACCOUNTING IN THE 1920s

W<small>HEN I BECAME A PERMANENT MEMBER OF THE</small> audit staff of Arthur Young & Company in the mid-1920s, there were only two pieces of "firm literature": a thirty-four-page pocket manual inscribed "Arthur Young & Company—New York Staff Manual—Private and Confidential" and a set of Standard Working Papers.

I don't recall when the Staff Manual fell into disuse. Actually, I think it was used by staffmen more for information on such subjects as "Time and Expense Reports," "Traveling Time," "Regular Hours and Overtime," and "Vacations" than it was for information on the conduct of engagements, which was stated in very general terms.

As far as I can remember, the Standard Working Papers were

seldom referred to. This is what the Staff Manual had to say about them:

> Upon application to the Office Manager, Seniors in charge of engagements may borrow (and must return) a set of "Standard Working Papers." It is not expected that this standard form of working papers can be adhered to in all cases, but experienced Seniors and studious accountants of a lower grade will recognize the general principles outlined, which must be maintained. The plans indicated in such working papers should be altered only when justified by circumstances.
> Seniors in charge will be so assigned only because of our belief or knowledge that they are entirely capable of conducting the engagement. The "Standard Working Papers" are not expected to curtail or limit the exercise of their ability in carrying the engagement to a complete and satisfactory conclusion, having regard to the requirements of the engagement.
> In other words, this Manual and the "Standard Set of Working Papers" are not expected to supply the ability and initiative that a Senior in charge must have to meet the calls that will be made upon him.

In those days there were no audit programs. All I recall seeing was an occasional memorandum pertaining to certain special features of an engagement.

Most audits in the 1920s were so-called balance sheet audits, and what we referred to as the "Federal Reserve Bulletin" was considered the authority to which accountants should look for guidance. This pamphlet was prepared by the American Institute of Accountants at the request of the Federal Trade Commission. It was subsequently submitted to the Federal Reserve Board and was adopted by that body as a semi-official pronouncement of what it regarded as the minimum requirements in balance sheet audits.

WHAT DID ACCOUNTANTS' CERTIFICATES look like in the 1920s? Early in 1927, David Himmelblau, then professor of accounting and head of the Department of Accounting at Northwestern University, published a book entitled *Auditors' Certificates* (The Ronald Press Company). The following four certificates, which are indicative of the type of certificates then being used, are taken from that book:

Accountants' certificates in the 1920s

We have examined the books of Armour and Company of Illinois, Armour and Company of Delaware, and their Subsidiaries, except The North American Provision Company, and have been furnished with the report and accounts submitted by the Independent Auditors of that Company. We certify that the accompanying Consolidated Balance Sheet as of December 29, 1923, has been correctly drawn up therefrom and in our opinion fairly sets forth the financial position of the combined Companies at that date.

PRICE WATERHOUSE & CO.

Chicago, Illinois
March 1, 1924

We have audited the books and records of the Reliance Manufacturing Company of Illinois and its Subsidiary Companies for the year ending December 31, 1925, and have prepared therefrom the above Consolidated Balance Sheet, which we certify is in accordance therewith and, in our opinion, is drawn up to correctly exhibit its financial position as at December 31, 1925. The inventories were taken by the Company's representatives and the quantities were not verified by us. We verified the clerical accuracy and satisfied ourselves that the prices used were the lower of Cost or Market.

ARTHUR YOUNG & COMPANY

Chicago, Illinois
February 3, 1926

February 6, 1925

We have audited the accounts of the

AMERICAN TELEPHONE AND TELEGRAPH COMPANY

for the year ended December 31, 1924, and have reviewed reports for that year rendered to the company by the associated and directly controlled companies.

We certify that the balance sheet and income statement as published herewith are in accordance with the books, and, in our opinion, set forth correctly the financial position of the American Telephone and Telegraph Company as at December 31, 1924, and the results of its operations for the year 1924.

LYBRAND, ROSS BROS. & MONTGOMERY

March 29, 1922

We have audited the books and accounts of the United States Rubber Company and its subsidiary companies for the year ended December 31, 1921, excepting those of certain of the foreign subsidiaries, as to which we have accepted reports of other accounting firms and, in some instances, reports of the companies, and

WE HEREBY CERTIFY that subject to the final determination of Federal Taxes, the accompanying general balance sheet, in our opinion, correctly sets forth the financial condition of the companies on December 31, 1921, and that the figures relating to the Income and Surplus accounts referred to in the text of the Chairman's report are correct.

HASKINS & SELLS

THE YEAR I GOT MARRIED was anything but an encouraging year for staff accountants. There was a long "slack" season which began early in 1926 and was very late in ending.

A slack season

This is what *The Journal of Accountancy* had to say in the spring of 1927 about that particular summer as it affected the great question of employment in the accounting profession:

> During the last summer in all parts of this country there was a general lack of demand for accountants which accentuated the unevenness of employment and of work. It is quite the usual thing to find the summer season a period of comparative inaction. Staffs are then reduced to their lowest numerical strength and the superfluous men are compelled to look for other sources of livelihood. But the summer of 1926 was dull and quiet beyond the ordinary, and so the old problem of the man who is not permanently and firmly established was given a new life and an increased urgency. There were firms which seemed to escape the general depression, but conditions which we have described did exist in the profession taking the country and the practitioners as a whole.
>
> It is difficult to assign a reason for the dullness of the past summer—it extended, by the way, well into the fall—but that is not our present endeavor. It may have been attributable to the hesitant condition of the financial world following the break in the long bull market. It may have been in part the result of a steadily decreasing volume of tax cases which made it necessary for many organizations whose chief function was the preparation and presentation of tax returns and claims to curtail their establishments. It may have been due to mere coincidence. Whatever its cause its effects were clear and thus the question of finding and retaining occupation revived.

Despite the problem of slack seasons, however, the accounting profession was making steady progress. September 1926 completed the first decade in the history of the American Institute of Accountants, which on September 19, 1916, had succeeded and

Developments in the accounting profession

absorbed its predecessor, the American Association of Public Accountants, established in 1887.

In September 1926 the Institute owned and occupied a five-story building at 135 Cedar Street, New York. It now boasted a total membership of 2,064, comprising 1,664 members and 400 associates.

The profession was making progress in the difficult matter of standards of examination. In 1926 the majority of the CPA examinations held throughout the country were conducted in cooperation with the board of examiners of the American Institute. In those states outside this cooperative scheme, the testing standards of the state boards of accountancy were generally considered to be good, but of course there was a lack of uniformity and the significance of the certificates issued naturally varied according to the conditions prevailing in each state.

"Stop, Look, Listen!"

In the fall of 1926 an article which appeared in the September issue of *The Atlantic Monthly* caused a great stir in financial and accounting circles. The article was written by William Z. Ripley, professor of economics at Harvard University, and was entitled "Stop, Look, Listen!—The Shareholder's Right to Adequate Information." Professor Ripley had previously caught the ear of the public with another article, entitled "From Main Street to Wall Street," in the January issue of the *Atlantic*. These two articles were to have far-reaching effects. Indeed, George O. May observed years later that the genesis of the term "accepted principles of accounting" was closely related to these articles by Professor Ripley.

"Stop, Look, Listen!" was a vigorous attack on the inadequacies of financial reporting practices of the time. Ripley developed

118

his argument largely by criticizing actual examples drawn from the reports of a number of leading companies. Some of the more striking of these criticisms had been circulated in advance by the publishers. In addition to these general criticisms, Ripley launched a specific attack on the accounting treatment of no-par-value stock and surplus.

In search of possible remedies, Ripley considered various expedients, including audits supervised by shareholders, state legislation, efforts of such bodies as the New York Stock Exchange and the Investment Bankers Association, and finally Federal intervention. He concluded with the suggestion that the Federal Trade Commission was the body which could best deal with the situation and said that in his opinion it already had the necessary powers to do so.

Leaders in the accounting profession felt that Professor Ripley's September article should not go unanswered, so the Institute prevailed on George O. May, the senior partner of Price Waterhouse & Co., who was one of the truly outstanding figures in the U. S. accounting profession, to address its annual banquet, set for September 22nd, on the subject of "Corporate Publicity and the Auditor." May very wisely decided not to discuss Ripley's article in detail in his talk, although he emphasized in it that he dissented from Ripley on some of his facts and on some of his arguments, and that he disagreed entirely with Ripley's suggestion as to the role which should be played by the Federal Trade Commission.

May, in his address, made essentially three suggestions which he felt would bring about substantial improvement in financial reporting: (1) He said that auditors should "use their best efforts to ensure that directors publish accounts which conform to the highest established standards," and he suggested that auditors, in the past, had not done their full duty in this respect. (2) He recommended that independent audits be extended and that the public be more clearly informed of the significance of such audits and of the responsibilities of auditors. (3) He suggested that the American Institute of Accountants invite the cooperation of other bodies "in considering what are the proper responsibilities of auditors and what can be done to hold them to such responsibilities and to put them in a position to assume all the responsibilities which they ought to assume."

In elaborating on the second suggestion, May pointed out that more than ninety percent of the industrial companies listed on the New York Stock Exchange already had annual independent audits of their accounts. May also noted that under English law the independent audit had for many years been compulsory, and that in England the auditors shared with the directors the responsibility for the accounts as published. He said that while it was impracticable to bring about through legislation a situation in America similar to that which existed in England, he saw no reason why this could not be done in large measure through the cooperation of such bodies as the leading stock exchanges, the investment bankers, and the commercial banks which grant credit. Thus, he observed, the New York Stock Exchange, as to listed companies, could readily bring about, through its listing agreements, a situation similar to that which existed in England.

It was at a meeting of his partners in the fall of 1926 that George O. May, at the age of 51, arranged to relinquish active administration of his firm and assume a consulting role, the understanding being that he would devote a large part of his time to professional and public matters. I have often thought how wise that decision was: it was good for the profession, it was good for May, and it was certainly good for Price Waterhouse & Co. Early in 1927 May became an unofficial accounting adviser to the New York Stock Exchange. A year later the relationship became official.

It was in 1926 that the New York Stock Exchange appointed J. M. B. Hoxsey to serve as executive assistant to the Committee on Stock List. In this role, Hoxsey was to help substantially in bringing about improved standards of financial reporting, and he worked closely with May in these efforts.

SO MUCH FOR DEVELOPMENTS in the accounting profession; now let me return to our own firm. I have said that the national partnership of Arthur Young & Company began in 1921 with eight general partners, all of whom were Britishers. No change took place in the partnership for eight years. Then in 1929 an American, Warren W. Nissley, joined the partnership, bringing the number of general partners to nine. Warren was to play an important part not only in the history of the firm but in the development of the accounting profession.

Born in Middletown, Pennsylvania, in 1893, Warren Nissley graduated from Princeton University with a civil engineering degree in 1914. For the next several years, while he studied accounting at night, Warren held various positions with banks and utility companies. Finally he became a staff assistant with a small accounting firm, and in July 1921 he joined Arthur Young & Company.

Warren W. Nissley

I first met Warren in the fall of 1921. It was in the report department. We were all working late one night and Warren dropped in about eight o'clock to pick up the office copy of a report that had been typed for him. It was a report on a special investigation of one of the several colleges that Tom Clarke and Charles Judson had brought in as clients. The first thing that struck me about Nissley was his serious and reserved demeanor. He asked for the report, glanced at it thoughtfully, put it in an envelope, thanked us, and departed. I noticed that he was reading a textbook on accounting, which he left on the table as he scrutinized the report. Nissley was then 28 years old.

I recall nothing further about Warren Nissley until about two years later. I was in the men's room one day, smoking and gossiping with a bunch of other staff men, and the conversation drifted around to the relative abilities of various people in the organization. Everyone seemed to have an opinion about almost everybody else in the office, and it was interesting to compare these different viewpoints. On this particular day, one of the staff seniors, a controversial, argumentative Scot, said with a good deal of fervor, "Keep your eye on that fellow Nissley. He has a drag with somebody around here."

As I was later to learn, Warren Nissley had no "drag" with anyone. Whatever influence he had was attributable entirely to his very considerable ability. He was unpopular with a number of people, partly because he was so outspoken in his views—particularly in his view that the source of future American accountants should be graduates of U. S. colleges and not chartered accountants trained in Great Britain. Warren never was and never would be a conformist, in this or any other matter about which he felt strongly.

Warren Nissley's outstanding characteristic was his consuming interest in all things pertaining to the profession of accounting. Early in the 1920s he became convinced that the general public was not sufficiently aware of the importance and dignity of the accounting profession, or of the high qualifications required of those who practiced it. It was this conviction that impelled him to take a leading part in the profession's efforts to attract young men of the highest caliber to public accounting.

It was Nissley who conceived, organized, and promoted the Institute's Bureau for Placements, which in 1926 made the first organized effort on behalf of the accounting profession to attract U. S. college graduates to its ranks. Under his chairmanship, the committee supervising the Bureau published the first official Institute pamphlet on accounting as a career.

The Institute's Bureau for Placements acted as a clearing house between the accounting firms which agreed to cooperate and college students. The Bureau undertook to select candidates on the basis of their scholastic achievements and extracurricular activities, and after personal interviews. The firms, on their part, agreed to three things: (1) to pay the Institute a fee of $50 for every man engaged, (2) to employ men selected for a period of at least three years, and (3) to pay them a regular salary of at least $125 a month, with stated increases at the end of each year.

At least two men who are well-known partners in Arthur Young & Company today came to us as a direct result of the American Institute's Bureau for Placements: Ralph H. Galpin, who joined the firm in July 1926, and Harry C. Grumpelt, who came with us about two years later.

No one stands still in public accounting. Either he grows with the profession or he falls behind. Satisfactory completion of the job at hand is seldom enough; the accountant must do well that which is assigned to him and at the same time must be preparing constantly for the next job that he may be called on to perform. During the pressure of a busy season additional engagements and unexpected problems on old engagements call for shifting between assignments and the assumption of increased responsibilities by some in order that the work may go forward and adequate service be furnished to clients.

R. K. MAUTZ: *Duties of Junior and Senior Accountants*

CHAPTER NINE

LIFE ON THE AUDIT STAFF

It was in the fall of 1926 that life on the audit staff started for me in real earnest. From then on things became more and more hectic, and I seemed to have little time for anything but accounting. All of us on the audit staff traveled a great deal in those days, and we put in many hours of overtime. I liked everything about the life, and the long hours bothered me very little. What appealed to me most was the variety—never being completely sure where I would be a month hence or what kind of work I would be doing. I worried a good deal about all kinds of accounting problems, but I had a real sense of achievement when they were resolved in one way or another.

To give some idea of how much moving about we did in those days, let me describe my itinerary for the winter of 1929-1930. Soon after the New Year I was in Philadelphia in charge of the audits of the Midvale Company, the Alan Wood Steel Company, and the Philadelphia Coke Company. Before I had completed any of these audits I had an urgent request from New York to finish up as soon as possible and get down to Atlanta. In Atlanta I reviewed the final figures on a special investigation of Columbia Baking Company and wrote the report on it. From Atlanta I went to Orlando, Florida, to audit the New Ice Company, and from there I went to Ohio, first to Marion and then to Columbus, to audit a number of utility companies. When I got back to New York, sometime in the spring, I found the firm comfortably established at 1 Cedar Street, which we all agreed was a beauty parlor in comparison with our quarters at 82 Beaver Street.

The firm was apparently prospering. It was in the summer of 1930 that the New York office had what I believe was its first golf tournament. It was held on June 12th at the Clearview Country Club in Flushing, Queens, and was so successful that the partners decided to make it an annual affair if at all practicable.

We were unusually busy in the summer of 1931, and we all felt sure that there would be no golf tournament that year. It was finally held, however, on October 15th at the Bonnie Briar in Larchmont, with dinner following at the New York Athletic Club. Fred Colley, who did not play golf, got a bit "high" at the dinner that night and reminisced to the group about his early days in England and America.

In the 1920s and early 1930s the firm had considerable public utility work, and I had my full share of it. Many utilities changed hands in that period, and special investigations took us to a variety of places around the country. Most of the work was rush work, and much of it represented the first independent audits that had ever been made of the companies concerned.

The prize utility audit in the New York office was the annual audit (then June 30th) of Public Service Company of Colorado.

Practically every staffman wanted to be assigned to this engagement—first, because of the climate in Denver, which was delightful in July and August; second, because there were always plenty of good permanent staff assistants available in the summer months; and third, because the work could be done in a fairly leisurely manner, since it was highly unlikely that another client would be breathing down anyone's neck to start his work at that time of the year.

I was in charge of the 1932 audit of Public Service, and I found that the assignment lived up to my every expectation. I had four good assistants, one of them being Dick Barry, who is now a partner in New York. Altogether I spent roughly eight weeks on the engagement—six weeks in Denver and two in New York.

Our group got on well together, and we visited a number of the scenic spots and other tourist attractions around Denver. On the weekends we usually had cook-outs in the mountains. We ate steak and drank corn whisky diluted with large quantities of ginger ale and smoked our heads off. One day a couple of the company officials took us to Cheyenne to see the rodeo. This was an all-day excursion in perfectly delightful weather, with dinner afterwards in Denver.

I recall vividly a trip we made one Sunday to Lookout Mountain, near Golden, Colorado, where "Buffalo Bill" Cody is buried. We were all young enough then to feel a certain excitement at seeing the last resting place of that great adventurer and showman. As a boy I had seen "Buffalo Bill's Wild West Show" in Ireland, and I had never forgotten the thrill it gave me. (Whether what I had seen in Ireland was really Bill Cody's show or another that had adopted the name I'm not sure, but the association was vivid.)

Memories of Buffalo Bill

By coincidence, Arthur Brisbane, who wrote for the Hearst papers, had something to say about Bill Cody on the same weekend that we visited Lookout Mountain. I pasted his article in my diary:

MONTELLO, NEV., Aug. 6—This is written on the Union Pacific train carrying fast express to the Pacific Coast, and fast means fast. The train a little while ago ran ninety-five miles in one hour and six minutes.

The sun went down Friday slowly, "taking its time" as tho sorry to leave the beautiful hills and plains of western Wyoming, 6,000 feet above the sea.

You might well travel far to see such a sky—a pale, yellow blue, thin wisps of gray clouds stretching from mountain to mountain. You feel that you are really on solid ground, half a continent on either side, an ocean back of you, another bigger ahead of you. Everything is calm, restful. As it is now among these mountains, so it will be 10,000 years after you are dead.

To the north lies Cody, named for "Buffalo Bill" Cody. Only a few years ago he rode about here, killing bison to feed workmen building this Union Pacific, killing Indians to protect the workers. Later, when he had turned showman, and this writer saw him performing before Queen Victoria, he had written his story, "How I Slew Yellow Hand." Perhaps he has since met Yellow Hand, for we must assume that only one happy hunting ground is provided for Indians and whites, and perhaps Yellow Hand has forgiven him for making that story one-sided.

Experience in the oil industry

FOR A GREAT MANY YEARS, beginning in 1931, I had a wide variety of oil company assignments, from which I gained invaluable experience in that industry. In May 1931 I left for Independence, Kansas to assist in a special investigation of the Prairie Oil & Gas Company and the Prairie Pipe Line Company. This work was for our client Sinclair, which acquired the Prairie companies about a year after our investigation. The Prairie work kept me busily engaged morning, noon, and night from the latter part of May until the middle of August. I started off on Prairie Pipe Line Company and then was diverted with two assistants—Ralph Henkel from Milwaukee and Bob Coons from Kansas City—to audit a number of affiliated utility companies located in Amarillo, Lubbock, and Colorado Springs.

Special investigations can be exciting, and the Prairie investigation was no exception. Fred Colley was the supervising partner, and Gordon Steele was in charge of the field work. I saw a great deal of both of them. There were, I suppose, twenty of us in all in Independence, drawn from our offices in Kansas City, Tulsa, Milwaukee, and New York. When the field work was finished at the end of June, six of us moved to Kansas City to put the final figures together and write our reports. It was viciously hot both in Independence and in Kansas City.

As I think of the hours I worked in those days on the staff I'm amazed how energetic and enthusiastic I continued to be year after year. Still clear in my mind is the brief visit that Henkel, Coons, and I made to Colorado Springs in June 1931. We arrived there on a Thursday morning and worked very late on Thursday, Friday, and Saturday. We had promised ourselves a trip to Pike's Peak, so we arranged for a car to pick us up at 1 a.m. on Sunday morning. We worked until 10:30 Saturday night, lay down for an hour or so, and then started out in a Pierce Arrow with a uniformed chauffeur. Ralph Henkel felt the altitude and became sick as the car zig-zagged higher and higher, but we kept going and were well rewarded by the magnificence of the sunrise. It was a thrilling experience as we stood there shivering in the snow. We got back to Colorado Springs in time for breakfast and then went to the office to put in another full day's work. I can still remember how tired we were that Sunday night as we sat in our hotel room, sipping corn whisky and ginger ale to ease our weariness.

Later on in 1931 I took charge of a special audit of Tide Water Associated Oil Company, and early in the following year Fred Colley asked me to take charge of our first annual audit of Vacuum Oil Company. Standard Oil Company of New York, our client since 1921, had merged with Vacuum as of July 31, 1931, and I think I am correct in saying that Vacuum had not previously been audited, although certain of its subsidiaries in South Africa and Australia had.

It was a very large engagement. The Vacuum group comprised a large number of companies, both in the United States and abroad, and also a great many domestic divisions, all with separate sets of books. In those days books were not closed as promptly as they are today, and in many cases stockholders did not receive their accounts until some months after the year-end. Thus, in the case of Vacuum I did not start work at 61 Broadway until the first of March. Then it was a matter of working day and night until the final figures were approved. It was the middle of April when I finally delivered the Vacuum Oil Company consolidated accounts to my counterpart at Socony, an interesting and erratic Scot named Finlay Hunter.

In the fall of 1932 Fred Colley told me I would again be in charge of Vacuum under him, but early in 1933 he telephoned me one day when I was in Oklahoma to say that Hunter had died suddenly of a heart attack and that he and his partners had decided to put me in charge of both Socony and Vacuum. This was the beginning of an association with Socony-Vacuum Oil Company, Incorporated (now Socony Mobil Oil Company, Inc.) which was to last for many years.

It was a thrill to have charge of what by then had become one of the most important accounts in the New York office. There were many problems, both in Socony and in Vacuum, and I had so many arguments with company employees that I was sure I had had my first and last chance at the Socony-Vacuum work.

At Socony-Vacuum

But things turned out all right. A few days after we released the accounts, Fred Colley, in bubbling good humor, asked me to drop into his office to see a letter he had just received from the Socony-Vacuum comptroller. I don't recall ever having seen Colley more pleased. The letter read:

> May I at this time extend my sincere thanks for the splendid cooperation you gave us in expediting preparation of the 1932 figures. The members of your staff assigned to our audit worked long and faithfully, and we are particularly gratified with the excellent work of Mr. Higgins. He really showed unusual ability in grasping the many ramifications of our rather complicated system.

Colley talked to me at great length about service to clients and said there was no satisfaction in a professional man's life to compare with the praise that came from a well-satisfied client.

AS I LOOK BACK on this period of my life, it seems to me that I could not have been a very satisfactory husband. I was completely preoccupied with my work and it got the right of way over practi-

Meanwhile, at home . . .

cally everything else. As I think of those days now I am aghast when I realize that not only was I separated from Madge on two Thanksgiving Days and several New Year's Eves, but I was also separated from her on the Christmas of 1932 and the Christmas of 1933. What is worse, I think the separation from my family did not concern me nearly as much as it should have. I simply looked on it as a necessary and inevitable fact of life.

Possibly my casual attitude toward my family responsibilities had its roots in my upbringing in Ireland. Or perhaps it was simply my philosophic nature. Whatever its cause, I seem to have had the mistaken notion that at home there should be a definite division of labor, with the husband taking the role of provider and wandering around more or less at will and the wife taking complete responsibility for running the home and rearing the children. I'm sure that in that period of my life I had absolutely no conception of the idea of mutually shared family responsibilities.

On the other side of the coin, however, Madge and I did get to spend many long vacations together, a number of them in Ireland. We were there in 1928 and again in 1932. The latter trip was a long one, from September 9th until November 23rd.

I have always preferred to sail on smaller ships, when time permitted, and in the year 1932 time permitted. We sailed on the *Tuscania*, which took us directly to Belfast, and returned on the *Laconia*, which we boarded at Liverpool. The return trip took nine days because of scheduled calls at Cobh, Galway, and Boston.

Two days before we sailed for home, Madge's sister Winifred was married to Andrew Taylor, a young engineer, in Omagh Methodist Church. For days before the wedding there was great excitement, and women seemed to be all over the place. (Poor

Andy was not to live long. Some years later, when he was in his thirties, he entered the hospital for what was thought to be a routine appendectomy, but he died of a coronary a day or so after the operation. In addition to Winifred he left three young children.)

Most of that particular vacation was spent in Omagh at the Corker home, but we also visited Dublin, Belfast, and Dervock. Things seemed much as they used to be, although Grandfather Thomas Higgins was missing from Dervock. He had died in February of the previous year at the age of 86. When he died, the press described him as "a staunch Unionist in politics who rendered yeoman service for a great number of years to the North Antrim Unionist Association, of which he was a member, and who was always fearless in the advocacy of the views he held."

IN THE 1920S AND 1930S the American public seemed to have developed a great hunger for information of all kinds, national and international. There were forums and meetings and public debates of all sorts and varieties. Large crowds of people could be gathered to hear almost anyone, it seemed, on little more than a minute's notice.

I recall one night in Columbus, Ohio, around 1930 hearing a public debate on Prohibition between Clarence Darrow and Senator Brookhart of Iowa. Darrow was then in his early seventies.

I get to hear Clarence Darrow

Darrow was not one of my heroes, but I had heard and read so much about the man that I had a tremendous curiosity to see him in action. The big hall was filled to capacity, but I had succeeded in getting a good seat. What struck me first about Darrow was his absolutely unkempt appearance: his suit was large for

133

him and gave the impression of never having been pressed; he slouched in his chair in a dreamy, indifferent way, and his look seemed cynical and contemptuous. My instinctive reaction to Darrow was completely negative, and I imagine that he made the same initial impression on others.

On a purely intellectual basis Brookhart made, I thought, an excellent case for Prohibition, and Darrow really added nothing new or startling to the facts. There was this difference, however: Darrow understood people, individually and collectively; how they react; what they are like. Within a matter of minutes—and this was the amazing thing—he seemed to have the entire audience in the hollow of his hand.

After Brookhart had made his impassioned plea in favor of Prohibition, Darrow got up wearily and in a quiet, drawly kind of way began, "I am opposed to Prohibition because I like to take a drink." Then he paused a long while and continued: "Can you imagine a philosopher sitting down to write some great work with a pitcher of ice water beside him?"

His whole theme was that he was a drinking man, that he did it in a quiet, civilized way, and that fanatics in our government had no right under heaven to interfere with what was a very personal affair in his life. He said that Prohibition was a menace to the rights of the individual, imposed by an intolerant few who would hesitate at nothing to force their own convictions on the rest of the world. As he progressed in his talk the audience became spellbound; you could quite literally have heard a pin drop. I never saw such a demonstration of the power of personality. After that night I had a much better understanding of how Darrow could influence juries.

Actually, Darrow cared very little for intoxicating liquor. He made it quite clear in his autobiography that, while he occasionally took wine or whisky, he did not do so regularly or in any way that could possibly be called a habit, and he had never in his life drunk to excess.

A year or two after the Columbus debate on Prohibition I almost got to hear Winston Churchill. He had come over to America in December 1931 to give a series of lectures across the country, and I bought a ticket to hear him in New York. That did not come to pass, however, for he was struck by an automobile the day before his first scheduled lecture in New York and had to spend a while in the hospital as a result. The accident occurred as Churchill, after leaving the home of his good friend Bernard Baruch, stepped off the curb to cross the street. Apparently Sir Winston, thinking of British traffic which moves on the left side, became confused and looked in the wrong direction. The lectures were eventually given, but in the meantime I was off again on an out-of-town trip. I never did get to hear Churchill on the platform.

I don't get to hear Winston Churchill

As a year, 1929 has always been peculiarly the property of the economists. It was a year of notable economic events; indeed, in that year began the most momentous economic occurrence in the history of the United States, the ordeal of the Great Depression. In many ways this preoccupation with economics is unfortunate, for 1929 was a year of many marvels. In particular, it was one of those years that marvelously illuminate human motives and the very wellsprings of human behavior.

JOHN KENNETH GALBRAITH: *The Great Crash, 1929*

CHAPTER TEN

THE GREAT DEPRESSION

To REALIZE WHAT WAS HAPPENING TO THE stock market in the fall of 1929, it might be helpful to consider the front page of the New York *Times* of October 29, 1929. The headline of the lead article that day read:

> STOCK PRICES SLUMP $14,000,000,000
> IN NATION-WIDE STAMPEDE TO UNLOAD;
> BANKERS TO SUPPORT MARKET TODAY

The article itself began as follows:

> The second hurricane of liquidation within four days hit the stock market yesterday. It came suddenly, and violently, after holders of stocks had been lulled into a sense of security by the rallies of Friday and Saturday. It was a country-wide collapse of open-market security values in which the declines established and the actual losses taken in dollars and cents were probably the most disastrous and far-reaching in the history of the Stock Exchange.
>
> That the storm has now blown itself out, that there will be organized support to put an end to a reaction which has ripped billions of dollars

The Great Crash

from market values, appeared certain last night from statements by leading bankers.

Although total estimates of the losses on securities are difficult to make, because of the large number of them not listed on any exchange, it was calculated last night that the total shrinkage in American securities on all exchanges yesterday had aggregated some $14,000,000,000, with a decline of about $10,000,000,000 in New York Stock Exchange securities. The figure is necessarily a rough one, but nevertheless gives an idea of the dollars and cents recessions in one of the most extraordinary declines in the history of American markets.

It was not so much the little trader or speculator who was struck by yesterday's cyclone; it was the rich men of the country, the institutions which have purchased common stocks, the investment trusts and investors of all kinds. The little speculators were mostly blown out of their accounts by the long decline from early September. Thousands of them went headlong out of the market on Thursday. It was the big man, however, whose holdings were endangered yesterday and who threw his holdings into the Stock Exchange for just what they would bring, when hysteria finally seized him.

MARKET LEADERS HARD HIT

Shares of the best-known American industrial and railroad corporations smashed through their old lows of Thursday, and most of them to the lowest level for many years, as wave after wave of liquidation swept the market during its day of utter confusion and rout. As bid after bid was filled for stocks and more and more offered, stocks of the best grade dropped almost perpendicularly, with 2, 3, 5 and even 10 points between sales under probably the most demoralized conditions of trading in the history of the Stock Exchange and the Curb. United States Steel declined 17½, General Electric lost 47½, United States Industrial Alcohol, 39½; Standard Gas, 40½; Columbia Gas, 22; Air Reduction, 48⅞; Allied Chemical & Dye, 36; Baltimore & Ohio, 13⅝; A. M. Byers Company, 30¾; Chesapeake & Ohio, 23½; New York Central, 22⅝; Peoples Gas,

40½; Westinghouse Electric, 34¼; Western Union, 39½; and Worthington Pump, 29.

These are the blue chips of the market, seasoned stocks based on the country's leading industries, and which have led the way up the ladder of fluctuations over many months of the now thoroughly defunct bull market. They, and many others, are the issues in which speculation has been most rampant. But stocks of all kinds were affected by the market's second debacle. The good went down with the bad and levels undreamed of in Wall Street a month or so ago were crashed through before the resistless assault of a headlong and in many cases senseless wave of liquidation.

As I think back on that day and the weeks that followed, I don't recall anyone predicting the long depression that lay ahead. People in general seemed philosophic. The experts reasoned that good stocks and bad stocks had all been rising, and that in many cases market prices bore no relationship to either dividends or earnings. Inevitably, they said, security prices had to find their proper value.

I don't think I became acutely aware of the impact of the depression until the winter of 1930-1931, when I spent about seven weeks in Pittsburgh on the audit of a large manufacturing company. All of my five assistants were temporary men, and it was quite apparent that they were all hard-pressed financially. One of them came back to the office on a cold, damp Saturday afternoon very pleased that he had been able to buy a winter overcoat at what he said was a phenomenal bargain—$6, we afterwards learned. When we asked him where he had gotten the overcoat he said, with a look of triumph, that it was at a fire sale just a few blocks away. The coat was quite worn and tattered, but it served its purpose. I felt sorry for these men and I enjoyed my association with them. What they lacked in education and accounting training, which was considerable, they made up for in loyalty and sincerity and the common decencies of life.

Pittsburgh, of course, was hard hit by the depression. I was amazed at how many times, night after night, I was approached by prostitutes and panhandlers. They plied the same streets and made the same approaches. I got so that I could recognize almost any one of them a block away.

At Continental Oil

MY LONGEST ENGAGEMENT during the depression years was Continental Oil Company, in the winter of 1932-1933. This work had to do with a major downward revaluation of assets which was followed by the annual audit for 1932. The general decline in prices in the previous few years had resulted in assets being carried on the books of the Continental companies at amounts which were substantially in excess of estimated replacement costs. The management decided, therefore, to reduce the company's capital and to write off, against the surplus so created, the total deficit resulting from the major write-downs.

Quite a number of companies had similar downward revaluations during the depression years, but Continental is the only company I know of which considered carefully the book value of *every* asset carried on its books. The other companies simply chose a few major items for adjustment.

I left for Ponca City, Oklahoma, in the latter part of November 1932, and it was the end of February before I finished there. For the first month I was alone on the work. After that I began to build up a staff as the audit got under way.

I spent that Christmas in the Jens-Marie Hotel. The hotel clerk told me that I was one of six people there. I don't know what the others did for diversion, for I never saw hide nor hair of them. Perhaps they were merely figments of the clerk's imagination, designed to keep me from feeling quite so sorry for myself on Christmas Day.

The Continental work was interesting. The revaluations were made by representatives of the company's various departments, and I and an internal auditor had to question each of these people carefully to make sure that the bases for their revaluations were reasonable, and then we had to check their figures for accuracy. In the process I got to meet all of the company's officials and department heads, and many of their families as well. Altogether, the revaluations and certain other adjustments added up to approximately $61,000,000.

An interesting question was raised about the revaluation by the New York Stock Exchange. This had to do with the producing properties, which had been valued at the lower of cost or estimated eventual "payout" discounted to present value. George O. May, as accounting advisor to the Exchange, took the strong position that the basis used was not sound and that all properties should have been valued consistently on a payout basis, which would have meant writing up certain of the properties above cost.

A meeting to decide the issue was held on May 2, 1933 at the New York Stock Exchange. The following persons were present:

Richard Whitney — President, New York Stock Exchange
Frank Altschul — Chairman, NYSE Committee on Stock List
J. M. B. Hoxsey — Executive Assistant, NYSE Committee on Stock List

George O. May — Price Waterhouse & Co., Accounting Advisor to the Stock Exchange

George Whitney ⎫
Thomas S. Lamont ⎬ J. P. Morgan & Co.

Lansing Reed — Davis, Polk, Wardwell, Gardiner & Reed

James J. Cosgrove ⎫
R. L. Bosworth ⎬ Continental Oil Company

W. D. McGregor ⎫
T. G. Higgins ⎬ Arthur Young & Company

While undoubtedly May was technically correct, no one at the meeting except Hoxsey reacted favorably to the idea of write-ups. George Whitney said very firmly that, in the light of things as they were then, nobody could be sure that the write-downs were sufficient, and that from a conservative point of view it would be thoroughly unwise to have any write-ups of any kind. After the pros and cons had been discussed at some length it was finally decided not to adopt May's suggestion but instead to furnish certain additional details about the producing properties to stockholders and to include these same details in the listing application.

This work on Continental in the winter of 1932-1933 was my first contact with that company. As in the case of Socony, it was the beginning of an association that was to continue for many years.

In those days, the top officials of Continental, some twelve to fifteen men, used to lunch together each day in a comfortable room at the top of the building in Ponca City. After a year or two on the work I was invited to join this group. This was an invaluable experience for me, for in the course of these luncheons I learned a good deal about the day-to-day problems of a large oil company. Dan Moran, the president of Continental, always sat at the head of the long table, and it was he who dominated every conversation. He was one of the most dynamic men I have ever known. Although he had a strong temper, he usually kept it in subjection—but when it did break forth, he was tremendous in his wrath. Right or wrong, Dan Moran was always colorful; he was never dull.

I got to know "D. J.," as they used to call him, very well. He was a terrific worker, and never spared himself. In many ways he was a perfectionist: the offices, the refineries, the service stations all had to be spotlessly clean, and he would get terribly annoyed at anyone who kept an untidy desk.

THE FOLLOWING WINTER I had another fairly long engagement which kept me out of town, mostly in Kansas City, for almost two months. This was a special investigation of a pipe line company in which a number of major oil companies were interested. I felt flattered because Dan Moran had suggested that I be placed in charge of the field work.

Jim Burton took charge of the investigation, and he spent a week with me getting the work lined up, after which I carried on alone with a number of assistants. We visited four points: Chicago, Tulsa, Ponca City, and Kansas City. Jim was then 47 and in his prime; I was 33. We naturally saw a great deal of each other on that trip and really got acquainted for the first time.

Getting to know Jim Burton

We spent some interesting evenings together. I recall that one night in Ponca City, for want of something better to do, we went to see a Mae West movie in the local theater. I also recall that Jim and I both took our first airplane flight that year—a very bumpy trip, in a very small plane, from Kansas City to Tulsa.

When Jim Burton and W. D. McGregor had first talked to me about the special pipe line investigation, they had estimated that it would take approximately three months. This was around November 1st. Knowing that this job would be followed by several weeks in Ponca City on the Continental audit, I persuaded Madge to make a trip to Ireland to visit her parents. She was gone for four months.

Just before we started out on our trip Jim, in the presence of W. D. McGregor, talked to me about my satisfactory progress with the firm and said that, as from January 1, 1934, I would share in the profits of the New York office. He also said that, through a rearrangement of office space occasioned by the death of Fred Colley, I and two other men would share a large room at the end of the corridor.

Fred Colley dies

Fred Colley was just 61 when he died. He was in Wimbledon, England, at the time. Death frequently comes as a shock, but it should not have been so in his case because he had for years been troubled with hypertension, to which he paid little heed. When he said goodbye to me just before he sailed for England he was quite depressed, and I thought I had never seen him look so ill.

In the two years before he died, Fred Colley had become very friendly and considerate to me. I remember particularly one evening we spent together just a few months before he sailed for England. This was at a dinner of the Pilgrims Society, at which Ramsay MacDonald, the British Prime Minister, spoke. Fred's guest that evening was his son-in-law, and we all had a very pleasant time.

Most special investigations take longer than anticipated, but for what I believe was the first and only time in my accounting career I concluded the pipe line investigation long before the estimated finishing date. The result of this was that I spent from December 22nd, when I returned to New York, until January 13th, when I left for Ponca City, in a hotel in New York. That particular holiday season was a jolly and boisterous one for most people, for on December 5th Prohibition came to an end, somewhat less than fourteen years after it had been instituted.

DURING THE DEPRESSION Madge and I suffered virtually no financial hardship. Although my annual salary was reduced in 1932, the cut was more than offset by the substantially lower cost of living.

It is hard for us now to realize what prices were like in those days. In January 1931, for example, my room rent in the William Penn Hotel in Pittsburgh (then, I believe, the leading hotel in that city) was $2.83 per day on a monthly basis. The following year my room rent in the Jens-Marie Hotel in Ponca City was $2.50 per day. In 1931 I bought two business suits from one of the best men's clothing shops in New York; each suit cost $38, and one of them included two pairs of trousers.

The low cost of living

One Saturday afternoon when I was walking towards the William Penn Hotel in Pittsburgh I saw an advertisement in a window announcing a weekend excursion to New York on the Pennsylvania Railroad for $6, round trip. I did not think I could afford to miss such an opportunity, so I bought a ticket then and there and took the excursion—twelve hours on the train on Saturday night and twelve hours back on Sunday night!

The firm in the depression years

HOW DID OUR FIRM fare in the depression? I don't have any information on the partners' stock market losses, but the following summary of chargeable hours will give some idea of how our offices were affected. Quite aside from the effects of the depression, it is interesting to note how small our firm really was in those days:

Chargeable hours (in thousands)

	Total	New York	Chicago	Other offices*
1927	475.8	177.3	192.9	105.6
1928	501.4	189.5	208.1	103.8
1929	599.4	208.7	262.8	127.9
1930	625.6	228.9	250.1	146.6
1931	657.1	239.3	251.6	166.2
1932	477.7	161.5	195.1	121.1
1933	340.5	136.2	110.2	94.1
1934	363.9	142.2	119.2	102.5
1935	553.2	258.1	160.0	135.1
1936	547.9	253.2	155.1	139.6

*"Other offices" include Milwaukee, Kansas City, Los Angeles, Dallas, Pittsburgh, Tulsa (from 1929, when it was opened), and Detroit (from 1925, when it was opened, to 1933, when it was closed).

The firm was forced to take drastic steps to cope with the situation caused by the depression. There were reductions in staff, cuts in salary, and so-called Hoover vacations (four weeks' vacation with two weeks' pay). The salary reductions for the most part occurred in the spring of 1932. They ranged from $15 to $50 per month for staff, and from $1 to $3 per week for typists and office help. In some cases further salary reductions were made effective in 1933. Some of the staff did not again reach their 1931 salary levels until three to five years later.

Audits in the depression years were in many cases extraordinarily difficult. Inventories, particularly in manufacturing companies, and receivables created many problems. I recall making an audit of a fairly large lumber company whose treasurer seemed awfully optimistic about everything. We had to qualify our opinion because of what we felt was an inadequate allowance for receivables, and as a result we lost the audit. Quite by coincidence, I happened to meet my counterpart in the successor firm a few years later, and I asked him about the adequacy of the reserve. He replied that it was a good thing we had qualified our opinion, for charges for bad debts from our time were by then six times the amount of the allowance which had caused our qualification—and accounts, he said, were still being written off.

The depression hurt the Chicago office more than our other offices. This was because of the loss of the Insull work, the bulk of which had been done by Chicago (although New York had audited the eastern subsidiaries, which were quite important).

Changes in management frequently result in changes in auditors, and it was inevitable, I suppose, that we would lose the Insull work when Insull's utility complex collapsed and he lost control. This happened in the spring of 1932. We had done work for Insull companies for more than twenty years.

Since the Insull system was an important client of the firm, and since it is now over thirty years since the Insull crash, it might be appropriate at this point to say something about Samuel Insull and his utility "empire."

SAMUEL INSULL came to the United States from England in 1881, when he was 22 years old. He became private secretary to Thomas A. Edison and for some time held high positions in a number of

Samuel Insull and his empire

Edison companies. At the age of 32 he became a vice president of General Electric Company, and later he resigned to become president of a small utility in Chicago. Shortly thereafter, Insull began to build what was eventually to become a huge utility empire.

The following description of the Insull empire is from a study by Arthur R. Taylor, entitled "Losses to the Public in the Insull Collapse: 1932-1946," which appeared in the Summer 1962 issue of *Business History Review*:

> During the 40 years beginning in 1892, Samuel Insull had built a complex of utility and related properties whose power lines and gas mains stretched from Maine to Texas and from Wisconsin to Florida, serving over 5,000 communities in 32 states. The principal corporate sinews holding this vast body of properties together were issues of common stock. Super holding companies owned the common stock of giant companies, which owned the stock of large operating and holding companies, which in turn owned those of large operating companies, which owned the common stock of the thousands of small rural operating companies which formed the heart of the system. The more than two thousand securities issued in the building of this system were owned by more than 600,000 shareholders and 500,000 bondholders. At the very top of this multilevel structure were two great investment trusts, Insull Utility Investments, Incorporated, and Corporation Securities Company of Chicago. Owning a great deal of one another and of companies on other levels, they formed the key to the ownership of the entire system. The personal holdings of the Insull family and its associates were primarily concentrated in the investment trusts, which had been formed in 1929 to perpetuate the management and policies of one man, Samuel Insull.

When the empire collapsed in 1932, Insull went to Greece and later to Turkey. He was brought back to the United States, where he and seventeen others were charged with using the mails to defraud and with other crimes. All were acquitted. Insull spent most of his remaining years in Europe and died in Paris in 1938.

To give some indication of the important companies included in the Insull complex, here are the names of the twenty largest companies, in terms of the value of securities in public hands: Insull Utility Investments, Inc. and Corporation Securities Company of Chicago (both investment trusts), Commonwealth Edison Company, Public Service Company of Northern Illinois, Middle West Utilities Company, Peoples Gas Light & Coke Company, Central Illinois Public Service Company, Northern Indiana Public Service Company, North American Light & Power Company, Jersey Central Power & Light Company, Chicago Rapid Transit Company, Public Service Company of Indiana, Midland Utilities Company, Public Service Company of Oklahoma, Midland United Company, Wisconsin Power & Light Company, Central Maine Power Company, Virginia Public Service Company, Central Power & Light Company, and Kentucky Utilities Company.

Although our firm was the principal auditor for the Insull companies, another national firm was joint auditor on Middle West Utilities Company, and still another was the sole auditor for Corporation Securities Company of Chicago. In addition to the work of these three national firms, three local firms also did certain work. One acted as joint auditor on the Midland group of companies. The other two did a considerable amount of income tax work for some of the companies.

For the reader who would like to know something more about Samuel Insull and his "empire," a most interesting book on the subject is *Insull,* by Forest McDonald, published by the University of Chicago Press in 1962.

What part did accounting practices play?

WERE UNSOUND ACCOUNTING PRACTICES a major contributing cause of the enormous stockholder losses of the depression days? There seems to be little agreement on this question.

In a speech in 1937, Robert H. Montgomery, then president of the American Institute of Accountants, had this to say:

> As alluded to elsewhere there is a feeling abroad that public accountants are able to protect investors from mistakes which they would not make if they would pay more attention to our reports. I hope that is true, but the implication is dangerous.
>
> We have to deal with conflicting elements, with the passion for quick profits and the assurance of safety. It is true that business practices and ethics are growing better, but I doubt if there is any change today, as contrasted with fifty years ago, from the conflicting elements I have mentioned. What can we or could we do with the stock which sold at $225 a share in 1929 and $2.25 a share in 1932. What could and what did a Congressional committee do? In my opinion, the Congressional committee which recently purported to investigate the transactions of bankers, brokers and investment trusts did little more than to rehash old stuff. Little of anything constructive was accomplished. Some of the witnesses attempted to point out that good management could not manage if hampered at every turn with intolerable restrictions.
>
> Real protection to investors would be to explain that a stock earning $2 a share selling at 100 probably is too high, but who can argue with one who tells you that nevertheless it will sell at 150?

In the same year George O. May, in a lecture at Harvard Business School, said this:

> When with the passage of time it shall become possible to review dispassionately the history of the depression, it will, I think, be found that inadequate or misleading reports of established businesses played but a relatively unimportant part in causing the catastrophic losses that were sus-

tained. The speculative fever which produced also the Florida land boom (in which corporate reports played no part whatever), the pyramiding of holding corporations, unsound treatment of stock dividends, and belief in a new economic order encouraged by persons high in the political and economic world were far more potent influences. However, the temper of the times demanded control of the dealings in corporate securities, and of corporate reports, and it was felt, with reason, that confidence would not be restored until a drastic measure designed to create this control had been enacted. Time was pressing, and it may well have been thought impracticable to defer action until a carefully considered measure could be framed and a body competent to administer it satisfactorily created.

Accounting has come a long way in the past thirty to thirty-five years. Practices that were countenanced in the 1920s and 1930s are no longer permitted. And yet, despite this progress, there are still many alternative and undesirable accounting practices that are permitted only because they are "generally accepted."

The term "generally accepted accounting principles" was not used in the 1920s, but "general acceptance" was the criterion used in passing on the fairness of financial statements. Accountants then asked themselves, "Does this accounting principle have support in practice?" Even if a well-known textbook or a prominent CPA had spoken against the principle in question, in the usual case accountants eventually, if reluctantly, bowed to usage.

The criterion of "general acceptance"

It was the theory of "general acceptance" that, in the 1930s, permitted electric and gas utilities to follow practices which have since been discarded. Notable examples were recording unrealized appreciation of asset values, treating stock dividends as income, and providing depreciation on a "retirement reserve" basis.

Many accountants did not like the idea of recognizing appreciation of investments (some of which were in unconsolidated subsidiaries or other affiliates) by accounting for stock dividends as income, yet the practice was "generally accepted." It is interesting to note that as late as 1941 a well-known textbook* had this to say about the receipt of stock dividends:

> While the practice of taking up stock received as dividends at no value is conservative and strictly logical, it has probably been "more honored in the breach than in the observance" recently, except as to large distributions, in the nature of stock split-ups. A number of corporations have adopted the policy of paying current dividends, from current earnings, wholly or partially in stock, and it has become fairly general practice to take up such stock dividends as income upon receipt, at current market values, but not in excess of the amounts charged against surplus by the issuing corporations. It is probably generally regarded as proper, in case the dividend stock is sold immediately upon receipt, to take the entire proceeds into income. There would seem to be little justification for treating as income in connection with the receipt of a stock dividend (except in the case of a stock dividend from current income of a wholly-owned subsidiary company) any amount greater than the excess of the market value immediately after the distribution, of the stock held at that time, plus the cash received if the dividend stock has been sold, over the total market value immediately before the distribution, of the stock held at that time. At the time this is written, the question as to whether stock dividends are ever income to the recipient until sold is being considered by a committee of the American Institute of Accountants. It is to be expected that a pronouncement on the subject will be made in the near future.

What was the reasoning behind the "retirement reserve" basis of depreciation in utilities? It was simply this: that as long as property was maintained in good operating condition it did not depreciate (although it might become obsolete) and that all that was

---

*W. H. Bell and R. S. Johns, *Auditing*, Prentice-Hall, Inc., Englewood Cliffs, N. J., 1941 (revised edition).

necessary was to provide a "retirement reserve" to meet losses when property was retired. The provisions added to these reserves, which were frequently based on percentages of revenue, were usually considerably less than depreciation on a straight-line basis.

Most accountants would have preferred to have depreciation provided on a straight-line basis, but there was ample support for the retirement reserve basis. This support was not just in practice: the National Association of Railroad and Utilities Commissioners and most utility commissions approved retirement reserve accounting.

We are troubled today because we think there is insufficient guidance as to the nature of generally accepted accounting principles. Yet in the 1920s and 1930s there was virtually no guidance. In 1933, the American Institute of Accountants established a seven-member Special Committee on the Development of Accounting Principles, made up of the chairmen of certain other committees. Beginning in 1936, a successor committee, similarly constituted, was called the Standing Committee on Accounting Procedure. The twenty-one-member Committee on Accounting Procedure came into existence in 1938 and continued until 1959. During its lifetime, it issued fifty-one Accounting Research Bulletins. Today, the Accounting Principles Board is the senior deliberative body of the Institute. Obviously, not all the problems of defining generally accepted accounting principles have been solved, but there is far more authoritative guidance today than was available in pre-depression days.

And yet, despite the progress made since the 1920s, many CPAs today feel that the accounting profession should be moving much faster in improving accounting principles and reporting standards.

Upon their success in living up to the new responsibilities about to be placed upon them depends in great measure the future of the profession. If they will discharge their duties "in all cases with proper honesty, efficiency and independence" (to quote a striking phrase from the recent report of the investigators of the cause of the Kreuger & Toll debacle) they will firmly establish the position of the profession as one of the main safeguards of the investor.

From an editorial in
The Journal of Accountancy, February 1933

CHAPTER ELEVEN

THE YEARS 1933 TO 1940

T HE YEAR 1933 WAS AN IMPORTANT TURNING point in the history of Arthur Young & Company. In the spring of that year the senior authority passed from Arthur Young, who was then 69, to a committee of four partners. (This committee was usually referred to as the Executive Committee, until 1956, when the present name, Management Committee, was adopted. To avoid confusion, however, I shall use the name Management Committee throughout this account of the committee's early years.)

Arthur Young's place in the firm prior to this changeover has been well described in the book, *Arthur Young and the Business He Founded*, which Jim Burton wrote in 1948:

> I should like to give some account of Arthur's place in the firm as it was in the 1920s. I think I can recall it clearly through the years, particularly as his place did not change much during that time. He was primarily the source of unity in the firm. Even in New York, partners tended to look on their own work as being a separate unit and the contact with other

Arthur Young's place in the firm

offices through the country was limited. Arthur visited the other offices periodically and kept our own office from developing into a series of pockets rather than a unified firm. He was our main client contact. Some business came to us from work we did well. Then, as now, a satisfied client often recommended our firm for additional work; but the base of all our business in those days was contact with personal friends or acquaintances of Arthur Young.

Arthur Young was also, in many respects, our report department. Any report on a new or tricky matter the partners referred to him before it was typed, and he spent every morning reading the reports that had been issued the previous day. His reading of these reports was never cursory. If an expression was not clear, he would ask the partner just what was meant and often suggest an alternative expression to make the matter clear to the average business man. He was not so much interested in technical accounting procedures, but he was very much interested in seeing that these special procedures were in accord with common sense.

Arthur had the final word on the settlement of any accounting problems in the office. The people involved would gather around his table where he heard all sides of the story and questioned the various partners (or in some cases clients) until the matter was entirely clear to him. His usual procedure was to endeavor to get an agreement of all parties without his specifically giving a decision, but he never hesitated, in a case where this was impossible, to outline his own point of view and state that this would be the firm's policy in the particular case under discussion. After his total deafness made this impossible we used to submit in writing all aspects of the problem, and he would study the whole matter and give his considered opinion. The only exception to this procedure was the problem of any client Will Sutherland was connected with. Arthur, in those years, seldom questioned a decision made by Will. This was based on confidence well deserved by Will through many years' work with Arthur.

There was one matter that Arthur had very little to do with, namely, the internal organization of the office. He assumed that this was the problem of his partners. That is probably why organization per se of the office for a long time lagged behind the efficiency of the individuals in the organization.

In the twenty-five years that followed, my esteem for Arthur grew steadily. This is not to say that I always agreed with him or he with me. We had differences of opinion, particularly in the early days—probably in most cases I was wrong but I was, like Arthur, a Scot with a good conceit of myself.

Arthur was very active for the first eleven years I was associated with the firm, although since then his activity has gradually lessened, partly owing to his increasing deafness, which by 1932 was practically total, and partly owing to the burden of increasing years. His keen interest in the firm, however, has been shown throughout the period.

It was Jim Burton's idea to have the senior authority in the firm pass to a committee, and the changeover came about in the following way.

In 1932 Arthur Young, thinking of the future of the firm, began to have some doubts as to whether the organization he had developed, in which complete control rested in one man, was the ideal form of organization to carry the business along in future years. The partnership agreement at that time provided that Arthur Young should have complete control in every respect, and that, in the event of his death, Will Sutherland, as previously mentioned, should succeed him.

Arthur discussed the matter at some length with Jim Burton a number of times. Jim finally made a specific suggestion: namely, that Arthur should continue to exercise complete control over the firm's affairs so long as he was alive, but that thereafter there should be a Management Committee consisting of two partners each from the New York and Chicago offices, who would succeed to Arthur's responsibilities as senior partner.

Beginning of the Management Committee

Arthur turned the matter over in his mind and, according to Jim Burton, came to two firm conclusions which he immediately proceeded to put into effect: first, that the proposed Management Committee should begin to function at once and not upon his death; and, second, that the committee should consist of the younger members of the firm and that he himself, in New York, and Will Sutherland, in Chicago, should merely be consulting members whose advice he hoped would be asked but who would have no effective vote in the reaching of decisions.

Through an amendment to the partnership agreement, the committee operation became effective on March 31, 1933. The original four members of the Management Committee were J. C. Burton (age 47) and W. D. McGregor (45), from New York, and Harry Boyack (53) and J. P. McGregor (56), from Chicago. Arthur Young, as I have said, was then 69 years old; Will Sutherland was 55. No chairman was named, but Jim Burton's strong leadership qualities quite evidently manifested themselves from the very start.

The first meeting of the newly formed Management Committee was held in April 1933. Coming as this meeting did in the midst of the depression, it was only natural, I suppose, that its tone should be pessimistic. Among the decisions reached were (1) that the Detroit office, which had been opened in 1925, should be closed because the Detroit Guardian National Bank, our principal Detroit client, had become bankrupt; (2) that the Dallas staff should be radically reduced, the consensus of the committee being that there were no men on the staff who could not later be replaced with men of equal ability; (3) that the Los Angeles office should be advised that the committee expected the two Los Angeles managers to carry on with a minimum staff, and that probably no staff except themselves would be necessary for the next eight months; and (4) that the salaries of local partners in New York and Chicago should be reduced, the amount of the reduction being left to the discretion of the general partners in each office. (In those days the managerial class in the firm consisted of general partners and local partners. The general partners shared in the profits of all offices, but the local partners shared only in the profits of the office in which they worked. In a legal sense, the local partners were actually employees, and later in the 1930s the term "local partner" was superseded by the term "manager.")

At this first meeting of the Management Committee, it was decided to invite Frank Ahlforth of the Chicago office to join the partnership as of July 1, 1933. In those days the firm's accounts, which were on a calendar-year basis, were closed twice a year: on June 30th and on December 31st. As a rule the second six months of each year, with the long slack season in the summer months, showed a loss, so Frank started out his career as a partner with a charge to his account at the end of 1933 for his proportionate share of the firm's loss.

THE EARLY 1930S were particularly difficult years for accounting firms. Just at a time when most accounting firms were struggling to overcome the effects of the depression, they had a great deal of additional responsibility thrust upon them, almost overnight.

New responsibilities for the accounting profession

This period of increasing responsibility really started in the spring of 1932, when the New York Stock Exchange decided to

159

ask all corporations applying for listing, except certain railroads, to agree that future financial statements would be audited by independent public accountants. The Exchange followed up on this decision by announcing that after July 1, 1933 all listing applications would have to contain accountants' certificates. The announcement stated that the scope of the audits should not be less than that contemplated in the pamphlet, *Verification of Financial Statements*, issued by the Federal Reserve Board in May 1929. Shortly after this action by the New York Stock Exchange, the Curb Exchange (the forerunner of today's American Stock Exchange) followed suit.

The action of the New York Stock Exchange was undoubtedly the result of a number of considerations, but it was popularly believed at the time that two factors were controlling: (1) the failure of Kreuger & Toll, some of whose securities were listed on the New York Stock Exchange, and (2) the increasing cooperation between the Stock Exchange and the American Institute of Accountants, committees of which had recently been exchanging advice. (It was the Institute that had prepared the pamphlet referred to in the New York Stock Exchange announcement.)

The Kreuger case

The speculation and fraudulent financial practices which wrecked the Kreuger match trust and brought about Kreuger's suicide in 1932 shocked the whole financial community. In the recent book, *Kreuger: Genius and Swindler* (Alfred A. Knopf, 1960), Robert Shaplen describes the extent of Kreuger's global manipulations as follows:

... After five years of investigation of the financier's four hundred companies around the world by batteries of accountants and lawyers, who

160

conducted the biggest post-mortem of its kind ever made, the final rendering showed that Kreuger, between 1917 and 1932, had inflated earnings on the books of his various real and unreal companies by more than a quarter of a billion dollars. During that period he had received about six hundred and fifty million dollars, mostly from securities he floated and partly as loans from banks, but at the time of his death his companies' net assets came to but two hundred million dollars, which was half of what the statements he drew for them were claiming. The shrinkage was due in part to the low market values of 1932, but most of it was the result of Kreuger's having paid large dividends out of capital over so many years. Many of the millions Kreuger got his hands on simply disappeared and probably will never be traced. . . .

Whatever had happened to the missing Kreuger millions, his death left a general legacy of ruin which included lost personal fortunes the world over. . . .

An editorial in the February 1933 issue of *The Journal of Accountancy* said of the accountants' report of the Kreuger case that it "reads like a combination of the Arabian Nights and the Financial Chronicle." Pointing out that the report dealt "with matter-of-fact figures and with the wildest dreams of imagination," the *Journal* editorial presented the following excerpts:

> The perpetration of frauds on so large a scale and over so long a period would have been impossible but for (1) the confidence which Kreuger succeeded in inspiring, (2) the acceptance of his claim that complete secrecy in relation to vitally important transactions was essential to the success of his projects, (3) the autocratic powers which were conferred upon him, and (4) the loyalty or unquestioning obedience of officials, who were evidently selected with great care. . . . The absolute powers with which Kreuger was vested gave him complete domination of the en-

tire group . . . Indeed he conducted the entire business as though he was accountable to no one . . . Closely related to the causes already mentioned are the complicated and confused bookkeeping in regard to many important transactions and the gross inadequacy of the documentary evidence in support of accounting entries which our examination has disclosed. The frauds could not have been consummated without assistance —witting or unwitting—of some of his associates, including some of the officers of the holding and financial companies, nor could they have been concealed if either the audits of the companies had been coordinated under a single control or the audits, though not so coordinated, had been carried out in all cases with proper honesty, efficiency and independence. It is apparent that the employment of different auditors for different closely associated companies, restrictions in the scope of examinations, subserviency if not complicity on the part of some of the employees and some of the auditors, and forgery of documents in order to meet demands for evidence confirmatory of book entries, all contributed to prevent such audits as were made from resulting in exposure. The history of this group of companies emphasizes anew the truth that enterprises in which complete secrecy on the part of the chief executive officer as to the way in which important parts of the capital are employed is, or is alleged to be, essential to success are fundamentally unsuited for public investment, since such secrecy undermines all ordinary safeguards and affords to the dishonest executive unequalled opportunities for the perpetration and concealment of frauds.

It is interesting to recall the reactions of some of the country's leading companies to the new requirement of the New York Stock Exchange. One large company let it be known publicly that the magnitude of its activities was such that it would be impractical for it to submit its fiscal affairs to independent audit. Other companies pointed out that it would be ridiculous to require outside audits of companies which had able comptrollers and chief accountants, and particularly of companies which had their own staff of internal auditors. Within a year or two, however, all of these companies gave way, one by one.

Not long after the action of the New York Stock Exchange, accountants became very much aware of certain important happenings in Washington, where Franklin D. Roosevelt's "New Deal" legislation was being enacted at a very rapid rate. The Banking Act of 1933 divorced commercial banks from affiliates which handled the underwriting of securities. Then came the Securities Act of 1933, the Securities Exchange Act of 1934, the Public Utility Holding Company Act of 1935, and the Investment Company Act of 1940.

Important happenings in Washington

Accountants were particularly apprehensive about the increased responsibility imposed upon them by the Securities Act of 1933. They talked about the point beyond which it might be unsafe for an accountant to venture. They reasoned that an accountant could raise his fees substantially and carry large amounts of insurance but still be inadequately protected against not only negligence but inadvertence. Most accountants felt that the law was unjust.

This is how George O. May expressed this general feeling:

> I cannot believe that a law is just, or can long be maintained in effect, which deliberately contemplates the possibility that a purchaser may recover from a person from whom he has not bought, in respect of a statement which at the time of his purchase he had not read, contained in a document which he did not then know to exist, a sum which is not to be measured by injury resulting from falsity in such statement. Yet, under the Securities Act as it stands, once a material misstatement or omission is proved, it is no defense to show that the plaintiff had no knowledge of

the statement in question or of the document in which it was contained, or that the fall in the value of the security which he has purchased is due, not to the misstatement or omission complained of, but to quite different causes, such as the natural progress of invention, or even fire or earthquake. The Securities Act not only abandons the old rule that the burden of proof is on the plaintiff, but the doctrine of contributory negligence and the seemingly sound theory that there should be some relation between the injury caused and the sum to be recovered.

Throughout this hectic period the firm was helped considerably by the able leadership of Jim Burton. Blessed with amazing powers of concentration, he could make a decision rapidly and then apparently put the matter completely out of his mind. Jim was the one in New York who distinguished the essential from the nonessential and had the courage to insist on the essential.

Warren Nissley's crusades

AT THIS TIME Warren Nissley was making himself felt in the profession. The additional responsibilities which accountants were being required to assume made Warren more vigorous than ever in his campaign for getting better-educated people into the profession. During this period, he made a number of important speeches in which his theme generally was (1) the need to raise the educational requirements for CPA candidates, so that in the near future a college degree would be mandatory, and (2) the need to develop professional schools, at both the undergraduate and the graduate levels, where through formal education, with emphasis on the humanities, young men might be adequately prepared for a career in public accounting. Warren said that he did not know of a single college in the United States which considered that its principal job, or even one of its major jobs, was to train young men for a career in public accounting.

In one of his speeches, Warren used the following table to illustrate the need for raising the educational requirements of future CPAs:

	CPAs admitted to the Institute from 1917 to 1934 inclusive			
	Ten years ended 1926		Eight years ended 1934	
Educated in the U.S.	Number	Percent	Number	Percent
Not high-school graduates	240	27.5	73	10.4
High-school graduates	278	31.8	316	45.2
College graduates	179	20.5	227	32.4
Total	697	79.8	616	88.0
Educated outside the U.S.				
Not high-school graduates	91	10.4	9	1.3
High-school graduates	71	8.1	64	9.1
College graduates	15	1.7	11	1.6
Total	177	20.2	84	12.0
Grand total	874	100.0	700	100.0

Warren further pointed out that, of the institutions attended by the 227 U. S. college graduates during the eight-year period ended 1934, only fourteen colleges supplied five or more graduates each, as follows: New York University, 38; Harvard University, 17; University of Pennsylvania, 17; University of Illinois, 15; Columbia University, 7; University of Washington, 7; University of Wisconsin, 7; University of California, 6; Dartmouth, 6; Northwestern University, 5; University of Maryland, 5; University of Michigan, 5; University of Chicago, 5; University of Texas, 5.

Around this same time Warren became deeply concerned about the inadequacies of the financial reporting practices which then prevailed and the apparent lack of independence on the part of certain accounting firms. He took very much to heart the following comments which James M. Landis, then chairman of the Securities and Exchange Commission, made in a speech in December 1936:

> The impact of almost daily tilts with accountants, some of them called leaders in their profession, often leaves little doubt that their loyalties to management are stronger than their sense of responsibility to the investor. Such an experience does not lead readily to acquiescence in the plea recently made by one of the leaders of the accounting profession that the form of statement can be less rigidly controlled and left more largely to professional responsibility alone. Simplicity and more adequate presentation is of course an end much to be desired, but a simplicity that misleads is not to be tolerated.

When Warren Nissley was on a crusade, his tenacity was terrific. We in the New York office had accounting principles morning, noon, and night. A lunch with Warren in those days was a substantial mental exercise. This aggressiveness of Warren's paid off, however; the profession took heed. It was to a great extent due to Warren's crusade that, at the American Institute's Council meeting in September 1938, the Committee on Accounting Procedure recommended an increase in its own size and the establishment of a research division, with paid assistants, with a view toward eventually formulating pronouncements on specific procedures and practices. As a result of this suggestion, the Committee on Accounting Procedure was enlarged from seven to twenty-one members, representing accounting firms of various sizes and including some teachers of accounting. Thereafter the Institute's Executive Committee approved a plan for the employment of research assistants.

NOT LONG AFTER THIS the financial community and the accounting profession received a terrific jolt from the McKesson & Robbins scandal, when it was revealed that audited financial statements included assets, which, through undiscovered fraudulent practices, had been substantially overstated. The scandal broke into the headlines early in December 1938, and from then on rumors flew thick and fast. The press and others were generally critical of the accounting profession. Almost immediately the Securities and Exchange Commission undertook an extensive investigation, with the announced intention of (1) determining whether or not the audit which had been made had met the prevailing and generally accepted standards of audit procedure and (2) determining whether these standards were adequate to assure the reliability of published financial statements.

The McKesson & Robbins scandal

In February 1939 the following editorial comments appeared in *The Journal of Accountancy*:

> The Institute has offered its wholehearted cooperation to the Commission in its review of presently accepted standards of procedure. At the time this magazine goes to press, the testimony has already made one thing clear: the auditors, regardless entirely of whether they shall finally be held to be at fault, were confronted by one of the most amazing and skillful frauds in the history of American business. Persons who occupied responsible positions in the company are alleged to have conspired in an elaborate and complicated scheme which included the forging of an un-

believable number of documents—credit reports, letters of confirmation from supplier's warehouses, invoices, orders, receiving tickets, shipping notices, bills of lading, bankers' statements, inventory tally sheets, inventory summaries, and book entries.

In the light of circumstances so unusual, one might predict that such a case could never occur again. Yet the fact remains that auditors had been misled and that a published balance sheet had contained substantial overstatements of assets. The need for a critical review of audit procedure was evident. Members of the Institute from all parts of the country were demanding some public statement by the executive committee to clarify the position of the profession as a whole. After extensive deliberation, the executive committee issued a short statement to the press on December 28th, simply saying that in the interest of the public and the accounting profession the Institute would review customary auditing procedure in the light of the McKesson & Robbins case to determine what, if any, changes should be adopted; that a standard of accounting procedure had been in existence for many years in written form in the bulletin, *Examination of Financial Statements by Independent Public Accountants* (a copy of which was sent to every newspaper which received the release); that the McKesson & Robbins case was an extraordinary one in which there was testimony indicating collusive fraud on the part of high officers and the forging of accounting records, and therefore should not be emphasized unduly in consideration of proper auditing procedure in the great majority of cases; that the problem of auditing was to find means of affording adequate protection at a cost which would not constitute an undue burden on honestly administered companies.

The principal purposes of this statement were to inform the public that certified public accountants are members of a well-organized profession which recognizes its responsibilities in this case, and that the profession had not neglected its duty to set up standards of procedure and to publish them for the information of the financial community. At the same time it was made clear that the profession was ready and willing to re-examine these procedures and to change them if they could be strengthened.

In the SEC hearings, twelve prominent accountants testified at considerable length. This testimony, which amounted to more than 1,500 pages of stenographic transcript, was viewed by practicing accountants and teachers as a veritable mine of information concerning practices and procedures in the accounting profession.

The Institute deserves a great deal of credit for the speed with which it moved to correct the apparent inadequacies of then currently accepted auditing procedures as evidenced by the McKesson & Robbins scandal. On May 9, 1939, the Council of the Institute adopted the report of the Special Committee on Auditing Procedure, which in effect made mandatory the observation of physical inventories and the confirmation, by direct communication with debtors, of accounts receivable balances.

WARREN NISSLEY'S CRUSADING SPIRIT was good not only for the accounting profession but for our own firm as well. In the mid-1930s the New York office, largely under Warren's leadership, began to recruit good college graduates.

We were getting much more organization-minded in New York. On December 17, 1936, the first monthly meeting of partners and managers was held in the New York Athletic Club. By coincidence, the meeting took place on Arthur Young's birthday —his seventy-third—and he attended that first meeting. It had been Jim Burton's idea to have such a monthly meeting, and he had been toying with the idea for fully a year before the first meeting was held.

There were nineteen people present at the meeting: five partners and thirteen managers from the New York office, and Tony Murison from London, who happened to be in New York at that

The first monthly meeting of partners and managers in New York

time for American experience. These monthly meetings were to benefit the New York office immeasurably.

Jim Burton, who presided at the meeting, opened it with the following statement:

> The business of an accounting firm is dependent on the ability not only of the partners who are supervising engagements but also of the managing accountants who have a much more direct touch with the actual conduct of audits undertaken by the firm. We feel that you gentlemen have a large amount of responsibility for the quality of work done by the firm. My partners and I have felt that while we have had occasional social meetings with you and while we have talked to each of you individually on specific engagements, we never have had any meetings for discussion of the principles and practices of our profession.
>
> I feel that an exchange of viewpoint is of the utmost value to all of us. The problem that comes up with one accountant is often of great value in preparing another accountant in a similar problem that may come up with him in the future. With the increased responsibilities of accountants under the Securities Act of 1933 and the Securities Exchange Act of 1934, and with the increased interest of the New York and other stock exchanges in accounting practice and procedure, it is essential that our accountants, and particularly those who are in charge of the larger engagements or groups of engagements, should know what other people in the profession are doing and what other people in the profession are thinking.
>
> I know, of course, that many of you, and indeed most of you, by study of current literature, are keeping in touch with such matters, but we have felt that an open forum of this sort might be of benefit to all of us.
>
> Our proposed plan is to have a meeting of this sort once a month, that the discussion and business should be limited to 1½ hours, during which time we hope to keep our discussion strictly to business but during which we hope to have the maximum contribution by each of you to the success of each meeting—by questions, by discussions, by statements. At the end of the meeting, we hope to have a quiet dinner with the whole proceedings being over by eight o'clock on each occasion.

After we get through the particular subject of this meeting, I hope we will still have time to hear suggestions as to any change in the form of these meetings; if there is not time for any prolonged discussions and if no ideas have occurred to you now, I hope if you have any thoughts on the subject prior to the next meeting, you will not hesitate to bring them to the attention of me or any of my partners.

In the spring of 1937 Warren Nissley talked with Jim Burton about the great need to develop college graduates as fast as possible so that they might undertake responsible work. After this matter had been discussed at some length with the other partners, it was decided that the way to bridge the gap between theory and practice was to run a staff school. This staff school—the firm's first—was held in Arthur Young's office in the summer of 1937. The instructor was a staff senior, William Abernethy, a Scot. The school was attended by fourteen men, and it ran for six weeks. Five of those fourteen men are still with us today, in 1965, and are well known throughout the firm: John J. Catterall, Walter M. Daly, John J. Deering, Frederick E. Horn, and William C. Ings. *The first staff school*

Three years later, in 1940, it was decided to resume the firm-wide annual meetings of partners and managers which had been discontinued during the depression. There were about forty men present at the 1940 meeting, which was held in the Palmer House, Chicago, from June 17th through June 19th. The afternoon of the third day was given over to golf.

Warren Nissley was very much interested in this 1940 meeting and participated vigorously in the discussions. He had just become a member of the firm's Management Committee, whose membership had been increased from four to five, and he was becoming more and more active in firm affairs. *Warren Nissley joins the Management Committee*

It was as a result of the death of J. P. McGregor of the Chicago office, in December 1939, that the opportunity arose for Warren to become a member of the Management Committee. A few months after McGregor's death, Warren discussed with Jim Burton the question of McGregor's successor on the Management Committee. Warren observed that, by virtue of seniority and partnership participation, he was the next logical candidate, but that if the geographical pattern of the original committee was followed the firm would undoubtedly look to Chicago rather than New York for McGregor's successor—which, Warren pointed out, made little sense from an organizational viewpoint. Jim Burton talked with me about the matter, and I imagine he talked with Arthur Young and W. D. McGregor and wrote to Harry Boyack about it. Later Jim told me that he would propose that the membership of the committee be increased to five.

At the next meeting of the Management Committee two decisions were reached: (1) that the membership of the committee would be increased from four to five, and (2) that the committee would recommend to the partnership that the two vacancies be filled by the election of Will Sutherland and Warren Nissley, with the proviso, however, that Will, who was then 62, should serve on the committee for only one or two years, "pending the selection of the most suitable of the younger partners in Chicago."

IN THE PERIOD covered by this chapter my personal life became more enjoyable. I had assumed responsibility for a number of sizable audits in the New York area, and these kept me much closer to home than I had been in the past. Although I worked as many hours as ever before and had a great deal more responsibility, I had much more flexibility in the use of my time.

It was in this period that our two daughters were born—Sheila in 1936 and Eileen four years later, in 1940. Children make a big difference in any married couple's life, and so it was with us. Madge and I began making all sorts of plans for the future. I found myself reading reviews of children's books and listening to children's records. For years we all listened with delight to a recording of verses set to music from Robert Louis Stevenson's *A Child's Garden of Verses*, and to countless other records. When one evening in December Madge and I listened on the radio to the farewell address of Prince Edward, who until that morning had been King Edward VIII, Sheila was in our arms; and when, months later, we got up at 4:30 a.m. to listen to the London broadcast of the coronation of George VI, Sheila was again with us. We were a happy family.

Our family grows

Madge and I wanted to introduce our first-born as soon as possible to all our relatives, so in May 1937 Madge and Sheila sailed for Ireland with the understanding that I would follow after as soon as I could. I was very busy that summer, but I finally managed to get away in July, and after a refreshing voyage on the *Berengaria* I joined Madge and Sheila in Ireland.

It was in that summer of 1937 that I first visited our offices in Paris and London. William Carter, an English chartered accountant, was then in charge of the Paris office, with Maurice Durando as his right-hand man. The Paris office in those days was under the supervision of the London partners, so Charles Tyrrell and Tony Murison came over from London to participate in the discussions of our mutual problems.

The war clouds were gathering in Europe then, but like most people I was not at all aware of it.

Not long after I got back from Europe, Jim Burton told me

that one of the matters on the agenda for the fall meeting of the Management Committee was the question of my admission to the partnership. This came as a complete (and, of course, a very pleasant) surprise to me. We had never discussed this question before, but the tenor of Jim's remarks that day led me to believe that my admission had in fact already been agreed to by the individual committee members, and that clearing it through the Management Committee was a mere formality.

I am admitted to the partnership

So that fall, when we were all assembled at a banquet in the Waldorf-Astoria celebrating the fiftieth anniversary of the American Institute of Accountants, Jim Burton announced that I would join the partnership on January 1, 1938, and then he promptly ordered champagne for everyone.

It is interesting to recall what the managerial group in the firm was like in 1938, when I became a partner. There were sixteen partners, including myself (eight in New York, seven in Chicago, and one in Kansas City), and there were twenty-four managers (twelve in New York, three in Los Angeles, two each in Chicago, Kansas City, and Milwaukee, and one each in Pittsburgh, Dallas, and Tulsa).

Bad news from Europe

I HAVE MENTIONED the firm-wide annual meeting held in Chicago in June of 1940. In many ways that meeting was a gloomy one, for the war news was very bad indeed. Just a few weeks earlier the evacuation from Dunkirk had occurred, and as our meeting began the news arrived that the Petain Government had asked for an armistice and had ordered all French forces to cease fighting.

Within a matter of weeks I received the following two letters from the men who were in charge of our Paris office. They are, I think, self-explanatory.

15 GROVE PARK GARDENS
CHISWICK W. 4

July 30, 1940

Dear Tommy:

It really was a pleasant surprise to get your letter, written as it was in the midst of the great rush. I meant to have replied months ago but my good intentions were always frustrated by either work or war.

After the breakthrough in the north, I began to make inquiries as to how a foreigner (and incidentally an ally) could get out of the country. The authorities required ten days to make out an exit visa, so Mollie and I filled up the required forms. As the ten days dragged out, a period that seemed so many weeks, the Germans were getting nearer and nearer, and during those hot nights we would wake up and hear the firing in the distance, often accompanied by nearby bombing and anti-aircraft fire. At last we got our visas, and I was then able to get tickets for a boat train leaving in five days' time and seats on an airplane leaving in six days' time. I thus made sure of getting away by either route unless they were cancelled or the Germans arrived in Paris before the date of departure. All airplanes had been cancelled for five days! On June 8th, I went to the railroad office and cancelled my tickets as we heard that by this route the journey took three days which, with two babies in very hot weather, would have been a nightmare. All the same our only hope now was the airplane. On Sunday, June 9th, we arrived at the air offices at 7:45 a.m., where they kept us until 10 and then drove us out to the aerodrome which, by the way, had been bombed to hell. The office was a tent and we sat in long grass by our airplane right away in a corner of the field. After three hours' wait, they started to take out baggage and told us they must drive us back to Paris as we could not fly to London. The Germans were then 35 miles away! However, after a snack lunch, they rushed us back to the aerodrome and we flew off. We left on June 9th and the French Government left Paris the next day for Tours, so we were just in time. Here I should add that reservations were liable to be cancelled at the last moment if any important officials or a "mission" had to go to London. What with that and the advancing Germans, you can imagine the constant nervous strain we endured with two babies on our hands. Mollie was wonderful throughout. I have to admit that I have never had so much "wind-up" in my life owing to the constant dread of being taken prisoner and separated from Mollie and the babies. As a pilot in the last war, I have had narrow escapes and have been machine-gunned by Hun fighters several times, but my wind-up then was nothing in comparison.

As for looking round our very nice home, I can assure you we just could not. We buried most of our silver in the cellar and packed some of our clothes and the babies' things. All my books collected since I was a boy and all our furniture, etc. and my fine wine cellar are left behind. God knows what has happened to it all and, if we can train ourselves to do so, we ought to try to forget it all. As for the cost of replacement in these days of leaping prices, I just cannot imagine it.

There is much more to say but I will not bore you further. Here we are in my mother's home where fortunately there is just room for us but, of course, it is harder, much harder, for Mollie than it is for me. We both agree, however, that it would be foolish to start our own home just yet. Having lost one, it would be just too bad for the second to be bombed!

London office has been very kind to me and have at once taken me back into the fold.

As for Paris office, we are completely cut off and France is as far from us as Germany. Durando *may* try to carry on if there is any work for him as he is French.

Please remember me very kindly to all the partners.

With all best wishes to you and your family.

Sincerely yours,
Bill [s]
(W. C. Carter)

August 6, 1940

Dear Mr. Higgins:

As I had the pleasure of meeting you when you were in Paris a few years back, I am addressing you this letter, but it is to give the New York office information regarding the Paris office and its staff.

You will perhaps have had news by now of Mr. Carter and will have heard that he and his family were able to return to England on the Sunday preceding the occupation of Paris. I have just heard that a letter arrived shortly after, informing us of their safe arrival. Now, of course, we are completely cut off from each other.

My family was able to escape from Paris on that disastrous week, my wife and her mother by car, my boy of 18 and myself by bicycle riding some 300 miles to a small village not very far from Vichy where the French Government is at present located.

I have received news that Morel, whom you will recall having also met in Paris, is still under the colors in unoccupied territory. His wife was taken away to the country with considerable difficulty a week before she gave birth to a baby girl. I hear that fortunately both mother and baby are well.

Our secretary also left Paris for Brittany but was able to return fairly promptly and is now keeping the office open. She informs me that many of our clients have reopened their offices. I am endeavoring to return to Paris as soon as possible but it is not an easy task at the present moment. As soon as I get back, I will resume work and take charge of the office. If the mail is still accepted in New York for England, or as soon as it is resumed, will you kindly inform Mr. Carter, care of the London office, of the contents of this letter, but please in your reply do not refer to this other than that you have taken care of the matter.

Yours very truly,

M. Durando [s]

Young accountants and accounting students by the thousands are being and will be transformed into fighting men. Hundreds of others have placed their professional skill at the disposal of governmental war agencies and war industries, and many others will respond to continuing calls from those quarters which cannot be ignored. Those who are not called must spread themselves thin enough to do the accounting work which is indispensable to the effective operation of our economy—the economy which supports the whole war effort and feeds and clothes the citizens who must remain at home.

From an editorial in
The Journal of Accountancy, April 1942

CHAPTER TWELVE

THE WAR YEARS: 1941 TO 1945

On July 1, 1941 I had rounded out twenty years with Arthur Young & Company. I had been a general partner of the firm for three and a half years.

During this twenty-year period, the number of general partners in the firm had increased from eight to seventeen. I was number eleven in the "participation" ladder. The amount of my participation in the firm's profits at that time was $6,000 salary plus 4 percent.

Of the original eight partners, only four were still active on July 1, 1941: Arthur Young (who was then 77), William Sutherland (63), Jim Burton (55), and W. D. McGregor (54). Two of the original eight partners had died—Fred Colley in 1933 and J. P. McGregor in 1939—and the other two, Tom Clarke and Harry Boyack, had retired in 1941.

Tom Clarke retired from the partnership for reasons of health on January 1, 1941, and unfortunately died within the year. Harry Boyack retired on June 30th. Although Harry was in good health, he seemed to lose interest in things when J. P. McGregor died.

Harry and Jim McGregor had been close personal friends, and McGregor's death in 1939 evidently had a profound effect on Harry. Although he was only 60 at the time, he began to think seriously of retirement. Harry was a bachelor, and had always lived modestly; by even higher standards than he was accustomed to, he was a wealthy man.

So about a year after Jim McGregor's death, Harry Boyack notified the Management Committee of his intention to retire on June 30, 1941. I first learned of this decision from Harry himself. We were having a partners' dinner at the Metropolitan Club, and after dinner, while some of the partners were playing cards and others had gone off on the town, Harry chatted with me. He said that McGregor's death had forced him to do some serious thinking about how he himself wanted to spend his remaining years. "Jimmy," he said, "worked hard all his life, day in and day out. He made money. He had a beautiful home and a good family. But he didn't live to enjoy any of these things he had worked so hard for." Harry paused, and said, "I've decided that I don't want the same thing to happen to me."

Shortly after Harry Boyack had made it clear that he wished to retire from the partnership, Will Sutherland announced his wish to resign from active membership in the Management Committee and to serve as a consulting member only. Thus, at the Management Committee meeting held in June 1941, the resignations from the committee of Harry Boyack and Will Sutherland were accepted, and the committee decided to recommend to the partnership the election of Frank Ahlforth and A. V. McPhee, both of the Chicago office.

At this time Ahlforth was 45 and McPhee was 44. They were both extremely able men and carried heavy responsibilities in the firm for many years.

FRANK AHLFORTH was born in Moline, Illinois in 1895 and at the age of 11 moved to California with his parents. He returned to Chicago in 1917 and was employed by Deloitte, Plender, Griffiths & Company from October 1917 to April 1918, when he enlisted in the U. S. Navy. J. P. McGregor was then in charge of Deloitte's Chicago office, and when Frank returned early in 1919 he found that McGregor had joined forces with Arthur Young & Company. Frank looked up Jimmy and started with our firm in March 1919.

Frank Ahlforth

Frank progressed rapidly. He became a local partner on January 1, 1927 and, as I have said, a general partner on July 1, 1933. He became administrative partner of the Chicago office on July 1, 1941, when he became a member of the Management Committee.

For twenty years Frank played an active part in the profession, both through the American Institute and through the Illinois Society of CPAs, of which he was president for the fiscal year 1942-1943. In May 1928 he received the Elijah Watt Sells award for having achieved the highest grade in the Institute's CPA examinations that year.

A. V. McPhee

I FIRST MET A. V. McPhee in Kansas City in the winter of 1933. He was making an audit of what we referred to in those days as "our branch offices," while I was engaged in a special investigation. The picture of McPhee which I have carried with me over the years is of a big, red-headed friendly individual who wore his clothes casually and paid a lot of attention to his pipe.

Mac was born in Alpena, Michigan in 1897, and it was in Alpena that he received his early education. It was his ambition as a youth to become an engineer, so he entered the Engineering College of the University of Michigan in 1916. In May 1917, however, he enlisted in the Army and saw service in France with the 125th Infantry of the 32nd Division. Upon his return to civilian life in August 1919, he decided against devoting four more years to the study of engineering, largely because he wanted to marry the present Mrs. McPhee. He returned to the University of Michigan, however, and graduated in June 1921 with an A.B. degree. It was William A. Paton, then a young professor of accountancy at Michigan, who interested Mac in the idea of a career as a public accountant. Mac started with Arthur Young & Company in November 1921.

In addition to our close collaboration on administrative matters, Mac and I worked together for four successive years on the audit of International Minerals & Chemical Corporation (formerly International Agricultural Corporation), whose fiscal year ended on June 30th.

International moved its head office from New York to Chicago in June 1941. At McPhee's suggestion, I continued to give a good deal of attention to the work through fiscal 1944. I should point out that while McPhee was in a secondary position until 1945, when he took over from me, this was only because he felt I had the confidence of the client. There was never any doubt in my mind that McPhee was a much better accountant than I was.

THE YEAR 1941 was a busy one for all the New York partners, and in the fall of that year it became apparent that W. D. McGregor was feeling the strain. Always noisy and boisterous, he was even more so then. Jim Burton became worried at the thought of McGregor entering the winter's rush in that state, so he suggested to me that McGregor and I go off someplace together, possibly on a cruise. I felt a loyalty to McGregor, of course, but it did not stretch that far. Burton then talked to McGregor but, as might be expected, Mac flatly refused to go off on a cruise, with me or anyone else. Burton was equally positive, however, and in those days he had a trump card he could play. This card could not be played too often, but when it was played it was very effective. That trump card was Arthur Young, with whom Jim then had considerable influence. Jim talked to Arthur and convinced him that it was an absolute necessity that McGregor get away for a rest. It was difficult, if not impossible, to argue with Arthur. Aside from the fact that he was completely deaf, everyone had a deep respect for him. He was so gracious and so utterly selfless in all things that one just hated not to do what he wanted. So McGregor quickly succumbed, and after that, of course, I did not have a chance. Almost immediately Mac and I went over to the Grace Line office to see what cruises were available. We had no difficulty in finding one to our liking.

A cruise with W. D. McGregor

So on October 31, 1941 Mac and I sailed on the *Santa Paula* on a twelve-day Caribbean cruise. Our families came to see us off, and they all seemed to think it was an enormous joke, our taking a vacation together.

At first Mac and I were anything but enthusiastic, but within forty-eight hours sunshine and music and a recurring thirst all combined to make us one with the spirit of the ship.

On the first night we were both invited to have cocktails with the captain. There were about eighteen of us, and we sat at a long narrow table at the head of which sat the captain. I was amazed at the purser's memory for names and faces. As each person entered the room he asked his or her name and then made the introductions to everyone else. Not once did he have to pause to recall a name, and some of the names were quite difficult.

In those days Mac had a great passion for martinis, and one of the first things he did was to get acquainted with the bartender to make sure that he understood how to get the martinis exactly the way Mac liked them. The bartender did well by Mac and me, and Mac was soon loud in the man's praises.

The *Santa Paula* made four stops on the cruise: Curaçao in the Netherlands Antilles, La Guaira and Puerto Cabello in Venezuela, and Barranquilla in Colombia. We both disembarked at La Guaira and took a two-day 160-mile automobile tour of the Andes. This was a very pleasant diversion. We stayed overnight in Maracay and rejoined the ship at Puerto Cabello.

I believe that this cruise of the *Santa Paula* was her last or last but one pleasure trip until after the war. On November 30th she took off on a secret voyage to West Africa with 500 aviation technicians and a great deal of equipment. From the outbreak of war until V-J Day she covered in all some 240,000 nautical miles. She shuttled a great many times between the United States and North Africa while the African campaign was under way, and she was among the first transports to enter Palermo harbor in the Sicilian campaign.

The Caribbean cruise was good for Mac. For the next three or four years there was to be little let-up for him or anyone else. Neither Mac nor I realized, of course, how close the United States was to war when we started out on our cruise.

I was in the dining car of a train en route to Holt, Alabama when I first learned about Pearl Harbor. The news of the Japanese attack came to us from the steward, who went from table to table giving what little information he had about the attack. When I arrived at the railroad station in Birmingham the newsboys were all shouting their extras. I wished I could have been almost any place but Holt, Alabama.

I have said before that McGregor always gave a great deal of personal attention to his clients. This was especially true during the war years, when those clients actively engaged in the war effort had a number of difficult problems. One of these clients was Todd Shipyards Corporation, which Mac had handled for more than twenty years and which was called upon for important work as soon as the war clouds appeared. Mac gave so much of himself during the war years that I don't believe he ever fully recovered from the strain.

I HAVE OFTEN THOUGHT that Warren Nissley's most productive years were from about 1938 to 1948. By 1941 he was carrying a

Busy years for Warren Nissley

great deal of responsibility—in the firm, in the profession, and for a while in the Government.

When Tom Clarke retired at the beginning of 1941 a number of his clients—one of them Radio Corporation of America—were turned over to Warren. This, together with special work that arose from the war, added considerably to Warren's burden of responsibilities. In addition to his client work, Warren put in a great deal of time during the war years on various Institute committees and subcommittees, including those on national defense, war activities, accounting procedures, aptitude tests, and personnel.

It was during this period that Warren became very interested in the work of the Institute's Committee on Selection of Personnel. One of the main tasks of this committee was to develop some practical means of helping accounting firms and collegiate schools of business to more accurately identify and select those individuals who had the potential to give the quality of service needed in the profession. It was Warren who spearheaded the creation of the original Strong* Interest, Orientation, and Levels I and II tests which have since become familiar throughout the accounting profession. During this period quite a number of people in our firm—myself included—served as guinea pigs to establish some of the norms that were used in evaluating these tests. After the program got under way, Warren worked very closely with Professor Ben Wood, director of the Institute's testing program, to continue improving the tests.

During the war years Warren served as special consultant to

---

*Dr. Edward K. Strong was a psychologist who developed the widely used vocational-interest test bearing his name.

186

the War Department, in which role he did at least two important things: (1) he assisted in putting civilian-operated pilot-training schools on a sound financial basis and (2) he improved the procedures for renegotiating war contracts.

The civilian flying-school program played an important part in the winning of the war. By helping to solve the financial probbems of the civilian contractors and by making it possible for them to substantially expand their training program, Warren unquestionably performed a very useful service. In the beginning, the contract flying-school program was available only to Air Corps cadets, but later it was expanded to include women pilots, glider pilots, liaison-type-aircraft pilots, and aviation cadets of allied nations.

ABOUT THE TIME that Warren Nissley was active in Washington, Herman Ward, now a member of the firm's Management Committee, received an interesting assignment. I'd like to say something about this assignment here, because it typifies some of the peculiar accounting problems that arose during the war.

Herman Ward at Lockheed

The assignment originated one day in June 1941 when a call came into the Los Angeles office from our client Lockheed Aircraft Corporation requesting a good man to make a systems investigation. Herman Ward, then a manager in the Chicago office, turned out to be the "good man." He was loaned to Los Angeles to make the investigation, with the definite understanding tht he would be back in Chicago to handle important audits at year-end. As things turned out, however, Herman was not to return to the Chicago staff for that particular year-end or any other.

The early summer of 1941 was a growth period for Lockheed, as the British Government had placed orders for a substantial number of bombers. Lockheed planned to handle some of these orders through its subsidiary, Vega Aircraft Corporation, and a new plant had been built for this purpose adjacent to the Lockheed airport in Los Angeles.

This was the first attempt in the United States to mass-produce large airplanes on an assembly line. (Our client Vultee Aircraft Company had been producing small trainers in this manner for a year or two.) Everything was to be performed by the most modern methods of manufacture, including the maintenance of materiel control records on punched-card equipment. However, it soon became apparent that the proposed system was not providing information such as the scheduling of materiel to meet production requirements, the amount on order, when it was promised, usage to date, and spoilage factors.

An argument had developed among the management group at Lockheed as to whether or not the machine system was functioning properly. The difference of opinion was so sharp that management decided to get outside help to settle the matter, so Arthur Young & Company was asked to provide a systems expert.

When Donald MacTavish, who was in charge of the Los Angeles office, took Herman Ward out to meet the Lockheed people, Herman wore his sailor straw hat to be well-dressed. Donald didn't have to tell anyone that Herman was from the East: few people wore hats of any kind in Burbank, to say nothing of sailor straw hats. It didn't take Herman long to throw away that hat.

The investigation soon disclosed that the machine system was inadequate for the job, and that the men whose responsibility it was to make sure that the parts and materiel were on the assembly line on schedule, and who had to defend themselves if production was held up, were maintaining their own set of manual records in addition to the machine records. Apparently, very little use was made of the machine records. Herman so reported and, in general, indicated the type of records that should be designed and used. As a result of this report, the firm was requested to plan and install a complete materiel control system. By the time Herman had finished this materiel control assignment, December 7th—Pearl Harbor Day—had come and gone, and the U. S. Government was frantic for fighters and bombers. Orders poured into the Vega plant. These included orders for such important planes as the P-38 fighter and the B-17 bomber. (As an aside, it should be mentioned that the United States was very fortunate that Lockheed and Vega had moved into high gear before our country became involved in the war. Hundreds of lethal weapons were delivered to the armed services from six months to a year earlier than they would have been delivered if it had not been for Lockheed's earlier work for the British Government.)

The frantic production efforts at the new plant focused considerable attention on the production control system, which was blamed for many production bottlenecks. So Herman stayed very close to Lockheed's production department for some months. In the meantime, two other Los Angeles clients—Consolidated Vultee Aircraft Corporation and the Ryan Aeronautical Co.—also needed "systems" assistance (what we would call management services work today), and it was not until the end of 1943 that

Herman was again available for audit work. His first audit assignments were the Lockheed and Vega audits as of December 31, 1943.

My responsibilities increase

DURING THE WAR YEARS, and increasingly afterwards, Jim Burton was in the habit of dropping into my office each morning, after reading the incoming mail, to discuss matters. I became a sort of right-hand man to him in internal office affairs—personnel, assignments, bulletins, office records, and so on. The arrangement was never official; it was simply something that evolved over a long period of time. It all started, as I recall, by Jim's using me as a sounding board on the abilities of certain staff men. I knew the staff very well, partly because of my familiarity with the personnel records from my days in the bookkeeping department but primarily because of my close working contact with them. Because I handled a number of large engagements, practically everyone on the staff had worked with me at one time or another.

Jim Burton was particularly interested in the monthly meetings of partners and managers, and soon after they got under way in 1936 I became secretary of these meetings—a duty which I performed for several years. This role brought me into contact with Jim a good deal. He chaired the meetings, but I was the one who was charged with all the details, and it was up to me to brief him if that was necessary. I did the research. I examined every set of printed accounts I could put my hands on, clients' and nonclients'. I prepared the agenda. I wrote the minutes and from time to time defended (or at least tried to defend) what I put in them.

In June 1941 it was decided to move the firm's Home Office from Chicago to New York, and when the books came to New York in the following winter it was a natural extension of my responsibilities to have a hand in supervising the firm's accounts and all the details connected with them.

Life was not always easy. Sometimes I stubbed my toe badly. This happened once in connection with an "office letter," which, as we then used the term, was an informal means by which a partner could convey to the organization something of general interest that had come to his attention. One day I came across a set of printed accounts in which the auditors' certificate struck me as being unique. It was in effect a long-form report, but compressed into one page. I distributed an "office letter" in which I reproduced the certificate and wrote a covering note which simply said that the report had come to my attention and seemed to me to be quite interesting. In my simple way I had overlooked entirely the fact that the firm I quoted from was not in great popularity with many of our partners. At the next annual meeting of partners, which followed shortly after my office letter, all hell broke loose. I still chuckle when I think of that meeting, which was held at the University Club in Chicago. The following is from the minutes:

> There was a vigorous discussion on the subject of office letters and bulletins. The feeling was unanimous that bulletins are a decided advantage, but there was a difference of opinion on the subject of office letters. One partner took a strong position that the office letters were useless and an unnecessary effort, that he did not like the idea of these being issued on the responsibility of one or two individual partners, rather than having the consideration of all partners as the bulletins do. He particularly men-

tioned one which he said they had found damaging to the morale of their office, in that it quoted from the procedure of another accounting firm. No decision was arrived at.

After Pearl Harbor I seemed to become a sort of Jack-of-all-trades, and all kinds of problems found their way to my desk. Some of the things that gave me the greatest headaches had to do with the staff. First and foremost was the draft. While certified public accountants were included among a list of essential occupations in a Selective Service bulletin issued by national headquarters in March 1943, getting the facts across to certain draft boards was anything but easy. The chairmen of some draft boards (and, for that matter, the public at large) seemed to feel that the only way a man could serve the war effort was by carrying a gun. I appeared before many draft boards and prepared countless appeals. In the appeals I did my best—not always successfully—to demonstrate that the clients being served by the individual concerned were in activities essential to the war effort. These activities were spelled out in considerable detail. Sometimes the appeal was supported by letters from client officials.

Then there was the problem of salary and wage stabilization. This problem made itself felt in the winter of 1942-1943, when it was announced that salaries and wages were frozen as of October 3, 1942.

A fruitful expedition with T. T. Shaw

I remember quite vividly how we got our original salary schedule approved. On January 13, 1943 T. T. Shaw and I called on the regional office of the Salary Stabilization Unit to see how our application for approval of stipulated rate ranges was making out. (At that time, T. T. Shaw was one of our outstanding younger partners. At 38, he was in charge of the New York office tax department, and we had worked a good deal together on the Socony account.) Despite our urgent entreaties, however, T. T. and I failed to get past the receptionist; we could get absolutely no information.

When I reported back to Jim Burton, he was deeply concerned, and I too felt apprehensive. The proposed salary increases were important, but even more was the matter of the additional compensation called for by our managers' contracts. It was obviously quite risky to make any move without approval of the Salary Stabilization people.

The next day I suggested to T. T. that we go back to the Salary Stabilization office and sit it out in the reception room—all day, if necessary—in the hope that someone would eventually see us. So we arrived there about 9:30 a.m., and the receptionist gave us the same pat answer: namely, that Mr. S. would deal with each application as soon as possible but in the meantime could not see anybody. She said he had refused consistently to make exceptions to this rule. I told the receptionist that we were determined to see Mr. S., if only for a minute or two, and that, if she didn't mind, we would just sit there, on the chance that Mr. S. could eventually fit us in. She evidently *did* mind and told us we were wasting our time—although, she added, it was no concern of hers. T. T. was restless, but I whispered to him that Mr. S. would eventually have to go to the men's room and that that occasion might give us an opportunity to get a word or two with him.

At 10:15 a.m., word came out to the receptionist that Mr. S. wanted a large carton of coffee. I took this to be a good sign. I had the feeling that nature had very definitely put herself on our side.

I tried to engage the receptionist in conversation. She was snippy and very sarcastic about T. T. and me sitting there with no prospect whatever of seeing anyone. She said that Mr. S. did not even know we were waiting to see him. I tried to make a few wisecracks but they were lost on her. By 11 a.m., however, she began to mellow, and T. T. and I began to make some progress. At 11:15 a rather heavy-set individual came down the corridor and, with a determined expression on his face, headed in the direction of the men's room. "That," said the receptionist to us when the door to the men's room closed, "is Mr. S."

"It's now or never," I said to T. T., but I was not optimistic. Five minutes later, back came Mr. S. Much to our surprise, up jumped the receptionist, and going to meet Mr. S., she asked him if he would be willing to see T. T. and me for just a few minutes, since we had been waiting for two hours. He paused, but then agreed to see us, so T. T. and I walked with him into his office.

I said nothing to Mr. S. about our application. I simply asked him about his job and said something sympathetic about the problems he must have. He talked to us at considerable length, first about his present job and then about his previous experiences. It turned out that he had worked for some time for a small firm of accountants, so we had a point or two in common. We talked about audit procedures, defalcations, unreasonable clients, and so on.

Just a little before noon Mr. S., while still engaged in conversation with us, got our application out of a large pile and looked it over quickly. He appeared to think about it for a minute or two, said it looked reasonable to him, and then picked up a rubber stamp and literally covered the application with stamps of approval.

What a blessed feeling. I don't think I've ever experienced a greater sense of victory, before or since. I was to be in and out of that particular regional office many times in the next few years, for the technicalities of salary stabilization gave me almost unending concern until the end of the war. After that first meeting, however, the receptionist and I got along famously.

It is interesting to recall how we described managers and Grade A seniors for salary stabilization purposes at the end of 1942:

MANAGERS	Men who, after acting as Grade A seniors for a number of years, are able to assume general charge of large engagements having many divisions or branches or to accept responsibility for the simultaneous examination of a number of engagements. Partners in the firm are invariably selected from this group, and they are given many duties in behalf of the partners relating to the supervision of the engagements they cover and to the discussion with the clients of accounting and auditing problems that arise.	$3,000 to $6,000 per annum with participation in profits under contracts varying from $500 to $4,000 per annum.
GRADE A SENIORS	Men who (usually after about five years' public experience) can be sent out to make an examination of any client with instructions limited to the known special features applicable thereto, and who can prepare a report thereon prior to reviewing the working papers and the report with a manager or partner. These men almost invariably hold a CPA certificate.	$3,000 to $3,900 per annum.

Later on, we were to refine the manager classification to Grades A, B, and C for salary stabilization purposes.

A Lend-Lease engagement

ONE OF THE LARGEST AUDITS for which I had responsibility during the war had to do with work for the Office of Lend-Lease Administration and its successors, the Foreign Economics Administration and the Office of Foreign Liquidation Commissioner, Department of State. This was an interesting assignment.

Early in 1942 the Netherlands Government was actively engaged in obtaining war materials in the United States for the defense of the Netherlands East Indies. Then the Indies fell on March 6th, and the question arose of what to do about these materials, since obviously they could not be used for the purpose for which they had originally been intended. These war materials were in a variety of places. Some were in factories in various stages of completion, some were on docks or en route to docks, and still others were on the high seas.

After discussions between the United States Government and the Netherlands Government, it was agreed that the United States would take over all such materials (essentially at cost) and would assume responsibility for those contracts which the War Department felt should be cancelled. In order to expedite the handling of the materials and the payment therefor by the United States, it was decided that the Lend-Lease Administration alone would represent the U. S. Government, instead of having several U. S. agencies involved.

Dutch ships which were en route to the Netherlands East Indies on March 6th were instructed by radio to put in at the nearest friendly port. Thereafter, twelve of them docked in Australia. The war materials on these ships were urgently needed in Australia so, after discussions between representatives of the governments of Australia, the United States, and the Netherlands, it was arranged that the Australian Government, under the War Powers Act, would requisition all materials on board. Representatives of the armed forces of the three governments made allocations of the materials in a manner which appeared to them to be most advantageous to the defense of Australia.

In addition to the Netherlands Government materials described above, there were also materials in the hands of Dutch merchants in the United States who were engaged in importing and exporting goods. War materials in the hands of these merchants were also made available to the United States.

When the Lend-Lease Administration became aware of the enormous amount of work involved, both in seeing to it that the various materials were received by the United States and in determining their cost, it decided to seek help from one of the large accounting firms. So one Saturday in June 1942 I received a telephone call from a Lend-Lease official, and a couple of days after that I made a trip to Washington to see him. After a two-hour conference I dictated to a Government stenographer a proposed letter which was approved verbally by the official, and when I got back to New York I put the letter into official form. Within a week after that I started work at the office of the Netherlands Purchasing Commission in New York.

We all knew that this Lend-Lease engagement was a large one, but none of us realized that it would last some four and a half years. During this period we issued, in all, some eighty individual reports.

From my diary... TO GIVE SOME IDEA of the general pace and variety of my activities during the years 1942 to 1945, here are some entries from my personal diary for that period. These terse comments are fairly indicative of life as it was in those hectic days. In a few cases I have added comments or explanatory notes in brackets.

1942 *February 15 (Sunday).* Jim Burton, Margery Mellis, Betty Carson, and I all showed up at the office to close the firm's accounts for calendar year 1941. [The firm's Home Office books had just recently been shipped from Chicago so that this was the first closing in New York.] Arrived home in time to hear Churchill announce the fall of Singapore, which gave me a sinking feeling.

April 9. Madge and I took title to 711 Parsons Road, Ridgewood, New Jersey. [On the following day we moved there from 920 Morningside Road, Ridgewood, where we had lived since moving from Staten Island in September 1940. Our new house on Parsons Road had been built in a hurry. I had an agreement with the contractor that, if the war effort prevented the completion of the house within a specified time, there would be no obligation on my part to purchase it. The house was started just about the time of the attack on Pearl Harbor.]

April 25 (Saturday). All day until 7 p.m. with Harry Grumpelt and others on Socony 10K.

June 25. Started work on the accounts of the Netherlands Purchasing Commission, New York, "to determine the liability of the United States to the Netherlands Government for various war contracts being taken over."

July 29. Hugh [my brother] named chairman of Draft Board No. 3, covering Ridgewood, Glen Rock, Midland Park, and Paramus, New Jersey.

January 11. At New York Transit Company.

1943

January 14. The Salary Stabilization Unit of the Treasury Department, greatly to our relief, approved our application. The approval enabled us to give effect to proposed January 1 adjustments and to pay managers their additional compensation.

January 20. At Navy Building in Washington, where I had an appointment with an officer and a civilian of the Bureau of Yards and Docks. Agreed to audit certain cost-plus-fixed-fee contracts.

January 21. Appeared at draft board in Jackson Heights to try to have induction postponed for a staff man who has a definite limp from polio in early childhood. The board agreed to call him in March instead of February.

January 28. Frustrating experience at the Wage and Hour Division of the War Labor Board.

February 8. At Central Foundry Company.

February 13. In Chicago, arranging for audit of International Minerals & Chemical Corporation in connection with preparation of A-2 registration statement. Met Frank Weston at Palmer House to discuss work he is to do at Peru, Indiana, for Bureau of Yards and Docks.

February 27 & 28 (Saturday and Sunday). At Naval Base at Peru, Indiana.

March 14 (Sunday). All day at Socony until midnight, this following several similarly long days.

March 25-30. International Minerals in Chicago.

199

June 27 (Sunday). Worked practically all day at home on two reports for Navy.

July 2. Conference at Netherlands Purchasing Commission office.

August 16-21. In Chicago on annual audit of International Minerals & Chemical Corporation.

August 24. With Frank Weston in Washington (Bureau of Yards and Docks).

September 9. Italy surrendered yesterday.

September 13. Insurance medical examination. Blood pressure 116.

September 27-October 8. Vacation with Madge at Hot Springs, Virginia. Guests there included Duke and Duchess of Windsor (he is now Governor of the Bahamas), Cordell and Mrs. Hull (Hull, Secretary of State, is resting preparatory to his trip to Russia), and Justice (Supreme Court) Frank Murphy.

1944

March. Very busy on Socony, Standard-Vacuum, Central Foundry Company, etc.

March 21. First luncheon meeting of partners (held at The Recess).

June 6. Papers carried large headlines about Allies landing in various places in France. Went to Trinity Church at 1:30 p.m.; it was crowded. At 3 p.m. listened to a broadcast from the King of England on a radio in Jim Burton's room.

October 10-11. Testified for three hours at SEC hearing in Philadelphia on Tidewater Power Company.

1945

January 2. Session at regional office of Salary Stabilization Unit.

February 13. Saw Francis Quillinan (son-in-law of Al Smith and law partner of Senator Wagner) to seek his help in appealing decision of

Salary Stabilization Unit of Treasury Department limiting payment of additional compensation to a number of managers.

February 17 (Saturday). In office all day until 9:30 p.m. (did not go out for dinner) working on appeal against decision of Salary Stabilization Unit. Home at 11:20 p.m.

February 23. Went to 26 Broadway to talk to John Deering and Amos Stone. Stone, who is from Tulsa office, has just come back from a seven-week trip to Caracas, Venezuela, where he made an audit of Sinclair properties and also visited the Socony office.

Then to Buckeye Pipe Line Co.

March 4 (Sunday). Eileen's birthday. At Socony all day until 9:30 p.m. Home at 11:15 p.m.

March 20. Saw McArthur of White & Case [the firm's counsel] regarding forms to be filed with the New York State Unemployment Department.

March 31 (Saturday). Left office at 2 p.m. with Tom Dowd to visit his draft board in East Orange. Home at 5 p.m.

April 3. A good part of day fussing with an appeal against the classification of 1A in the case of Tom Dowd.

April 4. Spent two hours with Burton and Nissley, the latter having a strong viewpoint that we should employ a cost man and also a personnel director who would contact colleges and elsewhere to get new staff members.

April 9. Burton confined to bed with an acute attack of gout.

April 10. Carter, who returned to Paris a couple of months ago, cabled today from London saying he had returned for consultation and asking us what work we would be in a position to give him.

April 12 (Thursday). Met Madge at 57th Street, went to a movie, had dinner and then took a cab to the bus terminal on 42nd Street. As we alighted from the cab we were both stunned by the newspaper headlines: "The President Dies—End Comes Suddenly at Warm Springs—Death Due to Cerebral Hemorrhage." Bed at 11:45 p.m.

April 29 (Sunday). Father, in his 77th year, has major stroke.

May 4. Father passes away at 11:30 a.m.

May 7 (Monday). Father buried in Moravian Cemetery, Staten Island, where Mother was buried in 1928. As the funeral was leaving Stapleton, automobiles and boats were tooting to celebrate the radio announcement concerning the unconditional surrender of Germany.

June 19. Eisenhower welcomed in New York by huge crowds.

June 29. Settled annual accounts of Standard-Vacuum Oil Company.

August 7. New York *Times* headline: "First Atomic Bomb Dropped on Japan."

August 10 (Friday). Walking along Maiden Lane I overheard a man refer to a broadcast saying that Japan was willing to surrender "if the step would not prejudice the prerogatives of His Majesty as a sovereign ruler."

Little work done in office—all sorts of rumors flying about the end of the war.

August 11 (Saturday). Listened frequently to radio.

August 12 (Sunday). Reviewed prospectus of International Minerals and listened hourly to radio.

August 13. No word as yet about Japan.

August 14. Japan surrenders unconditionally.

August 20 (Monday). Erik Blomqvist asked permission (which was granted) to go on a four-month leave of absence to improve his health. He told Jim Burton that, should he feel no better at the end of the year, he would resign from the partnership.

September 22 (Saturday). Martin Ruggaber, our office manager, died in his sleep at 3 this morning, apparently of a coronary. He had had a coronary eleven months ago but came back after being off a month or so. He was 54.

November 19 (Monday). Burton and Nissley talked this morning to Tom Flynn to say that by unanimous consent of the partners they were offering him the position of office manager of the New York office. [In those days we used the title "office manager" to describe what we would call a personnel director today.] Tom said he would very much like a try at the job and would be available in a week's time.

Observe how all things are continually being born of change; teach yourself to see that Nature's highest happiness lies in changing the things that are, and forming new things after their kind. Whatever is, is in some sense the seed of what is to emerge from it.

MARCUS AURELIUS: *Meditations*

CHAPTER THIRTEEN

THE POST-WAR YEARS

I HAVE SAID THAT THE WAR TOOK A HEAVY TOLL on W. D. McGregor. It always seemed to me that he was never the same after it. One afternoon early in 1947, Jim Burton showed me a typed letter, addressed to him from McGregor, announcing Mac's resignation from the Management Committee. I was on my way to a client's office at the time, but that night I thought a good deal about Mac. I suddenly realized, really for the first time, that the older generation was moving aside and the younger generation, of which I was a part, was taking over. I was sorry to learn about Mac's resignation from the Management Committee, for it indicated to me that he would probably be retiring from the partnership, too, before long. At that time Mac was 59.

I had worked a great deal with McGregor, and I could not help thinking of all the times we'd spent together. Like all of us, I suppose, Mac comprised a rather curious combination of qualities. Everyone on the staff feared him because of his boisterousness and his temper, yet at the same time almost everyone liked him and had a strong sense of loyalty to him.

Around this same time Erik Blomqvist decided to retire from the partnership at the end of 1947. This was not entirely unexpected, for Erik had been having health problems for a number of years. It was not an easy decision for Erik to make, because he was only 56. Time proved that he made the right decision, however, for his health improved substantially in the years that followed. I was saddened by the news of Erik's retirement, for I had known him for more than twenty-five years and had done many a job under his supervision.

After receiving McGregor's written resignation from the Management Committee, Jim Burton wrote to Frank Ahlforth asking for his thoughts as to McGregor's successor. Jim showed me Frank's reply, which said he had always assumed that I would be the next committee member. So at the March meeting of the committee, two weeks after my forty-seventh birthday, it was decided to recommend to the partnership that I be elected to the Management Committee. I was duly elected and attended my first meeting in September 1947. At this point the five-man committee consisted of Jim Burton, Warren Nissley, Frank Ahlforth, A. V. McPhee, and myself.

I am elected to the Management Committee

One month after that meeting Jim Burton told me he was very concerned about Warren Nissley's health. Warren had just had a medical check-up, and the results were not good. The cardiogram showed a slight heart condition, he was very much overweight, and his blood pressure was over 200. A week afterwards Jim talked in general terms to one of his doctor friends and asked him what *he* would do if his successor had a health report like Warren's. Jim's friend said that, frankly, he would look for another successor.

After the medical check-up Burton, Nissley, and I talked about how we could ease Warren's load in the office. One of the things that took a good deal of Warren's time was the American Institute's Committee on Accounting Procedure. I volunteered to replace him on that committee and I also agreed to take over one or two of his clients. This committee work was to be my first professional activity of any kind. Until that time I had never attended a single committee meeting of either the Institute or the New York State Society of CPAs. I had been named to a petroleum committee of the New York State Society some years before, but I had had no interest in it and never attended a meeting. My first meeting of the Committee on Accounting Procedure was held in January 1948.

IN THE LATE FALL OF 1947 Arthur Young showed signs of failing health. What had appeared at first to be a common cold developed into pneumonia, from which he never really recovered. Toward the end of January I spent a weekend with Arthur at his home in Aiken, South Carolina, and it was clear to me then that things were not well. He was in bed all the time except for two twenty-minute intervals when he sat by the fire in his bedroom with me.

Arthur passed away on April 3, 1948 at the age of 84. Friends paid their respects at services both in Aiken and in New York, and he was buried in Bethany Cemetery, Aiken, on a hillside looking toward the valley. The service in Aiken was conducted by the Reverend F. Gault Robinson, a Presbyterian minister, and the memorial service at the Madison Avenue Presbyterian Church in New York was conducted by Dr. George A. Buttrick.

Arthur Young dies

Arthur's close friend, Father George L. Smith, also attended the Aiken service and offered the following prayer, which seems to me to capture, in a few simple words, the essence of Arthur Young, the man:

Almighty and Eternal God, we ask Thy grace and blessing upon the immortal soul of our beloved friend, Arthur Young, who was such an inspiration to all of us during his life; a man of sterling character, absolute integrity, and unfailing kindness, who never pitied himself because of his affliction, but who, in his daily life and living, exemplified the fulfillment of the great Commandment to love God above all things and to love his neighbor, regardless of differences in creed or status, as himself!

Eternal rest grant unto him, O Lord, and let the perpetual light shine upon him. May his soul rest in peace. Amen.

Jim Burton, McGregor, Ahlforth, and McPhee all attended the Aiken service. Warren Nissley, Sam Welldon (for years chairman of the board of the First National Bank), and I acted as ushers at the New York service.

On the day after Arthur's funeral, McGregor talked to me about how impressive the Aiken service had been and about his long association with Arthur and about the wonderful character of the man. Mac seemed completely relaxed, and he wandered on at great length. He ended up by saying that now that Arthur was gone he felt no further obligation to remain with the firm, and so he had decided to retire at the end of the year.

IN SPITE OF JIM BURTON'S EFFORTS to lighten Nissley's load, it seemed to be impossible for Warren to slow down. A perfectionist himself, he did not find it easy to delegate responsibility to others.

He seldom could read a document prepared by someone else without wanting to edit it from beginning to end. It seemed to be constitutionally impossible for him to rely on another person's judgment, no matter how trivial the matter, and he was never satisfied until he had looked into all the details of a problem himself. Needless to say, he took a great deal of work home with him.

Nobody was more willing to get involved in other people's problems than Warren. I recall many occasions when I asked his opinion on some matter and he wound up taking everything pertaining to the problem home with him and making an exhaustive study of it. This sort of behavior may have been fine when Warren was young, but it certainly was inappropriate for a man in his fifties with a heart condition.

Warren's next medical report was considerably better. His weight was down and so was his blood pressure. Before long Warren was working just as hard as he always had. Then, a little more than two years later, the blow fell.

On Sunday evening, January 15, 1950, I had a telephone call from Jim Burton, who told me that Warren had had a major stroke at four o'clock that afternoon, and that he was now in Nassau Hospital, still unconscious. As we later learned, Warren had slept late that morning, after being out at a party on Saturday night, ate a hearty combination breakfast-lunch at noon, and decided to work off the meal by raking leaves. He had been raking leaves for about two hours, it seems, when he began to feel dizzy. He managed to make his way back to the kitchen, where he collapsed and almost immediately became unconscious.

The death of Warren Nissley

Warren never regained consciousness, and he passed away at 8:30 p.m. on Tuesday, January 17th.

I suspect that Warren died as he would have wanted to, working right up to the end. I had seen a good deal of him at the office in the week preceding his death, and he put in a full day's work on the Friday before he was stricken.

When someone writes a formal history of Arthur Young & Company, Warren Nissley's contribution to the development of the firm will, I am sure, be viewed as a major one. All of us in the firm today are beneficiaries of all he did and all he stood for. Warren was not quite 57 when he died.

The following tribute to Warren appeared in the March 1950 issue of *The Journal of Accountancy*:

Warren W. Nissley was a remarkable man, and the accounting profession has suffered a bitter loss in his untimely and sudden death January 17, 1950.

He had been elected treasurer of the American Institute of Accountants a few months before, but this was only the latest in a long series of services to accountancy which began only a few years after he entered the profession in 1919.

He conceived, organized, and promoted the Institute committee for placements, which in 1926 made the first organized effort on behalf of the accounting profession to attract college graduates to its ranks, and published the first official Institute pamphlet on accounting as a career. He made personal studies of the extent to which college graduates were entering the accounting profession, which were published in *The Journal of Accountancy*. He advocated the formation of graduate schools of professional accounting similar to law schools, and worked actively at Columbia University toward that end. He conceived the idea of applying vocational interest and achievement tests to students who wished to enter the profession of accounting, and won the approval of the Institute council in the face of some opposition and a good deal of inertia. He raised $80,000 by voluntary contributions to launch the project, secured Dr. Ben D. Wood as director of the project, and supervised it as chairman of the committee on selection of personnel for five years. In this capacity he advocated a personnel-reference service, which would put college graduates who had taken the tests into touch with prospective employers. This service is just about to be launched by the Institute.

While Mr. Nissley's first love was the education, selection, and training of accounting personnel, he had a wider range of interests. He was one of the group which actively advocated and finally organized the research department of the Institute, under an enlarged committee on accounting procedure, which has published the Accounting Research Bulletins since 1938, and he served as a member of that committee for nearly ten years.

Mr. Nissley served his country in both World Wars, first as an artillery officer in combat service, and later as a special consultant to the Secretary of War.

Warren Nissley was a remarkable man because he combined extraordinary physical vigor with intellectual depth and originality. He was no conformist. He did his own thinking and said what he thought. Just a few days before his death he had prepared a paper which he had intended to present at a meeting of the New York Chapter of the Robert Morris Associates, national organization of bank credit officers. This short paper is so characteristic of the man that we have obtained permission to reprint it in this issue of *The Journal of Accountancy*. It shows a mind and a vitality which will be sorely missed.

THE DEATH OF WARREN NISSLEY was a blow to Arthur Young & Company, and particularly to the New York office.

Warren was the firm's Crown Prince. There wasn't the slightest doubt in anyone's mind that he would succeed to the top spot in the firm when Jim Burton retired at the end of 1951. Every sign pointed in this direction. Warren was involved in everything of importance that went on in the firm, was in charge of a number of important clients in New York, with close personal ties to many of their top executives, and was far better known in professional accounting circles than any other partner in the firm. Indeed, he was so prominent in the profession that many people assumed he *was* the senior partner of the firm.

It was a pity that Warren did not live long enough to become senior partner. If ever anyone worked for the spot, he did. So far as the firm and the profession were concerned, no personal sacrifice was ever too great for him; and he was, of course, a highly talented individual.

Warren died just on the eve of the firm's great expansion. How gratified he would have been to be a part of that exciting period in the firm's history; and how sad it was that he had to leave the stage at the time he did.

On the day following Warren's funeral service, which was held on Friday evening, I got into the office very early to tackle the backlog of work which had accumulated during the week since Warren was stricken. Some time afterward McPhee dropped in, then Jim Burton came, and finally Frank Ahlforth joined us.

Before Frank arrived, Jim asked Mac and me what we thought of the idea of asking Frank to transfer to New York—and, if this seemed like a good idea from the viewpoint of the New York office, what we thought the loss of Frank would do to Chicago. Mac and I both thought well of the idea. Mac also said that, although Frank's leaving would be a great sacrifice for Chicago, he was confident that with the assistance of Jim Groves he (Mac) could run the Chicago office.

Jim Groves, I might say, was a first-class man. He had good

presence and excellent business judgment, and he was well liked by his clients. Jim undoubtedly would have been on the firm's Management Committee himself had it not been for the fact that he and Frank and Mac were all pretty much of an age.

So when Frank Ahlforth joined us in my office, Jim asked him if he would be willing to transfer to the New York office to fill at least part of the void created by Warren's death. Frank never had any difficulty in distinguishing "yes" from "no," and in this case his answer was a definite "No"; nor did he waver at all when Jim added that he did not see how Frank could ever hope to be senior partner of the firm if he remained in Chicago.

Frank Ahlforth says "No"

In the context of things as they were that Saturday morning, Frank's coming to New York would have made sense. Frank was clearly next to Warren in seniority. He was 54 years old, he had been a partner for almost seventeen years, and he had been in charge of the Chicago office for close to nine years. Frank was an extremely able accountant with a quick, decisive mind and sound business judgment.

So the four of us spent that Saturday forenoon discussing the future of the firm and particularly the burden that would fall on a number of us in New York as a result of the loss of Warren Nissley. No important decisions were reached that day, but the discussions were the forerunners of others which were to lead in the months ahead to important decisions.

When Warren Nissley died there were a number of organizational problems facing the Management Committee. First and foremost was the need for the firm to expand. We knew we needed more offices in the United States, but we hesitated to open new ones because our work in the areas where we needed facilities was

Some organizational problems

not sufficiently large to justify anything but a small office. We had recently opened four new offices—in Caracas (Venezuela), Philadelphia, Houston, and Boston—but, although we had a good man in charge of each of them, we were very conscious of the fact that it would be some years before these offices would be large enough to enable us to specialize to the extent we felt we should.

In January 1950 we were satisfied, for the time being, with our facilities for handling work outside the United States, and at that time we had no thought of further expansion abroad. Briefly summarized, these facilities were: (1) a partnership agreement, since 1923, with Broads, Paterson & Co. of England, which gave us offices in London and Paris; (2) a partnership agreement, since 1944, with Clarkson, Gordon & Co. of Canada, which gave us representation in the key cities in that country; (3) our own office in Caracas, Venezuela; and (4) an understanding with another large accounting firm that it would handle our overseas work in places other than Europe, Canada, and the northern part of South America.

While these facilities seemed satisfactory to us in 1950, we did not then realize the extent to which our clients, in the years to come, would be expanding abroad. As the pace of this overseas expansion began to quicken, it became very clear to us that we would have to provide overseas facilities of our own and not rely on any other large firm, regardless of how reputable that firm might be.

Another problem before the Management Committee when Warren Nissley died was the matter of personnel recruitment and training. For a couple of years we had felt the need for an educational director, and in the spring of 1949 the Management Committee had authorized me to offer the position to Frederick E. Horn, with the promise of a partnership. Fred was then teaching at Columbia University, but he was well known to us, having been in charge of our New York office report department before he went into the service.

Fred did not feel he could come with us on a full-time basis in 1949, primarily because he wanted to get his Ph.D. He did, however, agree to serve as educational consultant and to become a member of a firm-wide educational committee which had just been formed with Tom Flynn as chairman. So at the time Warren died we felt that, while we had a long way to go, we were definitely moving in the right direction in the matter of personnel recruitment and training. (A little more than two years later, Fred received his Ph.D., and on September 1, 1952 he became the firm's first national personnel director.)

In the beginning of 1950 we were far from satisfied with our facilities for rendering management services. We had good men in some of our larger offices, but we realized that we needed an expanded staff of specialists to meet the ever-growing demands of our clients.

On the other hand, we were optimistic about our facilities for providing tax services. We had a staff of highly competent people in 1950 in our tax departments, particularly in our larger offices. T. T. Shaw, who was in charge of the New York office tax department, had no official firm-wide title at that time, but he was providing a leadership that we were fully confident would show results. As in the matter of personnel recruitment and training, we knew we still had a long way to go in the tax field, but we were satisfied that we were moving in the right direction.

Five important events

IN THE MONTHS THAT FOLLOWED Warren Nissley's death a number of important events took place. I mention five which stand out very clearly in my mind:

1. Effective February 1, 1950, the firm merged with two well-known local accounting firms: Wideman, Madden & Dolan, with offices in Toledo, Detroit, and New York; and Lunsford, Barnes & Co., with offices in Kansas City and Wichita.

2. The partnership agreement was rewritten as of February 1, 1950. Among other changes, the firm's fiscal year-end was moved from December 31st to September 30th, and the keeping of the firm's accounts was changed from an accrual basis to a cash basis.

3. In May 1950 an Advisory Committee was appointed to meet with the Management Committee twice each year. The need for a "junior Management Committee" of this sort arose from the firm's contemplated expansion, the growing importance of accounting standards, and the desirability of having certain matters studied in detail before consideration by the Management Committee. The members of the Advisory Committee were Paul J. Adam of the Kansas City office, who was then 40 years of age; L. B. McLaughlin, Chicago, 49; Harry C. Grumpelt, New York, 42; John P. Brown, Pittsburgh, 45; and Herman E. Ward, Los Angeles, 47. These were all men of great experience who were highly respected throughout the organization. Together they constituted a strong "second line" in the firm's administration.

4. In September 1950, J. C. Burton was requested to continue as senior partner for a three-year period beyond September 30, 1951, the date of his mandatory retirement under the partner-

ship agreement. (His period of active partnership was subsequently extended to September 30, 1956, the close of the fiscal year after Jim's seventieth birthday.)

5. In the New York office, Ralph E. Kent and Thomas D. Flynn were appointed as a two-man committee responsible for the supervision of all personnel functions, the management services department, the report department, the stenographic department, and the bookkeeping department. They were also responsible for keeping the firm's Instruction Book and Handbook up to date, and for the allocation and use of office space in New York.

THE TWO MERGERS which became effective on February 1, 1950 were the first in the firm's history.

The merger with Lunsford, Barnes & Co. was entirely Paul Adam's idea, and he thought it was a natural. The two senior partners of that firm wanted to retire—Lunsford because of age and Barnes because of failing health (he died in the June following the merger). Paul, on his part, wanted a larger office than the one he headed up in Kansas City, and he also felt that it would be advantageous to have a Wichita office because we had a substantial amount of work in that general area. Paul knew a number of the Lunsford, Barnes personnel, and he felt that they would add a good deal to our pool of talent. The merger discussions were under way when Warren Nissley died, and they were brought to a satisfactory conclusion a week or so afterward, largely by Paul Adam.

The merger with Lunsford, Barnes & Co.

Our contact with Wideman, Madden & Dolan came through the controller of a client who used to be on our Chicago staff and

The merger with Wideman, Madden & Dolan

who knew that we had important work in Toledo and Detroit but no offices in these cities. He had met Tom Dolan and was very favorably impressed with him and his firm. He saw mutual advantages in a merger, so he introduced us, with the thought that something might be worked out. This was in the summer of 1949.

That there were, in fact, mutual advantages to be derived from a merger soon became clear to both sides. Cyril Wideman, Jack Madden, and Tom Dolan were a formidable trio. They were enormously aggressive and had succeeded in building up a first-class organization over the years. They had good clients and a good fee structure, and they were progressive in their thinking. Tom Dolan in particular had a wide circle of business and banking friends across the country, especially in Ohio and New York, who looked to him continually for advice and ideas. Tom was particularly knowledgeable in that area which we refer to today as "buy/sell activities"—that is, the bringing together of companies for merger or acquisition purposes.

But the partners of Wideman, Madden & Dolan were frustrated. They had found, first of all, that they were failing to get certain work, which normally would have come to them, simply because they were a local firm; secondly, that it was difficult for them to retain a client once the company went public (underwriters then, as now, usually insisted on having the name of a nationally known accounting firm on the financial statements); and, finally, that it was becoming more and more difficult to service the increasing number of their clients whose activities were spreading out across the country.

The Wideman, Madden & Dolan partners also were very conscious of the advantages of having readily available to them facilities for personnel recruitment and training, and of being able to offer their clients specialized skills, particularly in the area of management services. They were also becoming aware, as they got older, of the advantages of having a larger "umbrella" to provide security for themselves and their group of loyal employees.

As far as we were concerned, we saw very distinct advantages in acquiring well-established offices in Toledo and Detroit, and we were also impressed with the opportunity of gaining outstanding professional talent at a mature level. We had learned from experience that to start an office from scratch in a new city often produces long-range problems, and we were also conscious of the fact that, regardless of our aggressiveness in recruitment and training, we would have a shortage of good people for some time to come.

Our discussions progressed leisurely. Burton, Nissley, and McPhee first of all visited Toledo and Detroit, and later on Frank Ahlforth and I made the trip. Cyril Wideman and Tom Dolan visited New York, Tom on a number of occasions. The more we saw of each other, the more we were convinced that a merger made sense for both of us.

Strangely enough, however, just when we were all set on a merger agreement at the end of 1949, Tom and Cyril decided not to go through with it. The sole reason for this decision was that Tom Dolan, who contemplated moving to New York, had begun to have serious doubts as to whether he could work with Warren Nissley when Warren succeeded to the top spot in the firm. Without our knowing it, these doubts of Tom's had apparently been building up from week to week as the discussions progressed. Tom Dolan and Warren Nissley were both, after all, extraordinarily strong personalities, and I suspect that Tom may have been right in assuming that they would eventually clash. Be that as it may, we parted fairly abruptly toward the end of 1949, and I, for one, thought that the merger door had been slammed shut for keeps.

Quite by accident, however, our paths crossed soon again in connection with a business deal of one of our clients in which Tom Dolan was actively involved. This was just about a week after Warren's death, and I suppose it was only natural that we would again start talking about the possibility of a merger. The discussions moved fast, and, as previously mentioned, the merger was consummated as of February 1, 1950.

Under the merger agreement Cyril Wideman, the senior partner of Wideman, Madden & Dolan, became a member of our Management Committee, and later on in 1950 Tom Dolan also joined the committee when he moved from Toledo to New York. Cyril continued on the committee until his retirement at age 65 in 1957, but Tom unfortunately had to resign for reasons of health some three years after the merger.

I was in Europe with my family in the summer of 1952, and just as I was boarding the *Queen Elizabeth* at Southampton I was handed a letter from Jim Burton which told me about Tom Dolan's most recent health report. In effect, the doctor had told Tom in no uncertain terms that his health was in jeopardy because of the pace he was keeping, and he urged Tom to seek a less strenuous career. Tom, according to Jim's letter, had reluctantly decided to accept the doctor's advice, although Jim had apparently urged him not to take any precipitous action. Jim had the feeling that the problem might be resolved by providing Tom with competent help to relieve him of a considerable amount of detail work. Tom, however, was unconvinced of the practicability of this idea.

I did my best to dissuade Tom, but it was hard to argue effectively in the light of the doctor's strong feelings. So some six months later, on February 28, 1953, Tom Dolan retired from the firm and from public accounting.

From the standpoint of Tom's personal life, and with the benefit of hindsight, I have no doubt that his decision was sound. Certainly his health seems to be holding up well today, and although I am sure that he occasionally misses public accounting, his business interests, which are many, keep him fully occupied.

Tom returned to live in Toledo when he left the firm, and this move must have been warmly welcomed by Mrs. Dolan. With the hours that Tom kept, life in an apartment in New York, away from her Toledo friends, could not have been very pleasant for her. We continue to see Tom Dolan frequently in New York and Toledo, although one is apt to run into him in almost any part of the country.

I have always thought that the Wideman, Madden & Dolan merger was very good for us. Not only were Cyril Wideman and Tom Dolan first-rate members of the Management Committee, but they came to us, I think, at a time when an infusion of new blood was badly needed. It was good to have inquiring minds question our ways of doing things. Tom and Cyril approached our operations just as if they were investigating a proposed acquisition for one of their clients.

It was our satisfactory experience with Wideman, Madden & Dolan that convinced us that our contemplated domestic expansion could be helped substantially by merging with reputable local firms in those areas where we needed new or enlarged offices, and it was our satisfactory experience with Broads, Paterson & Co. in England and with Clarkson, Gordon & Co. in Canada that convinced us that we could best handle our overseas work by making ties, wherever practicable, with reputable local concerns. And this is the course we have followed.

In the 1950s and 1960s we merged with a number of well-known local firms in the United States, and overseas we made ties with several leading local national firms. These overseas ties have taken the form of joint partnerships except in those cases where the laws of the other country have precluded international partnerships. Where this has been the case, we have entered into representation agreements which provide for the local firm to handle work in its own name but on our behalf.

The Advisory Committee

NOW LET ME SAY a word or two about the Advisory Committee which was established as an aid to the Management Committee in 1950, and about the responsibilities which were delegated to Ralph Kent and Tom Flynn in New York.

I have already mentioned the considerations behind the decision to establish the Advisory Committee. Under the able chairmanship of Paul Adam, the committee members were an enthusiastic and energetic group who interested themselves in just about every aspect of the firm's operations. At the very outset, the committee was asked to study, and to make recommendations to the Management Committee on, the following matters:

1. Expansion into new territories, through mergers or otherwise.

2. Unification of office procedures, standardization of equipment, etc.

3. Improvement of published accounts.
4. Territorial supervision of SEC work.
5. Personnel hiring and training policies.
6. Public relations.
7. Requirements for registering the firm in various states.
8. Supervision of periodic audits of each office in the firm.

During the first few years that this committee was in existence, it made numerous recommendations to the Management Committee, most of which were approved. As other committees were established, however, to serve as direct subcommittees of the Management Committee on such subjects as personnel and accounting and auditing procedure, the role of the Advisory Committee diminished accordingly, and its influence declined. The Advisory Committee was finally discontinued in 1958.

The decision to appoint Ralph Kent and Tom Flynn to serve as a two-man office management team in New York proved to be a very good one. Each of these men brought different qualities to the job, and in addition to complementing each other they worked exceedingly well together. It was one of those cases, which occur every now and then, in which one and one add up to substantially more than two. Year after year Ralph's and Tom's responsibilities increased.

Ralph Kent and Tom Flynn in New York

Although Ralph Kent and Tom Flynn were obviously outstanding men, they were at the same time thoroughly representative of the younger group in the firm in the 1950s—the good college graduates whom we had started to go after aggressively in the mid-1930s. Kent, a graduate of Ohio State University, was 34 in 1950; Flynn, a graduate of Princeton and of the Columbia School of Business, was 37.

Jim Burton looks ahead

AS I THINK BACK to the year 1950 it seems to me that Jim Burton showed a great deal of wisdom in the way he handled himself after Warren Nissley's death. A man with a lesser sense of organizational responsibility might have taken the opportunity to establish himself as the indispensable partner in the firm—as in fact Jim was, at least for a while. But Jim was concerned with the perpetuation of the firm, and not with his own glorification. He was absolutely selfless in that respect. Since the death of Arthur Young in 1948 he seemed to feel responsibility for the firm's future in a much more personal sense, even though it was always his habit to be thinking of the years ahead.

Jim took a dim view of his own life expectancy—quite unjustifiably, I thought at the time. He was overweight, as he had been most of his life, and he had recurring attacks of gout; but, aside from these problems, he struck everyone as being in excellent shape. At 64 he was still enormously energetic, and he had the same quick perception he always had.

Jim was an excellent committee chairman. I never ceased to marvel at how adroitly he could dispose of issues and how quickly he could produce the minutes of Management Committee meetings. We committee members would spend all day together, discussing and arguing matters, and as people on committees sometimes do we at times would wander all over the map. By 5:30 p.m. all of us would be weary, and with a great feeling of relief we would all settle down for a pre-dinner cocktail. All of us, that is, except Jim Burton. He would withdraw to one of the other rooms in the suite, call for his secretary, and start dictating the minutes. Not long after the ice arrived he would rejoin the group, full of boyish enthusiasm. The minutes were usually typed that same evening, and would be available for the committee's review early the following morning.

I was always amazed how few changes, editorial or otherwise, were necessary in the minutes that Jim prepared. The reason for this was that Jim not only had amazing powers of concentration but also had an extraordinary ability to express himself with precision and clarity.

So when Warren Nissley died, Jim, with his thoughts on the future, began to withdraw more and more into the background—always, however, keeping his finger on the pulse of things. In this period in the 1950s Ahlforth, McPhee, and I became, for all practical purposes, the firm's administrative committee. There was nothing formal about this; it was simply something that evolved as Jim tried to keep away from details.

The three of us worked very well together, even though we did not always see eye to eye on everything. We kept in close touch with one another by letter and by phone, and I always made it a habit to drop into the Chicago office whenever I was in that general area. When the three of us agreed on any matter—a merger, for example—Jim Burton seldom questioned our decision. He went on the theory that we were the ones who would have to live with the situation, so we should be the ones to make the decision.

One day early in 1954, on my way to Oklahoma, I dropped in on Ahlforth and McPhee. After we had disposed of a number of problems, both of them talked to me about the future of the firm and said that they thought the time had arrived when the succession should be clearly indicated. They made the suggestion that I be named vice chairman of the Management Committee, which, they said, would put me in a position analogous to that of an executive vice president in a corporation. They also added, however, that they thought this whole matter was primarily a New York problem, and that they would support any arrangement that was agreeable to Jim Burton and me. I did not think there was any particular urgency about indicating the succession —our setup in New York was working well—but Frank and Mac felt that the younger people in the firm should know with some assurance who it was that would succeed Jim.

At that time I was preoccupied with a number of pressing client problems, in Oklahoma and elsewhere, so I put the matter on the shelf until I returned to New York some two weeks later, when I talked to Jim. Jim never took long to make up his mind. His reaction was immediate. He said that he was all in favor of making the succession clear, that I held the senior position in the firm in everything but name (he had cut his participation below mine in 1951), and that he could think of no reason why it should not be formalized. He then suggested that he resign from the chairmanship of the Management Committee and assume an advisory role somewhat similar to that which Arthur Young had taken at the time the committee came into being.

Since I was personally involved in the matter, I did not feel that I should participate in discussing it any further, so I suggested that Jim talk it over with Ahlforth and McPhee in Chicago, who had brought the question up in the first place. Jim did this, and then he got in touch with the other members of the Management Committee: Cyril Wideman, Paul Adam, and Herman Ward (the latter two having joined the committee the previous October).

So, effective October 1, 1954, Jim Burton resigned as a member of the Management Committee and its chairman, and the committee then offered him a position, which he accepted, as honorary chairman and honorary member of the committee for one year, with every right to participate in discussions but no right to vote. Jim also agreed to continue as an active partner until September 30, 1956, the end of the fiscal year in which he became 70. With the reorganization of the committee, two additional members came on: Ralph Kent and Tom Flynn.

It was with mixed feelings that I succeeded to Jim Burton's position in the firm. I was naturally pleased to get the spot, but I regretted that Jim's long period in the firm was coming to an end. He was a colossus among accountants—a man both representative and unique.

I become senior partner

I have always felt that, if it had not been for a setback in his health, Jim Burton could have continued almost indefinitely as an advisor to the firm. He was an excellent sounding board on almost any subject, was always receptive to new ideas, and was amazingly progressive in his own thinking. Unfortunately he was not to continue in the role of advisor for very long. One day in his office in the summer of 1956 he suffered a cerebral accident, to use the modern medical term, and as it turned out he was not to return to the office again. Although he made a reasonably good recovery from his illness and usually attends our annual meeting in Hot Springs, Virginia, he has never felt equal to conversing with more than a few people at a time or to mingling in large crowds.

Religion is any activity pursued in behalf of an ideal end, against obstacles and in spite of threats of personal loss, because of conviction of its general and enduring value.

JOHN DEWEY: *A Common Faith*

CHAPTER FOURTEEN

RELIGION

During the years 1946 to 1954 I gave a great deal of my leisure time, particularly over the weekends, to church work. Religion has been an important influence in my life, and this is probably as appropriate a place as any in my story to say something about the matter.

Ten years ago, nobody could have persuaded me to put anything in writing on the subject of religion. I was taught in my youth never to argue about the matter. Said my elders: "No one ever wins a religious argument, and the result is almost always unpleasantness and hurt feelings."

It is not my intention, however, to argue anything here. I am not looking for converts. I simply want to say something about what I consider to have been an important element in my life.

I persuaded myself to write this chapter because of my feeling that people have become much more tolerant of variations in religious belief, and especially of religious skepticism, than they used to be. In my youth an agnostic was associated with evil. At best, he was viewed as an egotist or a cynic, or someone who was simply perverse by nature. Today, it seems to me, there is much more general acceptance of the idea that religion is an evolving process, and that progress in any aspect of life, including religion, requires that accepted beliefs and attitudes be questioned. Certainly it is much more widely understood today that, while some people can accept the tenets of their Church with ease, others find any kind of religious belief terribly difficult.

Religion in my youth

As I have said, I grew up in a religious atmosphere. My parents were devoted to their Church, and as children we attended both Sunday School and Church services. Religion was a constant topic of conversation at home, and a frequent one in the community as well.

In addition to his keen interest in the Church of Ireland, Father was interested in revivalist meetings. When one of the well-known evangelists came to town to conduct a mission, Father could usually be found among the congregation. Quite frequently he would take me along.

The revivalist meetings always drew large crowds, and as a child I was deeply impressed with both the preachers and the gospel hymns. As I grew older, however, I began to waver. I fluctuated between a craving for the certainty of the evangelists and some of the very darkest doubts about religion and everything connected with it.

I wasn't long in America before I realized that there was nothing unusual about my doubts. Not only laymen but even some of the clergy appeared to have some of the same doubts that I had.

In those days, the press used to give much more coverage to religious matters than is customary today. A Brooklyn newspaper, for example, used to print a sermon every Monday.

There was a great deal written about the controversy between the Fundamentalists and the Liberals in the Protestant churches, and I remember well some of the things that excited my interest: (1) the publicity given to five public debates between Charles Francis Potter, a Liberal, and John Roach Straton, a Fundamentalist, concerning evolution, the infallibility of the Bible, the virgin birth, the divinity of Christ, and the Second Coming; (2) the trial of John Thomas Scopes, a school teacher in Dayton, Tennessee who was charged with teaching evolution in contradiction of the creation narrative in the Bible; and (3) a succession of tilts between Bishop William T. Manning of New York, a vigorous defender of religious dogma, and some of his Liberal-minded clergy.

It was in the fall of 1927 that I tuned in on Station WJZ on our small radio one Sunday afternoon and found myself listening to the Vesper Service at St. George's Church in Stuyvesant Square (on East 16th Street). It soon became very clear to me that Dr. Karl Reiland, who gave the address, was a Liberal, and a vigorous one at that. The next Sunday, Madge and I attended the Vesper Service and shortly after that we joined the Church.

I discover the Liberal churchmen

From Reiland I went on to hear other Liberal preachers, and for ten years making these rounds in Manhattan was to occupy a good part of those Sundays when I was not on the road. Madge was a good soldier and usually came along on these pilgrimages of mine.

To me, essentially a country boy not far removed from Ireland, New York's Liberal churches were peopled with giants. Even today, more than thirty years later, I still remember the thrill of listening to those stalwarts of their times.

There were about a dozen individuals who influenced my religious thinking tremendously. These men were not confined to any denomination, and in fact one of them was a rabbi, the Reverend Stephen S. Wise. I don't know how it came about, but by some means or other the collective influence of this group of men seemed to create in me a kind of inner harmony which has never left me. If my forefathers were alive today, perhaps they would say I had been "converted." I don't know.

What were the outstanding qualities of these Liberals of their day? They had a number of points in common. To a great extent they were in rebellion against the status quo in religion. They said what they thought, and they had the courage to doubt. They were not bound by orthodox tenets or established forms. All of them had great vitality. In a sense they were religious infidels, for they had broken with tradition. Yet despite these common characteristics, all of these men were strong individualists. Put them in a room together and I suspect their thinking on specific questions would have varied all over the lot.

In the years I'm speaking of (the 1920s and the 1930s), I got more out of St. George's Church than any other church—our daughters were baptized there—but I think I learned more from John Haynes Holmes of the Community Church than I did from anyone else in the ministry. This was due entirely to the way Holmes went about preparing and delivering his sermons. He put a terrific amount of work into these sermons, and they showed it. They were always lucid, concise, and beautifully organized. After a sermon was delivered, it was printed and sold at a dime a copy, so that one knew exactly what Holmes was thinking, week after week. Holmes was tremendously stimulating; one might disagree with him occasionally, as I did, but he was never dull.

What did Holmes preach about? All kinds of things. Here are the titles of eight of his sermons:

"St. Francis of Assisi—What He May Teach Us for These Times"
"Science, Psychology, Religion—To Which Shall We Turn for Guidance?"
"What Can 'I' Do to Save This Desperate World?"
"What Shall I Do if I Must Deal with Death?"
"Theologies and Ideologies"
"The Affirmations of Life"
"Spiritual Power—What It Is and How It May Be Used"
"Substitutes for Religion—Why Don't They Work?"

Holmes's background was Unitarian, but with the passing of the years his Community Church became nondenominational. He had no physical church when I used to go to hear him. His church had burned down some years previously, and during the long period until a new church could be built his services were held in Town Hall.

As I have said, St. George's impressed me very much as an institution. It was not only that Karl Reiland was a scholarly and fearless Liberal preacher, but he was backed up by outstanding laymen, some of whom were well-known public figures. I grew to admire the religious devotion of these men and their sense of civic responsibility.

I view the 1920s and 1930s as the period when I received my religious instruction. It was entirely a one-way street, however: I was on the receiving end; I gave nothing in return except money and, regrettably, not very much of that; I took no part whatever in any church activities.

St. Elizabeth's in Ridgewood

Shortly after our family moved to Ridgewood, New Jersey, in 1940, I began to develop a different attitude toward religion. Living in the midst of a parish, I soon became aware of the many problems that every church confronts. I recognized that my first responsibility was to my parish church in Ridgewood, and also that the time had come when I should start giving instead of receiving.

Like most Episcopal churches in the suburbs, St. Elizabeth's Church in Ridgewood is a fairly small church, and I saw the need for lay workers at all levels.

One evening in the fall of 1946 I had a telephone call from the Reverend Alexander M. Rodger, who told me that I had been suggested as a vestryman and asked whether I would serve if elected. Without a moment's hesitation I said that I would be honored to do so. In the succeeding years, I served in various capacities and went on to become junior warden and then senior warden. As senior warden I worked closely with the Rector. It was with real regret that, after some eight years on the vestry, I had to give up all activities in the Church because of major health problems, which I will talk about in the next chapter.

What I believe

IT IS NOW TWENTY-FIVE YEARS since I quit making my pilgrimages to churches in New York City, and some ten years since I was active in St. Elizabeth's in Ridgewood (although I still attend services there, and Madge and I count the Rector and his wife among our dear friends). Let me try to summarize, very briefly, some of the things I believe today, and some of the things I still have doubts about.

To begin at the beginning, what do I mean by "religion"?

There are, of course, many definitions of the term, but I personally prefer that of John Dewey, which is quoted at the beginning of this chapter. The following quotation, from a sermon preached by John Haynes Holmes in 1944, is, I think, a logical extension of Dewey's approach:

> Let me begin by pointing out that religion has always been presented from one or the other of two points of view. That is to say, there have been two theories about religion. One is the supernatural theory. Religion is something that is divinely bestowed upon us from without, or from above. It is an inspired revelation of the mind of God through the mouth of some holy prophet, or the pages of some holy book, or the dogmas of some holy church. In this sense, religion is unique and strange—a miracle that renews itself, from hour to hour, in the soul of the believer. The other theory is the natural theory. Religion is something that belongs to human nature, and therefore has its origin within the soul. It is a part, and the highest part, of man's day to day experience with the world and with his mind. From this point of view, religion is not unique or strange at all, but as normal as sleep at night or waking in the morning—as nourishing as bread, as quickening as water, as wholesome as fresh air. There is nothing miraculous about it, apart from the daily miracle of life itself.
>
> It is needless for me to explain to you that it is this second theory of religion which I accept. My whole approach to this problem is humanistic rather than theological. I start my thought with man and not with God—with this earth and not with heaven—with the facts of human experience and not with the myths of divine revelation. If religion is to be found anywhere, it is to be found in the heart of man—in the joys and sorrows, the dreams and visions of that heart. That it ends there, I do not believe for a single moment. The heart of man is like a key that opens the doors of "many mansions"; the experience of man is the turning of that key. Before we get through, this experience will take us into the very presence of God. Which means that religion has to do with God as well as man! But this does not mean that religion suddenly goes supernatural. It remains natural because it begins with the heart of man—and there finds God.

Which reminds me of the familiar saying, that "religion is the life of God in the soul of man"!

In what do I believe? I believe in a supreme Power; a Power greater than ourselves; a Power that makes for good. I also believe in the Church as an institution.

Do I believe in an omnipotent God? I do not. I think a good case can be made for the idea that the principle of evolution applies to the Creator as well as to his creation. Such an approach helps me to understand the existence of evil.

There is, I suppose, very little of the supernatural in my religious thinking, as compared with most people's. To me, belief in such things as the virgin birth and the physical resurrection is simply not essential to a religious faith. Such doctrines seem to me to have no relevance to either the problems of the world we live in or man's quest for the divine.

Next only to my family, the most precious thing in the world to me is freedom of thought—freedom to inquire, freedom to doubt, freedom to say that one doubts, not only on this or that subject but on all subjects. The importance of this is clearer to me today than at any time in my life. Everything else seems secondary. The fact is that we cannot find truth if we silence those who try to use their powers of reason and who agitate for their beliefs, however contrary to our own these may be.

I believe in the power of personal example. Few of us realize how we can influence people—not by preaching at them, but by the way we handle our frustrations, by our attitude toward life and our ideals.

I also believe that one of the greatest satisfactions a person can have comes from dedicating some part of his life to a cause that is bigger and more important than himself or his possessions.

Do I believe in a life after death? I don't know. I think I have read all the arguments pro and con, and have pondered them all, but I still must say that I simply don't know. I used to think about this question a great deal thirty years ago, but now it never enters my mind—why, I'm not really sure. Possibly it's because there now seems to me a certain completeness about this present life. It is popularly believed that the idea of life after death is especially appealing to old people, but I am beginning to doubt that this is so. Old people want rest, they want relief from suffering or poverty, they want to avoid punishment (if they happen to believe in Hell)—but all of these things are quite different from wanting another go at the kind of life we know on this planet.

I personally feel a deep need to worship, and I believe that the Book of Common Prayer, used in Episcopal churches, is ideally suited as a basis for worship. I admire the cadences of this great book, and the way it compresses into restrained and dignified language man's yearnings and aspirations. One of the great advantages of written prayers over extemporaneous prayers, it seems to me, is that they curb the excesses to which religious emotion sometimes runs.

Despite my great reverence for the Prayer Book, however, I believe the time has long since come for this four-hundred-year-old work to be brought up to date. I am on the side of the growing number of people who believe that the Church (and I am thinking primarily of the Episcopal Church) places too much emphasis on the recitation of formulas and declarations of assent. It is true that the Prayer Book has been revised from time to time, but the fact remains that it is still molded by a mode of thought which belongs to an age long past.

I listen to the recitation of the Creeds and, like many others, ask myself a number of questions: Why must the Church insist that each member of the congregation, Sunday after Sunday, recite the Creeds? How many of the people who recite the Creeds, Sunday after Sunday, believe literally what they say? Why should the Church strain a man's loyalty and sincerity in this way? How many people are kept away from church because they view the Creeds as preconditions which commit them to propositions for which they see really no evidence at all? Does the recitation of a creed, after all, have anything to do with the essence of religion?

Sunday after Sunday, too, I listen to the Lessons that are read in church: the first from the Old Testament and the second from the New Testament. Sometimes these Lessons carry a message for all ages; often, however, they do not. Frequently I find myself wondering what relevance a particular Lesson has to my (or anyone's) everyday experience and relationships. Why cannot there be a Lesson, not necessarily from the Bible, concerning man's involvement in the world here and now and the kinds of decisions he has to make today and tomorrow and the next day?

From what I have thus far written in this chapter, the reader will conclude that I am an agnostic about most of the things in which the Church—and, more specifically, the Episcopal Church, of which I am a member—believes. How, then, do I justify having taken a leading part in the life of that Church? And why is it that I would like to do so again? Quite simply, because I believe that truth (including religious truth) is progressive, and because I would like to be a part of that progress. What men a hundred or two hundred years from now will believe I do not know, but I am inclined to think that they will look back on many of our present religious beliefs and practices as mere superstitions, just as we today look back on many of the religious beliefs and practices of our forefathers. In this sense, I suspect that many of today's clergy, of all faiths, are to some extent agnostics as far as the official doctrines of their churches are concerned.

LATELY I HAVE BEEN READING with great interest about the discussions that took place at the 1964 sessions of the Vatican Council and of the Episcopal Triennial General Convention in St. Louis, Missouri. The question that almost every church appears to be facing today is essentially this: Shall the Church accommodate itself to the modern world?

The current ferment

Opinion on this question is, of course, sharply divided. At the St. Louis convention a great deal of excitement was generated by California's Episcopal Bishop James A. Pike, who is an outspoken critic of what he terms "outdated, incomprehensible, and nonessential" church teachings such as the doctrine of the trinity. Some of his fellow bishops think that Pike is a secret Unitarian; some of them think he should be tried for heresy; and a few, apparently, think that he is trying to become a martyr.

But the stir that Pike has created in America is nothing compared to the stir in England that followed the publication there of a book by John A. T. Robinson, Bishop of Woolwich. Entitled *Honest to God*, this little book, published by Westminster Press in 1963, has been discussed on television and radio, in newspaper reviews, and in sermons. Both the book and its author have been denounced and praised by thousands. A leading Church publication said, "It is not every day that a bishop goes on public record as apparently denying almost every Christian doctrine of the Church in which he holds office." And a newspaper reviewer described it as "an agonizing and unusual spectacle—a bishop groping for truth, admitting that he does not know all the answers."

Shortly after *Honest to God* was published, another book, containing reactions to Bishop Robinson's views, was published under the title *The Honest to God Debate* (Westminster, 1964). Then, still later, Bishop Pike published his book, *A Time for Christian Candor* (Harper & Row, 1964).

Anyone who reads these three books is bound to have his thinking stimulated. Admittedly, all of these books raise more questions than they answer, but the important thing is that the questions are being publicly examined.

What Bishop Pike says in the Preface to his book seems to me to be very true:

> We are in the midst of a theological revolution. It is not that the present well-known attempts to rethink and restate the Christian faith are entirely original, either in approach or in content; a good deal of all this has long been in learned books and in seminary lectures. But now more than ever, the process is going on *in public*.

An inspiring layman

I HAVE MENTIONED my belief in the power of personal example, and some of the inspiring laymen I met at St. George's Church. In closing this chapter, let me mention one of these laymen who inspired me—and, I'm sure, thousands of others. The man I refer to is Charles Culp Burlingham, who was a warden of St. George's for twenty-five years and who was senior warden when he died in 1959 at the age of 100.

People used to say, "Mr. Burlingham, how have you managed to live so long? Do you drink? Do you smoke? Do you have any advice to offer?" To which Burlingham would reply, "Yes, I do have advice: Just keep breathing."

That exactly was Burlingham's creed, and it was good advice for anyone. What, after all, is the essence of life? It is effort; it is functioning; it is constructive activity and growth of mind and personality.

This is what the New York *Times* said in its editorial columns when a great soul passed away:

When Charles Culp Burlingham was past one hundred years of age he was still one of the most active and influential men in the City of New York. He was blind and could not hear well, but the room where he sat, during those last glowing days of his, was a place of pilgrimage. Indeed, it was more than that. "C.C.B.", as hundreds of persons thought of him, was not merely a man whom one aimed to please by a personal call. He was a man to whom one went for wisdom down almost to the day of his death, which was last Saturday. Nor was this wisdom of Mr. Burlingham's traditional or derived from the past. He constantly renewed his ideas. He managed to know what was in the latest books and argued about their qualities. New friends, new ideas, new books, but not new principles—these concerned Charles Culp Burlingham.

The remarkable thing about him was not his great age but how magnificently he used every one of his adult years. He did not try for public office, did not pursue fame, influenced many a good cause, but never sought personal advantage.

He was no long-faced reformer. He worked by wit, by humor, and by the charm of an utterly unpretentious complexity. In spirit he was one of the youngest adults in our city. His death in his one hundred and first year cannot be thought of as tragic, but many will be sad to think that they can never again go to ask "C.C.B." about something.

*How sickness enlarges the dimensions
of a man's self to himself!*

CHARLES LAMB: "The Convalescent"

CHAPTER FIFTEEN

A NEW LOOK AT LIFE

In the story of my life, the year 1955 has just about as great a significance as the dividing line between B.C. and A.D. has in the history of the world. Although I was blessed with good health until my middle fifties, I was made very much aware, in that year, that I would have to proceed in the future with a good deal more caution than I had been accustomed to exercising in the past.

I suppose the average person, when he is confronted with the knowledge that he has an acute medical problem, thinks back to the various signals that might have indicated to him that he would not live forever. So, at any rate, it was with me.

The first alarm that I had—a false one, as it turned out—came at age 46, when an insurance examination indicated that I had an "enlarged heart." I took the insurance at a higher rate and did nothing about my "heart condition" until some years later, when I again applied for insurance, this time with a different company. In my application I mentioned my "heart condition," of course,

A false alarm

and was promptly requested to get a certificate from a recognized cardiologist. I went to a reputable cardiologist, who, after taking a number of X-rays of my heart and lungs, said that there was nothing wrong with my heart. He wrote to the insurance company accordingly, and I got the insurance at normal rates. When I asked him what had gone wrong in the previous examination, he said that it might have been either of two things: an incompetent technician or faulty instruments.

Beginning in 1950 I had a routine physical examination each year in fulfillment of our firm's requirement of annual check-ups. These routine examinations disclosed no abnormal findings of consequence, although in 1952 the doctor told me that his fluoroscopic examination had disclosed an abdominal hernia. He suggested I have a support made and wear it continuously, so from then on I wore a support.

Sometime around the beginning of 1954 I became aware that I was getting rather short-winded. I noticed it on the golf course and on my way to work, as I climbed the slight incline that leads from Hudson Terminal to Cortlandt Street. Madge said my stomach was distended and that I should cut down on starches; she said I ate four times as much bread and potatoes as she did. So I cut down on starches.

In Ireland in 1954 Madge's relatives talked to her about my appearance. They said they were shocked at how I had failed in the two years since they had seen me. She explained to them that I had been working hard but that otherwise I seemed all right. Later, when she told me what they had said, I made light of it.

Actually it was a mistake for me to take a month off to go to Europe that summer. I had the devil of a time getting things finished up before I left, and while I was gone I was committed to write two papers, one on "Historical Costs vs. Current Costs" for the firm's annual meeting and the other on "Research and Development Expenses" for the Institute's annual meeting. It was not a pleasant or relaxing vacation.

That fall Madge became aggressive about my seeing her doctor. I resisted as long as I could, but her persistence became so annoying that I finally made an appointment and saw him on December 30th.

When he asked me what my complaint was, I made light of my visit by saying I had been working hard and "didn't feel quite up to par." I added that I occasionally had a slight pain low down on my right side but otherwise had no physical problems of any kind.

The doctor gave me a superficial look-over and asked me to come back in a couple of weeks for a more complete check-up. My blood pressure was 122/74.

I saw the doctor again on January 6th, and on the following day I took off for Denver to spend the weekend discussing a proposed merger with the firm of Ralph B. Mayo & Co. Frank Ahlforth and Ralph Kent joined me there. When the merger agreement was signed, on January 10, 1955, I returned to New York.

A week later I went to Columbia Presbyterian Medical Center for tests. These tests disclosed a spasm in the colon. The doctor prescribed medicine to ease tension and said he would continue to watch me.

On February 6th I took off for my usual trip to the Southwest, but the trip covered more points than usual. There were eight stops in all: Ponca City, Bartlesville, Wichita, Kansas City,

Denver, Tulsa, Houston, and Chicago. I felt all right for the next week or two, but towards the end of February I developed a dull pain low down on my right side which seemed to extend around to my back. The pain covered a wide area, and I took a good deal of aspirin.

By this time I was in the clear with most of my year-end client problems, although I still had some matters to straighten up with John Deering on Socony and Standard-Vacuum. I cleared these with him on Saturday, March 5, 1955, and having done so telephoned the doctor to say I felt I was really in trouble. I think he may have been expecting such a call, for within a matter of hours I was in the hospital in Ridgewood for observation.

"Really in trouble"

During the next ten days I had all kinds of tests. On the third day one of the doctors asked me why I was wearing a support. I gave him the background. He asked me to stop wearing it.

At the end of the ten days my doctor told me that he and his associates were all in agreement that an exploratory operation should be performed. He said that, while they were by no means sure, they suspected a cyst in the vicinity of the pancreas.

I reacted negatively to the idea and asked for a consultation. The doctor readily gave me the names of three men who he said were outstanding and well known. After thinking about it overnight, I picked one of the three, only to discover that he was on vacation in Florida. When I told my doctor that I would wait until the consultant returned from Florida he was quite annoyed.

I returned to work and finally saw the consultant on April 7th. After a fairly simple examination and some searching questions, he decided to have me take one more test. When he had reviewed the results of this test he joined the other doctors in recommending an exploratory operation.

So on April 22, 1955, I had the operation. It was a long-drawn-out affair.

In the days that followed I learned, bit by bit, what my problem was. On the fourth day after the operation my surgeon explained that they had found a large fibrous vascular tumor, that they had removed it successfully, that it was essentially benign, but that unfortunately some of the cells were not benign.

A few days later I asked my doctor whether he and his associates were sure that all the malignancy had been removed, to which he replied, "No indeed—there is no such thing as certainty in a case like yours." Then I asked whether they could not have removed enough of the vein to preclude any chance of recurrence. "Well," he said, "we removed fifty percent of the vein, and that was as far as we felt we could go with safety."

Still later I got more details. Research had disclosed that there were only four cases on record that were exactly comparable to mine. What made the problem unique was the location of the tumor, the involvement of the muscles, and the type of operation employed. My doctor explained to me that he had written to each of the doctors concerned in the comparable cases, and that he and his associates would make every effort to benefit as much as possible from their experience. He added that, regardless of what they learned, they had good reason to believe that they could operate again in the event of a recurrence. By this time I had found out that the name of the vein was the inferior vena cava, one of two large veins which carry blood to the right atrium of the heart.

So, as I turned the matter over in my mind, the blunt facts gradually became clear to me. I had cancer of an obscure nature, and the doctors were by no means sure that all the malignancy had been removed. Possibly, it occurred to me, this was just another

The blunt facts

way the doctors had of saying that they were reasonably sure that some part of the malignancy had *not* been removed.

I was to find out that sickness can come quickly to anyone, doctors included. Within a year after my operation one of the three consultants suggested by my own doctor died of a coronary at age 58. Another of the three—the consultant I had chosen—ended up just a few doors from me in the hospital, before I left, with a suspected brain tumor. One evening I was strolling along the hospital corridor and a neurologist was there, directing my consultant to walk toward him and away from him, apparently to test his equilibrium. I tentatively asked my consultant how he was doing, and he tentatively asked me how I was doing, and, while we glanced at each other sheepishly, the neurologist, fully thirty years younger than either of us, continued to call out his commands in military fashion. I said to myself, "What a cockeyed world this is!"

I was some three and a half weeks in the Columbia Presbyterian Medical Center, and then I spent about five weeks, at home and in Bermuda, recuperating. I returned to the Medical Center for tests in the last week in June, and on the basis of these tests the doctors told me I could return to the office. I was shaky and nervous and short of breath, but I seemed to improve as the summer wore on.

BY SEPTEMBER I WAS OPTIMISTIC and in good spirits. A good part of my energy had returned, and I began making plans for an active fall. There was the firm's annual meeting in Hot Springs, the Institute's annual meeting in Washington, D. C., contemplated visits to Caracas, San Francisco, and Los Angeles, and finally heading up a canvass to enlarge the parish house of St. Elizabeth's Church in Ridgewood. I knew this last piece of work would be the toughest of the lot.

We had had endless discussions about the parish house problem during the preceding two years but were getting nowhere. In the fall of 1954 the chairman of the Expansion Committee resigned, and all our attempts to find a successor failed. Months went by, and then finally I volunteered to take on the job myself.

A tough job for my local church

As chairman I appointed three subcommittees: a Building Committee, a Finance Committee, and a Publicity Committee. This was early in the spring of 1955. Very soon we were in agreement on the plans, and then the Finance Committee came up with the idea that we should hire professionals to lead the fund-raising campaign. I was concerned about the possibility of an adverse reaction from our parishioners, particularly some of the older ones, but the Finance Committee stuck to its guns. The members said they were unanimous in their opinion. When they saw that I was clearly apprehensive, they volunteered to set up a meeting with a representative of the professional firm they had in mind.

So a date was set, and I and the members of the Finance Committee met with the professional. Before that night was over, I was fully convinced that, no matter what the older generation in the parish might think, hiring a professional was the way to get the job done.

We signed the contract, publicized the matter—and then the complaints began to trickle in. They were not as serious as I had anticipated, however, and I think that I and the others were able to convince most of those who complained that we were on solid ground.

Our professional advisor assured us that the entire job, including the preparation of the various mailing pieces and the face-to-face solicitation campaign, could be concentrated into a period of three weeks. He emphasized, however, that this would involve a great deal of work on the part of many people in the parish.

The professional arrived in Ridgewood early in November 1955, and the Rector, another member of the vestry, and I sat down immediately with him to make plans. I told them I would keep all my evenings and weekends free for the following three weeks.

The whole thing was an interesting and stimulating experience. During the three weeks more and more people in the parish got into the act, so that by the time we had our "loyalty" dinner just about everyone in the parish was enthusiastic about what we were trying to do.

The pledges, which were payable over a three-year period, were considerably in excess of the amount we had set as our objective. Not only that, but in the following year, when I was out of action because of my health problem, the parishioners were approached to continue their pledge payments into a fourth year, so that the church building could also be expanded and joined physically with the enlarged parish house. Most of the parishioners readily responded, and on May 25, 1957 the cornerstone of the parish house and church expansion was laid.

The professional fund-raiser had told us that increased giving by parishioners would cause them to take an increasing interest in the affairs of their local church. The intervening years have proved the truth of that prediction.

So the canvass worked out well for St. Elizabeth's Church and for its parishioners. All the parishioners, that is, except me. At the end of the three weeks I felt like a wet rag; I had about as much ambition as the lowest derelict in the Bowery.

Within a few days I learned that for the first time in my life I was faced with a blood pressure problem. My blood pressure had always been low, but now it had shot up above 200. I did not realize then that hypertension would be with me for the rest of my life.

On November 28, 1955, I went into the hospital in Ridgewood for tests, the results of which were discouraging. The doctor asked me to return to the Columbia Presbyterian Medical Center as soon as possible for additional tests, but I decided to put the matter on the shelf until I returned from a trip I had planned to the West Coast.

A trip to the West Coast

I WENT BY TRAIN to San Francisco and spent practically the entire time loafing in my bedroom. At first I felt miserable, but I perked up quite a bit during the trip. By the time I got to San Francisco I was beginning to feel that maybe I would live forever after all.

Herman Ward had been talking about the possibilities of a merger with Lester Herrick and Herrick, an old and respected firm in San Francisco, and on my first day there Herman and I lunched with Anson Herrick and his sixteen partners. Anson, whom I had known for many years, was then 72—and a very young 72 at that.

After lunch, Herman and I visited the Lester Herrick offices. Herman returned to Los Angeles that night, but I stayed on for two more days. On the next day I had a leisurely three-hour lunch with Anson at the Bohemian Club and that evening I had dinner with him and his wife, Louy, in their apartment. The Herrick merger was consummated within a matter of weeks, largely through the efforts of Herman Ward.

It could not have been an easy thing for Anson Herrick to consider a merger which would mean the end of a firm name he must have treasured greatly. Nothing has ever made me more proud of Arthur Young & Company, or more confident of its future, than the willingness of men such as Anson Herrick to cast their lot with us.

From San Francisco I went on to Los Angeles, and I returned to New York on December 10th. A week later I entered the Medical Center for observation and for some of the toughest tests I have ever taken.

The tests were inconclusive, and there was divided opinion as to whether or not there should be another operation. My surgeon was in favor of removing my right kidney immediately. His reasoning was that the kidney was not functioning well; that the malignancy, if it recurred, would probably be in the direction of the kidney; and, finally, that an exploratory operation would give the doctors a new look at the problem area, which he said was a necessity in my case.

The blood pressure specialist did not react well to the idea of an operation. He said that there was no clear indication of a recurrence and that the blood pressure condition might very well correct itself with the passage of time. In any event, he said, he did not think a delaying action would involve any great risk, at least for another year. Not surprisingly, I found myself siding with the blood pressure specialist.

So I was released from the hospital with the understanding that I would be watched pretty carefully in the succeeding months.

I was thrilled to get at least a few more months of freedom and proceeded to make the most of them. That spring I was out of town a good deal, as the following itinerary indicates:

A few more months of freedom

January — Wichita, Ponca City, and Bartlesville

February — Kansas City, Denver, San Francisco, Houston, and Dallas

March — Washington, D.C. for the American Institute's Committee Days

April — Atlanta; Clearview, Florida (attending the American Institute's Spring meeting of Council); and Caracas, Venezuela

May — Detroit, Chicago, Philadelphia, Pittsburgh, and Cincinnati; also attended the firm's Management and Advisory Committee meetings at the Seigniory Club, some 85 miles from Montreal

June — At Pocono Manor, Pennsylvania, attending the New York State Society's annual conference and at Hot Springs, Virginia, attending our own Managers Meeting.

On Saturday, March 24, 1956, Jim Burton celebrated his seventieth birthday. He was in Hot Springs at the time, and Ralph Kent, Tom Flynn, John Deering, and I, with our wives, surprised him by showing up in Hot Springs to mark the occasion.

At the end of January my blood pressure was down almost to normal, but shortly afterwards it started an upward trend. It continued quite high in the succeeding months.

In June my doctor discussed my problems with me at some length. He said that the tests made in Ridgewood the previous

253

week had disclosed nothing but a sluggish right kidney, and that his own feeling was that it was unnecessary to remove the kidney. He also said that he personally had no opinion as to the need, as a precautionary measure, for another exploratory operation, but that he would like to have the opinion of some outstanding pathologist. He mentioned the name of a pathologist who had retired from active practice but who, he said, was still very much in demand.

I heard nothing further until about a week later, when my surgeon asked to see me. He told me that he had consulted with three people: the retired pathologist who had been mentioned to me, the pathologist's successor at the Medical Center, and a woman doctor who he said had worked closely with both of these men for many years. All three, he said, were unanimous in recommending another exploratory operation as a wise precaution.

I entered Columbia Presbyterian on June 25, 1956, and a three-and-a-half-hour exploratory operation was performed on me on June 29th. The results of the operation were most encouraging. The doctors found no recurrence of the tumor and, after careful examination, decided against removing my right kidney. They did, however, remove my appendix, which was inflamed.

Encouraging news

When the news of the operation reached me I was naturally quite pleased. I realized, of course, that the possibility of recurrence would continue for several years, and I also knew that a defective kidney could affect my blood pressure and still might need to be removed. But this knowledge did not measurably detract from the relief of knowing that the operation had cleared up a good deal of the uncertainty about my problem. I figured I had freedom for at least two more years.

Sometimes people ask me, "How does it feel when you know you've had cancer and you know that there's a good chance of a recurrence?" Well, it's a lonely feeling; of course it is. But I suspect that for most people the problem is not nearly as bad as one might suppose. The fact is that no healthy-minded person, unless he is subject to continuing severe pain, can think very long about death. We are involved in life, and it is just about impossible to detach our thoughts from life. There is nothing logical about the will to live, but in illness one realizes what a terrific life force it is.

I have often thought of the truth of what Bernard Berenson once said: "Subjectively one never dies. It is only objectively that we expect to depart this life. Believers in immortality are therefore justified in practice. They will never know that they have died, for during the very last flickers of consciousness they were alive."

My weeks in the Harkness Pavilion of the Columbia Presbyterian Medical Center were in many ways quite pleasant. Naturally I felt (and acted) at times like a frightened rabbit, and I know that no matter how often I take certain tests I will always be scared to death of them. But modern medicine has come a long way, and I must say that my discomfort, even after the operations, was really very limited.

As I lay in Harkness I recalled a conversation I once had, when I was in my late forties, with Paul Knight, a well-known CPA. Paul, who unfortunately died some years ago, was in charge of the New York office of Arthur Andersen & Co. for some time. He was a delightful fellow, sound in his thinking and possessed of a wit that was most engaging.

Some years before our conversation Paul had had an illness that confined him to bed for several months. (I think it was a heart

Thoughts in solitude

condition resulting from rheumatic fever.) He explained to me that this long period of inactivity was one of the most rewarding experiences of his life. He said that from then on he had always felt that he would like to prescribe for all business men, and for a lot of other people too, three full months in bed, regardless of what the condition of their health might be.

I don't believe I got the full import of what Paul was saying at the time, but as I lay in Harkness Pavilion I began to understand. I think that what he was saying was that a long stretch in the orderly quietness of a hospital, or a bedroom at home for that matter, gives one an opportunity to sort out the pieces of one's life and get them in some kind of perspective.

It is hard to describe, but there is a kind of inner contentment that comes from being idle. One soon begins to realize that there is a difference between being lonely and being alone, and that the key to any man's life is to be found in what he thinks and does in his solitude. Perhaps it would not be such a bad idea for a man to have to spend some part of his life in isolation, thinking about the rules he lives by and his scale of the relative value of things.

A modern hospital is an enormously interesting institution, and I enjoyed my role as an unofficial observer. I got to know a number of very interesting patients, and of course I got to know many of the staff also. The two doctors who guided me through my difficulties are today my very dear friends.

A foolish resolve

Now I would not want anyone to think that one becomes divinely inspired merely by lying for a long stretch on a hospital bed. Far from it. At the time of my 1955 operation, for example, I made an unbelievably stupid decision: I decided to go on the wagon for life.

Alcohol had never been any problem for me—for years I had

256

drunk in moderation and with pleasure—but I reasoned that I could increase my efficiency terrifically by cutting out all liquor. I said to myself that when a person takes two or three drinks each night at dinner, as I did, this inevitably spells the end of any real mental effort for the rest of the day. I recalled how I had cut out cigarettes some twenty years earlier, and how the thought of smoking no longer occurred to me. So why not do the same with liquor?

I told each of the doctors in turn about my ambitious plan, and was surprised and disappointed when not one of them displayed any enthusiasm about the idea. They did not say I was wrong, nor did they say I was right; as the saying goes, they damned the idea with faint praise.

But I went on the wagon anyway. And when Madge and I attended cocktail parties in Bermuda and Ridgewood and elsewhere, and everyone else was enjoying dry martinis and whisky on the rocks, I marched around with a large glass of ginger ale in my hand, outwardly very smug but inwardly feeling that the very bottom had dropped out of my soul. It was only then that I realized the nothingness of cocktail conversations and how utterly boring the whole thing must be to non-drinkers.

I came off the wagon some six months later, quite unexpectedly. It was at a dinner where I had to make a speech. For the life of me I could not gather up enough energy to open my mouth, let alone make words come out. So away went the Puritan in me. I still remember the tremendous feeling of well-being that immediately came to me as the whisky warmed my soul.

As I look back on it now, I am inclined to think that going on the wagon hindered rather than helped my recovery. If I understand what I have since read, alcohol—in moderation—is never a shock to the heart but only to the equilibrium, and I never drank enough to bother my equilibrium. I have since proved to my own satisfaction that liquor helps a blood pressure condition and reduces tension. It may well be the safest of all the tranquilizers.

Where I did run off the tracks was in putting far too much emphasis on activity. One should not be active all the time—certainly not in the middle fifties and certainly not after a serious major operation. Life does not consist solely of action. As Aldous Huxley has it in his essay, "The Education of an Amphibian": "In all the activities of life, from the most trivial to the most important, the secret of proficiency lies in an ability to combine two seemingly incompatible states—a state of maximum activity and a state of maximum relaxation. The fact that these incompatibles can actually coexist is due, of course, to the amphibious nature of the human being."

Some people seem to think that Winston Churchill drank continuously. I suspect that he always was a heavy drinker, but nothing could be more absurd than to assume that the more he drank, the more productive he was. That is utter nonsense. Churchill must have disciplined himself rigidly to have accomplished all he did. I think he spoke true when he said, "I have taken more out of alcohol than alcohol has taken out of me."

Lord Beaverbrook knew Churchill very well from the days of the First World War. The following, from his remarks about Churchill in his book, *Men and Power: 1917-18*, is, I think, revealing:

> He lived well, and ate everything. He exaggerated his drinking habits by his own remarks in praise of wine and brandy. He appeared to smoke incessantly. Not at all. He smoked very little, although relighting a cigar frequently. His use of matches outstripped his consumption of cigars.

NINE YEARS have now gone by since my 1956 operation. Throughout that period, apart from hypertension, I have enjoyed good health. While for some time there was a recurring question as to whether my right kidney should be removed, the doctors are now satisfied that it is not aggravating my blood pressure condition.

Nobody likes medical problems, and particularly surgery; but, as I reflect on the matter now, I'm inclined to think that, on balance, my medical problems, coming as they did in my middle fifties, were beneficial. Not only did they force me to practice much more sensible working habits but they also forced me to delegate far more responsibility in the administration of the firm than I otherwise probably would have done.

Most important of all, however, my "new look at life" enabled me to see things in far better perspective and to realize that life can be good in all its phases, even in sickness.

The wise man looks ahead.
(Sapiens qui prospicit.)

Latin proverb

CHAPTER SIXTEEN

LONG-RANGE PLANNING

Early in 1957 it became clear that the firm had a number of organizational problems which required attention.

First and foremost was the need for a stronger Home Office organization. At the time I'm speaking of the firm was being run essentially through a Management Committee of nine partners and a fairly large number of supplementary committees. This was far from satisfactory. It was becoming more and more apparent how impractical it was for a policy-making group of nine otherwise busy partners to deal effectively on a day-to-day basis with operating problems as they arose.

Some years previously we had started moving in the direction of a Home Office staff, but we had not progressed very far. In 1952 Fred Horn was appointed national personnel director, and in 1954 Ralph F. Lewis was appointed head of the firm's management services activities and Frank T. Weston was appointed head of the firm's SEC and research activities. Ralph Lewis had joined the firm specifically to undertake the task of developing a national management services department; he had acquired a good deal of managerial and consulting experience before joining us. Frank Weston, in 1954, had been in charge of the Boston office since it was opened seven years earlier.

Certain other people were also working at the national level in 1957. While these were limited moves, they demonstrated to all of us the great advantages that would be derived from a strengthening of our top organizational layer. The problem, of course, was how to free up men to work at the national level without impairing our service to clients. All of our key people had close ties to important clients.

Then there was the problem of overseas work. In the postwar period more and more of our clients were expanding their operations overseas. It was becoming increasingly clear to us that if we were going to be able to serve these clients adequately we would need in the very near future to have facilities in all areas of the free world.

Next was the problem of communications. Our managerial group in the United States in the spring of 1957 had reached a total of 232, comprising 73 partners, 44 principals, and 115 managers. To make sure that the firm continued to speak with a consistent voice wherever a problem might arise would necessarily require a tightening of our lines of communication among individuals and offices through firm publications, meetings, and the like.

Finally there was the matter of public relations. Although we believed that Arthur Young & Company projected a favorable public image, there was a growing feeling that we should take some soundings to determine whether the facts coincided with our instinctive feelings.

The upshot of our discussions of these organizational problems was that the Management Committee appointed a Long-Range Planning Committee in the spring of 1957 and some eighteen months later engaged the services of Earl Newsom & Company, a well-known firm of public relations consultants.

THE LONG-RANGE PLANNING COMMITTEE consisted of three men: Herman E. Ward, J. Harold Stewart, and John J. Deering. All of these men were members of the Management Committee.

The Long-Range Planning Committee

At that time Herman Ward and John Deering each had some twenty years of service with the firm, but Harold Stewart was a relative newcomer. He had joined forces with us about a year earlier, in October 1956, when his firm, Stewart, Watts & Bollong, merged with Arthur Young & Company.

Herman Ward was appointed chairman of the Long-Range Planning Committee because he had an exceptionally strong organizational sense, and because of his many years of practical experience in systems planning. He was then 55 years old, had been in the Los Angeles office for sixteen years, and had been in charge of that office for about eight years.

Harold Stewart was 58 years old in 1957 and had been practicing public accounting for thirty-five years. A past president of the American Institute of Certified Public Accountants (as the American Institute of Accountants became known in 1956), he had also had extensive experience in Washington. In the Navy during World War II he acted as executive assistant to the director of the Navy Department's Cost Inspection Service. Later on, among other things, he acted as consultant to the Defense Department, served as assistant director of the Office of Contract Settlement, and presided over the Hoover Commission Task Force on Budget and Accounting. We felt that Harold Stewart, with his diversified experience, would add a fresh viewpoint to our problems.

John Deering, the third member of the committee, was added to insure that our international needs would have high priority in the committee's deliberations. For years John had been the firm's great traveler. Keenly interested in foreign affairs, he was one of the men hired by Warren Nissley in the summer of 1937 after graduating from Columbia University, and, as mentioned earlier, he had been a member of the firm's first staff school, which was run in that year.

The committee's report

THE REPORT of the Long-Range Planning Committee was submitted to the firm's Management Committee early in 1958. After carefully considering it and discussing it with individual members of the Long-Range Planning Committee, the Management Committee approved the report, with minor changes, in the fall of 1958.

The report was divided into seven parts: (1) organization of the firm's management, (2) maintenance of standards in auditing, reporting, and ethics, (3) services to the managements of clients, (4) expansion of the firm in the United States and policy on mergers, (5) international expansion, (6) personnel, and (7) professional activities in state and national societies.

The report was a long one, and there is no need to discuss it here in any great detail. I do want, however, to say something about the first part of the report—that is, the committee's recommendations as to the organization of the firm's management. This, in my opinion, was the most important part of the report, because its end result was to provide the firm with a strong organizational foundation.

The following, in summary, were the committee's recommendations concerning the firm's organizational structure:

1. That the plan of a Management Committee of nine members, elected for three-year terms, should continue, as should the selection of a chairman of the committee to serve at its pleasure.

2. That the general purposes of the Management Committee should be to fix and harmonize the policies and practices of the firm, and that it should appoint an Operating Committee of three and designate its chairman, who would be known as the managing partner of the firm. (The managing partner and the chairman of the Management Committee might be the same person or different persons.)

3. That the Operating Committee should be charged with complete responsibility for operating the firm and should have authority to do all things which in its opinion would be in the best interests of the firm except as such actions were reserved to the Management Committee.

4. That the Operating Committee should have such staff as it deemed necessary, which, in most instances, would comprise partners who had been selected for their particular capabilities; and that the managing partner should have reasonable authority for the making of day-to-day decisions in order to avoid unwarranted operation of the committee.

5. That the members of the Operating Committee's staff should generally be known as national directors; that they should report to the managing partner; and that the areas of activity covered by these national directors should be taxes, accounting and auditing standards, management services, personnel, the firm's internal procedures, accounting and finance, and overseas affiliations.

6. That a partner (or employee, if there was no partner) should be designated by the Operating Committee as the administrative partner (or employee) in each practice office, and that such administrative partner (or employee) should be charged with the responsibility for managing that office and should serve in this capacity at the pleasure of the Operating Committee.

The committee's report had this to say about the role of the administrative partner:

> He will be selected with primary emphasis on his administrative qualifications. He will be assisted in achieving an efficient office administration by attendance at firm-sponsored meetings and through literature distributed by the Home Office. He must be willing to coordinate the activities of the partners resident in the office, developing a good staff, but at the same time he must work for the interest of the firm as a whole. The plan permits local office autonomy so long as the practice is conducted according to the firm standards, coordinated with the practices of other offices, and conducted on a progressive basis. When any of these fails, it is assumed that the Operating Committee will make a change in the administration of the office.

When the report of the Long-Range Planning Committee was approved in the fall of 1958, it was recognized by the Management Committee that the report was not all-inclusive and that additions and changes would be necessary from time to time.

Two important changes were subsequently made. In the fall of 1961 it was decided to adopt a regional plan of operating the firm, and four members of the Management Committee were designated regional partners: Paul J. Adam, for the Southwest; George V. Carracio, Midwest; Ralph E. Kent, East; and Herman E. Ward, West. (In the fall of 1963 Tom Flynn succeeded Ralph Kent as Eastern regional partner.) Following this regionalization it was decided that the firm's Operating Committee could be discontinued with, in general, those Management Committee responsibilities previously delegated to the Operating Committee passing to the firm's managing partner (then Ralph Kent). Once this step had been taken, it was then decided that, in view of the increased responsibilities delegated to the firm's managing partner, he should be appointed for a five-year term so that a periodic review and evaluation of his performance would become a matter of routine for the committee. Ralph Kent's five-year term as the firm's managing partner began on October 1, 1962.

AS I MENTIONED EARLIER, the Management Committee engaged the services of Earl Newsom & Company in the latter part of 1958. The idea of having an outside public relations concern counsel with us originated with the firm's Advisory Committee. Initially, some of us on the Management Committee reacted negatively to the idea, but gradually we became convinced of its soundness.

The Newsom report on public relations

We settled on the Newsom firm because Harold Stewart, Ralph Lewis, and I all knew the firm and thought well of it and its partners. I had met Earl Newsom a number of times at a resort hotel in Maine, and later on, when I was on the American Institute's Executive Committee, I met his partner Arthur Tourtellot. Still later I read and was impressed with Tourtellot's booklet, *The General Recognition of Accountancy as a Profession.* So we all became convinced that an investigation by Newsom would be beneficial. Not only would it give us useful information about our own firm, but it would also increase our knowledge of how well the business community understood and regarded accountancy in general—what weak points needed to be strengthened and what strong points should be built upon.

Our specific request to the Newsom firm was to make an objective appraisal of Arthur Young & Company and on the basis of its findings to suggest steps that might be usefully taken, within the ethical bounds of the profession, to improve our public relations. We suggested that, in making the appraisal, the Newsom firm attempt to determine two things: (1) our standing within and outside the profession, particularly as to the qualities of independence, technical competence, and professional posture, and (2) our strengths and weaknesses, as a firm and as individuals, in creating the opinions which others held of us.

As part of their investigation the Newsom people used a firm of professional interviewers, considered highly competent in the conduct of depth surveys, and commissioned it to get a clear indication of the concepts held by the business community of accounting firms in general and the services rendered by them. The interviewees were carefully selected from financial institutions (including commercial banks, investment bankers, and insurance companies), from industrial and mercantile corporations, and from some utilities. Newsom assured us that the purpose and origin of the interviews were effectively masked and that the interviewers did not know that the investigation was being made on our behalf. We, on the other hand, did not know the identities of any of the people being interviewed, what companies they represented, or the responses that were made by particular interviewees.

The Newsom report, a lengthy one, was completed early in 1959. Its conclusions, briefly stated, were that, although we had certain special problems (which were spelled out in the report), our firm had an excellent reputation; that we shared in the exceptionally high opinion in which financial institutions and business concerns held the accounting profession; and that, generally speaking, the only ceiling on the growth of CPAs' services to American business appeared to be possible inadequacies of resources, in terms of knowledge and people, or passiveness in initiating strong relationships with business.

After the investigation was completed we engaged the Newsom firm on a retainer basis. This arrangement was continued until April 1961, by which time it had become apparent that any further benefit to be derived by us must come primarily from our own efforts rather than from further outside advice.

We will never be able to prove how much we gained from our association with the Newsom firm, but I personally believe that the benefits, although intangible, were quite substantial. At the very least, it confirmed certain things about which we had previously had only instinctive feelings, and it also forced us to think about a number of matters that we should have thought about long before.

*I hold every man a debtor to his profession;
from the which as men of course do seek to receive
countenance and profit, so ought they of duty to endeavor
themselves by way of amends to be a help
and ornament thereunto.*

FRANCIS BACON: Preface to *Maxims of The Law*

CHAPTER SEVENTEEN

PROFESSIONAL ACTIVITIES

THE ACCOUNTING PROFESSION IN THE United States has progressed enormously in my lifetime, and particularly in the past twenty-five years. Much of this progress has come about through the efforts of dedicated practitioners who have given freely of their time and talent in service to both the American Institute and the various state societies of CPAs.

For many years, we as a firm did not contribute a great deal to the profession, but in the 1950s and 1960s this situation changed markedly. Over the past fifteen years a great many of our people have contributed a substantial portion of their time to professional activity at both the state and national levels. The extent and quality of these contributions are well reflected, I think, in the fact that Tom Flynn, who for many years has carried heavy responsibilities in the firm, is currently serving as president of the American Institute. One does not attain this high office without having made a noteworthy contribution to the profession over a long period of years.

Although Tom Flynn is our first "home-grown" president, we are equally proud to number two past presidents of the Institute among the Arthur Young family: T. Dwight Williams, who was president in the fiscal year 1945-1946, and J. Harold Stewart, who was president in 1949-1950. Both Dwight and Harold held the office before they merged their practices with ours.

MY OWN PROFESSIONAL ACTIVITIES, as I have mentioned earlier, started fairly late in life. My activities in the American Institute of CPAs may be summarized as follows:

    Committee on Accounting Procedure — 1947-1954
    Council — 1954-1957; 1960-1963
    Council (as a state society president) — 1959-1960
    Executive Committee — 1954-1955
    Committee on Publication — 1954-1955
    Committee on Professional Ethics — 1955-1960
       (chairman — 1958-1960)
    Committee on Investments — 1955-1957
    Accounting Principles Board — 1959-1964
    Trial Board — 1962-1965
    Fiscal Committee of the Accounting Principles Board — 1963-1964
    Committee on Insurance Accounting and Auditing — 1963-1964
    Nominations Committee — 1963-1964

Throughout this same period I was active in various capacities —member of committees, officer, Board member, etc.—in the New York State Society of CPAs. In May 1958 I was elected to serve as first vice president of the Society, which meant that a year later I would probably be elected to serve as president. This is what happened, and I became president for the fiscal year 1959-1960.

When I became first vice president it became very clear to me that within a year my professional activities would be making serious inroads on my time. While I had been active for many years in both the New York State Society and the American Institute, I had been able to fulfill these responsibilities largely after office hours. Now it was clear that things would change, and change they did. In the summer of 1959 I found myself serving simultaneously as president of the New York State Society, chairman of the American Institute's Committee on Professional Ethics, and member of the Institute's newly created Accounting Principles Board. At that time I had also agreed to be an Institute delegate to the Asian and Pacific Accounting Convention which was to be held in Australia in the spring of 1960, to prepare a paper for advance distribution to those who would attend that convention, and to participate in a panel discussion at the convention itself. I was still tied to a number of important audit engagements, mostly in the Southwest, and I was devoting a good deal of time to the public relations study that was being conducted by Earl Newsom & Company.

The more I thought about these activities, the more ridiculous it seemed to me that I should continue to serve both as chairman of the firm's policy-making Management Committee and as managing partner of the firm. Even apart from the burden of my professional activities, it seemed to me that at age 59 the time had come for me to do something to make the succession in the firm clear to everyone in our organization. I had for years preached

I look ahead

the virtues of delegation and of planning for the future; why shouldn't I practice what I preached?

Since my illness in the mid-1950s, I had thought a great deal about how I should spend my last few years with the firm, particularly the years between age 62 and 65, and had concluded that two things would give me the greatest personal satisfaction: (1) to do everything within my power to provide for an orderly succession in the firm's management, and (2) to devote an increasing portion of my time to three aspects of the accounting profession that held my deep interest—professional ethics, public relations, and accounting principles. I had also convinced myself that, in the best interests of the firm, I should withdraw from the Management Committee at age 62.

AS I THOUGHT about these things, I realized that any reorganization of my activities would have to be related to the activities of Ralph Kent and Tom Flynn, who were then the administrators of the New York office. At that time each of these men, in addition to his office management responsibilities, had primary responsibility for a number of large and important clients.

I have said previously that Ralph Kent and Tom Flynn complemented each other in their abilities and interests. This is as true today as it was then. Although both men are remarkably effective in client matters, their other activities have taken them down different avenues. Ralph's efforts today are devoted primarily to the management of the firm; Tom, on the other hand, freed of deep involvement in day-to-day administrative problems, is able to apply his considerable talents to major client problems, professional matters, college recruitment, and training.

From their earliest days in the firm, Kent and Flynn worked well together, and it has always seemed to me that their combined talents and their respect for each other have added immeasurably to the strength of the New York office and of the firm as a whole.

In the spring of 1959 Tom Flynn and I talked at some length about the firm's organizational problems, as I described them in the preceding chapter. Tom and I agreed that, ideally, Ralph Kent should within a year or so be devoting perhaps ninety-five percent of his time to firm administration, as distinct from New York office administration, although we were both apprehensive about the problem of taking care of the clients then handled by Ralph. Tom's considered judgment, however, was that if he (Tom) were properly supplemented he could run New York office alone and thus free Ralph to concentrate on the management of the firm.

This whole matter was discussed quite exhaustively at the May 1959 meeting of the Management Committee. After exploring the pros and cons in some detail, the committee accepted my suggestion that I should withdraw as an active member of the three-man Operating Committee and that Herman Ward should immediately succeed me on the committee. Thereafter the committee named Ralph Kent chairman of the Operating Committee, with the request that he divest himself of all direct responsibility for New York office matters. Tom Flynn in turn was named administrative partner of the New York office, but the committee expressed the hope that he would have sufficient administrative assistance in this position that he could continue to devote a major portion of his time to client affairs, on a consulting basis, and to the continuance of his professional activities.

Ralph Kent becomes managing partner

By this action Ralph Kent, as chairman of the Operating Committee, became the firm's managing partner. This change in organization worked well from the beginning and strengthened our firm considerably. At the time of the change, Ralph was just 43 and had already won a great deal of respect throughout the firm. This respect was to grow from year to year.

I should add that at the May 1959 meeting of the Management Committee I suggested that the minutes show my stated intention of withdrawing from the committee at age 62. The committee disagreed with this suggestion and urged me then, and later when I raised the question again, to continue as chairman of the Management Committee and the firm's senior partner until my retirement at age 65. It is arguable whether this was a sound idea, but the other members of the committee were unanimous in their recommendation, and I'm sure they were sincere in their wish, that I continue as chairman until age 65.

My year as president of the New York State Society

I WAS, OF COURSE, QUITE PLEASED about this rearrangement of administrative responsibilities in the firm, and I proceeded to give a good deal of my time to the New York State Society. It is a wonderful experience to serve as president of a large state society of CPAs, particularly when the society has a competent full-time executive director such as the New York Society had then, and continues to have, in the person of Harry Howe. Harry and I worked very closely together during my year in office, and I hope he enjoyed the association as much as I did.

The Society accomplished a number of significant things that year (1959-1960), but it is well to point out that no single twelve-month period is any true measure of the work of a state society—or, for that matter, of the American Institute. Many of the objectives of these groups are such that several years of sustained effort are required before they can be achieved. This was true of the regulatory legislation in New York State which became law early in 1959, and it was also true of the revision of the Society's rules of professional conduct, which became effective in June 1960.

I think the toughest job I had to do during my year as president of the New York State Society was to serve as chairman at the meeting of the thirty-four-man Board of Directors which reviewed the revised rules of professional conduct. To get any large group to agree on a single rule of conduct is difficult enough, but to argue twenty-one rules to a conclusion is really something. I was very pleased with the results, although one change was made which troubled me then and still troubles me. This was the insertion of the words "in such a manner" in Rule 4, to make it read: "A member shall not engage in any other business or occupation conjointly with that of his professional practice as a certified public accountant in such a manner as would be incompatible or inconsistent therewith." I much prefer the language of the American Institute's Rule 4.04 on the same subject: "A member or associate shall not engage in any business or occupation conjointly with that of a public accountant, which is incompatible or inconsistent therewith." The absence of the words "in such a manner" in the Institute's rule indicates that it is the activity itself which is proscribed, and not the manner of its performance; and this, I think, is as it should be. Someday, I hope, the New York State Society's rule will be brought into accord with the Institute's rule.

The subject was ethics

IT NEVER OCCURRED TO ME that I would become a crusader for anything in life, yet I almost assumed such a role in battling for high ethical standards, both in our own firm and throughout the profession. I'm afraid some of my partners must at times have thought me another Don Quixote, tilting at windmills. I know some of them felt that, because I spoke and wrote so much on the subject of ethics, we had to be a lot holier than everybody else.

The fact is, however, that ethical concepts do not originate, nor will they long endure, in any large group without leadership. It is not enough to say, "Do not violate any of the profession's rules of conduct." If the senior people in a large professional firm do not make it clear where they stand on "borderline" practices—those many instances, in any field of endeavor, where what is permissible is not the same as what is right—these practices are almost certain to creep into the organization. Apathy on the part of the senior people may lead others in the organization to interpret "Do not violate" as "Do not get caught violating."

So I wrote and spoke a good deal on ethical matters. One of my memorandums on this subject was formally approved by the firm's Management Committee and incorporated in our firm literature. I also sent copies of the memorandum to the senior partners of the other large accounting firms.

Some of my ethical ideas were accepted; others were not. Thus, in 1959 I tried very hard to have the American Institute adopt a "notification" rule, the essence of which was that Institute members would not agree to perform services for the client of another public accountant without first notifying the other accountant. Although this proposal was approved by Council, it failed to receive the necessary two-thirds vote at the Institute's annual meeting. The battle was not entirely lost, however, for the New York State Society adopted the suggestion as part of Rule 7 in the revision of its rules of conduct which became effective in June 1960.

I don't suppose I'll ever forget the Institute's annual meeting in 1960, at which I tried to get approval of a new rule on independence. The practical effect of this rule would have been to bar any member of the Institute, after January 1, 1962, from certifying financial statements if the member was an officer or director of his client or if he had a direct financial interest, or a material indirect financial interest, in the client. Apart from making the motion for approval, as chairman of the Committee on Professional Ethics, I had virtually no part in the proceedings. After the motion was seconded, the whole affair got wrapped up in parliamentary procedure and emotion, and the chairman of the meeting was hard pressed to maintain some semblance of law and order. The long-drawn-out debate was finally resolved by the adoption of a substitute motion deferring action on the grounds that further elucidation of the pros and cons was needed. The vote for this substitute motion was 447 to 367, including proxies. It was the first time in twenty years that a paper ballot was required to determine the wishes of members present and those represented by proxies.

A new rule on independence

In some ways it was a pity that this emotional storm had to

develop, for the meeting had started out the previous day (Monday, September 26, 1960) on a very promising note. For the first time in the Institute's history its annual meeting was addressed by a President of the United States.

President Dwight D. Eisenhower spoke on the subject of fiscal responsibility and the role of the certified public accountant in helping the country to achieve it. I remember particularly one comment he made about CPAs in government:

> One of the more statistically minded people in the Government told me not long ago that I had appointed more certified public accountants to Government positions than any prior President. I certainly did not do this because they are accountants. I have been for all these eight years searching for talent—people of dedication, of training, of education, of capability—people who have a sense of civic responsibility. So, since I have appointed so many . . . persons who have been public accountants, I suppose it's a fair conclusion that your profession averages very high up among those that are so dedicated and so capable.

President Eisenhower was followed by Maurice H. Stans, then Director of the Bureau of the Budget and a former Institute president, who spoke further on the theme of fiscal responsibility. The Institute boasted the largest meeting attendance in its history, and the Academy of Music in Philadelphia was jammed with an enthusiastic audience of CPAs and others.

The Tuesday afternoon session was in sharp contrast to the Monday morning session. Right from the opening of the session it was clear that a battle was looming. Many CPAs were embarrassed at the emotional tone of the debate, for members of the press were present. As I look back on it now, however, it does not seem to me that any harm came to the profession. The press was intensely interested in the debate, and in the years to follow many articles about the profession appeared in newspapers and business periodicals around the country.

Immediately after the Philadelphia meeting I began to prepare an article entitled "The Need for a New Rule on Independence" for the January 1961 issue of *The Journal of Accountancy*. I was very pleased to have the opportunity to write this article, for I was firmly convinced that the need for the proposed new rule was urgent. The then-existing rule on independence (Rule 13) was both inadequate and inconsistent. It addressed itself essentially to those situations where a member or someone in his immediate family had (or was committed to acquire) a financial interest in a client company which was substantial either as to its capital amount or in relation to the member's own personal fortune. In such a situation, the rule forbade the member to express an opinion on the statements of the client company, if it was publicly owned, and required that he make disclosure of his financial interest if the statements were to be used for credit purposes.

The defects of this rule were quite apparent. First of all, the rule was inconsistent, in that it forbade a certifying CPA to have a substantial investment in a publicly owned client company but permitted such an investment if the company was closely held. Apart from this inconsistency, it was not clear just what was or was not a "substantial" investment. Any such determination would obviously have to be subjective, for it could hardly be expected that the member would disclose the amount of his personal fortune so that one could judge the effect his investment might have on his objectivity.

Defects in the existing rule

281

Another defect in the existing rule was that it was silent as to other client relationships. It made no mention, for example, of those situations in which a CPA was an officer or director of a client company.

Why was there such opposition to the proposed new rule? The fact is that in 1960 quite a number of CPAs were serving as directors of, or owned stock in, client corporations whose financial statements they certified. No one, apparently, objected to this practice: neither the local bankers, the minority stockholders, nor anyone else concerned. Why, then, these CPAs asked, should the American Institute force them to sever such relationships, which might be both prestigious and profitable? The answer, of course, was that the reputation of local CPA firms and practitioners was much less secure where such relationships existed. Also, it was well known in banking and financial circles that the larger accounting firms had found it advisable, years before, to require all partners to divest themselves of financial interests in client corporations. This was due in part to the SEC rule forbidding such relationships, but it was also due to the strong feeling which had been growing in the profession that such interests were, or could be, harmful.

The proposed new rule on independence was the result of careful deliberation. In addition to being reviewed repeatedly by the Committee on Professional Ethics it had been twice endorsed by the Institute's Council. It was virtually the same as the rule of the Illinois Society of CPAs, which became effective on June 1, 1954, and it was also virtually the same as the SEC rule, which was already complied with by all accounting firms which audited clients subject to the SEC.

In the months following the Philadelphia meeting, it became

apparent that opposition to the proposed new rule was gradually diminishing. There was a growing feeling that two things might enable the proposal to be approved at the next annual meeting in 1961: (1) making it clear to those in attendance at the meeting that the revised rule would apply only to members in public practice, and (2) changing the effective date of the proposal from January 1, 1962 to January 1, 1964, thus giving members ample time to make any necessary rearrangements with their clients.

This prediction proved correct, for the proposal met with only scattered opposition when it was again submitted at the annual meeting held in the fall of 1961. By a vote of 2,937 to 329, those attending the meeting approved submission of the proposal to the entire membership of the Institute for a mail ballot. Later the membership approved the proposal by a vote of 12,713 to 4,097, and on January 1, 1964 the new rule became effective.

The new rule is adopted

The adoption of the new rule on independence is fairly indicative of how the accounting profession's rules of conduct have evolved over a long period of time. Each step forward has meant discussion, argument, and education. New rules cannot and should not be hurried into being. The encouraging fact is that, despite the initial reluctance of many, practically all CPAs can be convinced that ever higher standards of professional conduct are in their best interests, both individually and as a group.

Since I consider the adoption of the new rule on independence to have been an important landmark in the history of the accounting profession, let me quote the rule as it was adopted:

> Neither a member or associate, nor a firm of which he is a partner, shall express an opinion on financial statements of any enterprise unless he and his firm are in fact independent with respect to such enterprise.

Independence is not susceptible of precise definition, but is an expression of the professional integrity of the individual. A member or associate, before expressing his opinion on financial statements, has the responsibility of assessing his relationships with an enterprise to determine whether, in the circumstances, he might expect his opinion to be considered independent, objective and unbiased by one who had knowledge of all the facts.

A member or associate will be considered not independent, for example, with respect to any enterprise if he, or one of his partners, (a) during the period of his professional engagement or at the time of expressing his opinion, had, or was committed to acquire, any direct financial interest or material indirect financial interest in the enterprise, or (b) during the period of his professional engagement, at the time of expressing his opinion or during the period covered by the financial statements, was connected with the enterprise as a promoter, underwriter, voting trustee, director, officer or key employee. In cases where a member or associate ceases to be the independent accountant for an enterprise and is subsequently called upon to re-express a previously expressed opinion on financial statements, the phrase "at the time of expressing his opinion" refers only to the time at which the member or associate first expressed his opinion on the financial statements in question. The word "director" is not intended to apply to a connection in such a capacity with a charitable, religious, civic or other similar type of non-profit organization when the duties performed in such a capacity are such as to make it clear that the member or associate can express an independent opinion on the financial statements. The example cited in this paragraph, of circumstances under which a member or associate will be considered not independent, is not intended to be all-inclusive.

After the Philadelphia meeting, as I thought about the possible effect of Rule 13 on my blood pressure problem, which seemed to be getting worse, I said to myself, "Never again will I become emotionally involved in such a highly controversial matter." To make sure I would carry out this resolve, I declined reappointment as chairman of the Committee on Professional Ethics. I did not feel badly about this decision, for I had then rounded out five years on the committee.

Never, however, is a very long time, and a word I should probably stop using. Before I realized it, I found myself very deeply involved in a much greater problem having to do with the Accounting Principles Board.

Although a great deal has been written about the investment credit, this story would not be complete if I did not say something about its effect on the work of the Accounting Principles Board and on the development of accounting principles.

THE ACCOUNTING PRINCIPLES BOARD of the American Institute came into being in 1959, and for the first few years everything went fine. The Board moved in very smooth waters. This placid atmosphere changed suddenly, however, toward the end of 1962, when quite a storm developed over what was the proper method of accounting for the investment credit provided in the Revenue Act of 1962.

The investment credit and the APB

There was nothing complicated about the investment credit. In general it represented a specified percentage of the cost of certain fixed assets placed in service after 1961. The credit served to reduce the tax liability of the year in which it arose and also served to reduce the basis of the property for tax purposes.

Although there was great diversity of opinion, both within

and outside the accounting profession, as to how the investment credit should be handled, the Board, after exhaustive discussion and by the required two-thirds vote, reached the conclusion that the credit should be taken into income over the life of the related assets. In reaching this conclusion it was the feeling of the majority of Board members that the best interests of the public and the profession would be served by recommending only one of the two alternative methods proposed.

But despite the Board opinion, some practitioners (including some members of the Board) and other businessmen continued to support vigorously what they referred to as the "48-52" method. Under this method, forty-eight percent of the investment credit (the maximum extent to which the credit could normally increase net income) would be taken into income in the year assets were placed in service and only fifty-two percent (the portion of the tax reduction that was merely temporary) would be spread over the lives of the assets.

Shortly after the Board issued its opinion (Opinion No. 2, December 1962), certain accounting firms let it be known that they would not insist that their clients follow the method approved by the Board. These firms contended that, until one of the two alternative methods became generally accepted to the exclusion of the other, auditors should not qualify their opinions on financial statements because of the use of either method. In support of their position, these firms pointed out, first, that the charter which established the Accounting Principles Board provided that the authority of Board opinions should rest on their general acceptability, and, second, that the opinion issued by the Board on the investment credit contained the same proviso.

In a release issued on January 10, 1963 concerning the investment credit, the Securities and Exchange Commission stated that because of the diversity of opinion existing among responsible persons it would accept financial statements which reflected the investment credit either on the basis recommended by the Accounting Principles Board or on the "48-52" basis. The release also stated that, since independent auditors might feel obliged to qualify their opinions on financial statements where the treatment of the investment credit ran counter to APB Opinion No. 2, it would accept qualified opinions in such instances.

The effect of the position taken by certain dissenting accounting firms was highlighted by an article which appeared in *The Wall Street Journal* on March 13, 1963. In this article the *Journal* reported that one well-known company had "boosted" 1962 net income $2,200,000 by "bunching 1962 tax-credit savings," while a well-known competitor had "adopted the spreading approach." As the article pointed out, both corporations were audited by the same firm of accountants. As the article did not point out, the auditing firm did not qualify its opinion on the financial statements of either company because of the handling of the investment credit.

In the spring of 1963 a great many CPAs—myself included—began to have grave doubts as to the ability of the Board to carry out its mission of narrowing areas of difference and inconsistency in accounting. Obviously some clarification of the Board's authority was urgently needed. It could make no sense to have APB opinions ignored on the grounds that they were not yet "generally accepted."

At the meeting of the Board held in Phoenix, Arizona in April

Some grave doubts about the APB

1963, a good deal of time was devoted to a discussion of the Board's functions and of the related accounting research program. On the afternoon of the second day a motion was adopted which in effect stated that the Institute's Executive Committee and Council should be requested to revise the existing standards of reporting so that they would be related to pronouncements of the Board.

The matter was again discussed at the June meeting of the Board, and following that meeting two recommendations were made to the Institute's Executive Committee: (1) that members of the Institute, in reporting on financial statements, should be required to direct attention to any material variation between the accounting principles followed and those principles which the Board had approved, and (2) that the auditing standards of reporting and the rules of professional conduct should be amended as necessary to provide that, in addition to the obligation of members to report departures from generally accepted accounting principles, they should also be required to report departures from opinions of the Accounting Principles Board.

The Executive Committee tackled the problem immediately, and it was on each meeting agenda from the summer of 1963 until it came before Council at its spring meeting in 1964.

While the matter was before the Executive Committee, the Revenue Act of 1964 changed the tax impact of the investment credit. The essential nature of the credit remained the same, but under the new Revenue Act the credit no longer reduced the basis of the property to which it related.

The Administrative Committee of the Accounting Principles Board met in March 1964 to discuss the problem of whether Opinion No. 2 was affected by the provision of the new Revenue Act relating to the investment credit. Before the meeting started, it was known that the SEC had decided to reaffirm the position which it had taken in Accounting Series Release No. 96 of January 1963, and it was also known that a number of companies were treating the investment credit as a reduction of current Federal income tax expense, disregarding Opinion No. 2. Also, everyone was well aware that many businessmen were dissatisfied with the lack of consistency within the accounting profession. These businessmen found it difficult to understand why some companies using the "flow-through" method for the investment credit might receive clear opinions from their auditors while other companies following the same accounting method might receive qualified opinions.

In the light of these facts, the Board's Administrative Committee drafted a proposed Opinion No. 4 which stated on the one hand that the Revenue Act of 1964 gave no basis for revising the Board's opinion as to the method of accounting for the investment credit. On the other hand, the proposed opinion noted (1) that the SEC had recently reconsidered and reaffirmed its previously expressed opinion on the treatment of the investment credit, (2) that the Board's review of experience since the issuance of Opinion No. 2 showed that the investment credit had been treated by a significant number of companies as increasing net income of the year in which the credit arose, and (3) that the authority of Board opinions rested upon their general acceptability and that, in the light of events and developments occurring since the issuance of Opinion No. 2, the Board had determined that its conclusions had not attained the degree of acceptability necessary to make the opinion effective. The proposed opinion then stated that the Board, in the circumstances, believed that while the spreading method recommended in Opinion No. 2 should be considered preferable, the "flow-through" method was also acceptable. The proposed opinion also pointed out that full disclosure should be made as to the method followed and the amounts involved, where material.

The required two-thirds of the Board members promptly approved issuance of the proposed Opinion No. 4. Five members dissented, agreeing that it was unwise for the Board to approve contradictory alternative accounting principles. Five of the eight members who assented with qualification disagreed with the opinion's expression of preference for the spreading method. The other three (myself included) based their qualification on the same general viewpoint that led five members to dissent. I suspect that many of those who assented without qualification had the same reluctance as I in agreeing to the issuance of Opinion No. 4. It is indeed anomalous to hold that buying an asset immediately creates income. It is equally strange to say to a company, as the opinion in effect says: "You may treat this item, even if material, as either income or corpus, and either way your independent auditor will give you exactly the same type of unqualified opinion."

An impossible situation

Opinion No. 4 did have this salutary effect: It made it crystal clear to almost everyone that the profession was in an impossible situation and that the Council had to do something immediately to clarify the Board's authority.

Although the Executive Committee was in agreement with the Board's objective, as described above, it decided, after a great deal of deliberation, on a somewhat different approach. The essence of the committee's substitute proposal was this: A pronouncement of the Accounting Principles Board would be considered as constituting the *only* "generally accepted accounting principle" in the subject area covered for purposes of expressing an opinion on financial statements within the meaning of the related rule of professional conduct and the first standard of reporting.

The Executive Committee's proposal had additional features of implementation, including a provision vesting a veto power in Council which would enable the Council, should it wish to do so, to rescind pronouncements of the Board.

The Executive Committee's proposal was vigorously discussed at the Council meeting held in Boca Raton, Florida in May 1964. Because of the complexity and importance of the issue, President Clifford V. Heimbucher ruled that debate would continue until everyone who wished had had a chance to speak. A total of forty-three persons, including members of the Accounting Principles Board who were present by invitation, participated in the discussion, which lasted almost ten hours.

As the debate progressed it became fairly clear that many members who basically were in favor of the Executive Committee's proposal were concerned about some of the features of implementation and some of the legal complications involved in incorporating them in an enforceable rule.

The long debate was finally resolved by the following substitute motion, offered by former President Louis H. Penney, which carried by a vote of 124 to 51:

RESOLVED—That it is the sense of this Council that reports of members should disclose material departures from opinions of the Accounting Principles Board, and that the President is hereby authorized to appoint a special committee to recommend to Council appropriate methods of implementing the substance of this resolution.

At its meeting in October 1964, the Council unanimously adopted recommendations in a report of a special committee to the effect that members should see to it that departures from opinions of the Accounting Principles Board (as well as effective Accounting Research Bulletins issued by the former Committee on Accounting Procedure) are disclosed, either in footnotes to the financial statements or in reports of members in their capacity as independent auditors. This action was made applicable to financial statements for fiscal periods beginning after December 31, 1965.

It is no part of this story of mine to get into the details of the subsequent work of the special committee. I do want to emphasize, however, the importance of the action taken by Council at its two meetings in 1964. Alvin Jennings, in an article which appeared in the August 1964 issue of *The Journal of Accountancy*, put his finger on the importance of the action taken by Council at its spring meeting. Here is what he said:

> I think we must all accept the clear evidence that the Penney substitute resolution was advanced and accepted as a compromise between the extremes. It specifically recognizes that the single most important matter is acceptance of an obligation to report departures. It does not rule out the possibility that in rare cases there may be substantial authoritative support for a principle which the Board has indicated an unwillingness to accept. At the same time, it gives opinions of the Board a somewhat higher status than it gives to "other substantial authoritative support." This higher status, which in my view is fully justified by the careful re-

search which precedes a Board opinion, comes about in this way: By requiring departures from Board opinions to be incorporated in the accountant's report,* the resolution puts a significant burden upon those who, in opposition to a Board opinion, would depend upon other support as the basis for an opinion as to the fairness of the financial statements. The professional, and perhaps the legal, implications of a failure to follow a pronouncement of the Board in the absence of clear indication that there is substantial authoritative support for a contrary view would appear to rule out capricious disregard of the official position of the Institute on any given accounting issue.

ON OCTOBER 1, 1964 I resigned as a member of the Accounting Principles Board, approximately one year before my second three-year term would have expired. My sole reason for resigning was that Board matters were demanding a disproportionate amount of my time, and I wanted to have greater flexibility in the use of my time during my last year as an active partner of Arthur Young & Company.

In the five years from 1959 to 1964 I gave a great deal of time to professional matters, as distinct from firm responsibilities. I wrote and spoke on just about every occasion that presented itself, and I must say that I enjoyed doing so. Whether my efforts did much good is hard to tell.

For example, I became interested in the ethical problems of

---

*At the fall meeting of Council it was decided that departures from APB pronouncements might be disclosed either in footnotes to financial statements or in the accountant's report.

advertising and after boning up on the subject on and off for a period of weeks wrote an article for *Printers' Ink*, the weekly magazine of advertising and marketing. The article was published in the March 31, 1961 issue of that magazine under the title "Can the Advertising Business Be Professional?" Although some knowledgeable people complimented me on the article and said it should do good, I have grave doubts as to whether it made very much impression on the vast majority of those readers to whom it was addressed.

I become an advocate of price-level accounting

In the early 1950s I became interested in price-level accounting. Like so many others I was initially very cynical about the whole idea, but I became a "convert," very largely through the efforts of Perry Mason, then a member of the Committee on Accounting Procedure and later a member of the Institute's staff. Perry, who has since died, was an extremely competent fellow. He was somewhat shy and withdrawn, but underneath his modesty there was a great deal of ability, and he wrote well and persuasively.

Perry had worked with Ralph Jones of Yale University on a price-level research project for the American Accounting Association, the results of which were published in 1955 and 1956 in a series of three booklets. I had heard Perry talk about the project, so my curiosity was aroused. I read and reread the booklets. The more I thought about them, the more I was impressed by what seemed to me their common-sense approach. I was particularly impressed with the case studies they included, which showed the effects of price-level changes for a period of years on four companies: New York Telephone Company, Armstrong Cork Company, the Reece Corporation, and Sargent & Company.

In the years to follow I wrote and spoke a good deal on price-level accounting. Here again, I'm not at all sure how persuasive I was, although I was more than gratified when the Accounting Principles Board, at a meeting held on April 28, 1961, took the action summarized in the following excerpt from its minutes:

> ... the Board ... agreed that the assumption in accounting that fluctuations in the value of the dollar may be ignored is unrealistic, and that therefore the Director of Accounting Research should be instructed to set up a research project to study the problem and to prepare a report in which recommendations are made for the disclosure of the effect of price-level changes upon the financial statements. In this study, special attention should be paid to the use of supplementary statements as a means of disclosure.

Later on, in 1963, this action resulted in the publication by the American Institute of the study entitled *Reporting the Financial Effects of Price-Level Changes*, prepared by the staff of the Institute's Research Division.

In this age of generalists there is a great deal of satisfaction in being somewhat of a specialist in at least one area. Until a few years ago I had read just about everything of any value on the subject of price-level accounting. It is an important subject, of crucial concern in certain areas overseas and worthy of full consideration by domestic companies.

ALL IN ALL, I think my outside professional activities did me a great deal of good, both as an accountant and as a person. It is a great challenge, and a great discipline, to thrash out controversial problems across a conference table, and then to have to reduce your thoughts to writing. There is a good deal of truth in the old saying that committee work is like a barrel—you get out of it just about as much as you put in.

Yet, rewarding as my professional activities and church activities have been, I have often wished that I could have devoted more of my time to the field of education. I have given a good deal of time to Mills College of Education, on whose Board of Trustees I have served for some nine years; but, while I have done my homework conscientiously and have attended most Board meetings, it has not been possible for me to give as much time or attention to Mills as I have given to professional and church matters, to which I was already heavily committed before I joined the Mills Board.

Mills College of Education

Mills is a fascinating college and renders, in my opinion, an outstanding service to the community. Its president, Dr. Amy Hostler, is not only a highly intelligent person but a very stimulating one as well, and the success of the college is undoubtedly due in large measure to her untiring efforts.

For the benefit of those who may not be familiar with it, Mills is a small, privately endowed, nonsectarian college which trains women to be teachers of young children from nursery school through the sixth grade. It offers a four-year liberal arts and professional curriculum leading to the degree of Bachelor of Science in Education. It has some 350 students, a faculty and administrative staff of 48, and two buildings on lower Fifth Avenue that house some of the most up-to-date teacher-training facilities in the country. In addition, a small but beautifully equipped dormitory has recently been completed on West 11th Street for 120 resident students. Though I would like to have done much more for Mills than I did, I still find some satisfaction in having played even a small part in what I consider to be a very worthwhile cause.

The firm is the unit of practice in the accounting profession. The way in which firms organize and conduct their practices, deal with their clients, plan for their own growth, recruit and administer their staffs, will largely determine the future course of the profession.

JOHN L. CAREY: *The CPA Plans for the Future*

CHAPTER EIGHTEEN

THE FIRM TODAY

I AM NOW IN MY FORTY-NINTH YEAR IN public accounting. I am, therefore, one of the ancients, one of the diminishing number of practicing accountants who started in accounting before America entered the First World War.

I am also one of the "old guard" in Arthur Young & Company. It is forty-four years since I began with the firm, twenty-seven years since I became a partner, eighteen years since I became a member of the Management Committee, and almost eleven years since I became the Committee's chairman. I am the only person left in Arthur Young & Company today who was with the firm in 1921, the year of my employment.

Of course, when I say that I am the only person left, I mean the only one still active in the firm. There are many retired partners and employees alive today who were with the firm in the 1920s and 1930s. Indeed, three of the original eight partners who formed the first national partnership in 1921 are still around and, considering their age, in reasonably good health. They are William Sutherland, who is now 87; Jim Burton, who is 79; and W. D. McGregor, who is 77.

LIFE HAS CHANGED a great deal, of course, in all of its aspects, since 1921. In thinking about all this change, I suppose it is only natural for me to have uppermost in my mind the changes which have taken place in Arthur Young & Company during that period.

The growth of the firm

First and foremost is the growth of the firm. In 1921 Arthur Young & Company had two "main offices," in Chicago and New York, and four small "branch offices," in Kansas City, Milwaukee, Los Angeles, and Pittsburgh. At that time there were eight national partners and about a hundred and fifty employees. In those days the firm's practice was entirely domestic, with most of the work centered in the Chicago and New York areas.

Today the firm's practice is international, and the work is handled through a network of offices throughout the free world. The truly worldwide character of the firm's practice today is well exemplified, I think, by a dramatic event which took place in 1964. In the fall of that year, representatives of Arthur Young & Company and of thirty-six associated firms from outside the United States met in Hot Springs, Virginia, to place their signatures on formal articles of association, the practical effect of which was to provide closer international ties and, as a result, better service to international clients. The practice of these firms (Arthur Young & Company and all the others) is spread over forty-four countries. In all, they have 131 offices, 475 partners, and more than 5,000 employees.

I dwell on size first because, in today's environment, any public accounting firm that serves large clients must itself be large. There are two main reasons why this is so. First, it is impractical to provide adequate service to the large, expanding corporation of today without a complement of highly skilled personnel in each of the corporation's key locations, regardless of where those locations may be. Second, it is essential in any dynamic public accounting firm today to insure a continuing supply of highly qualified personnel through an extensive program of recruitment and training. Such recruitment and training programs are extremely costly, and without a large volume of business few firms would be able to support them.

IN 1921, recruitment and training programs and firm literature, as we know these things today, did not exist. In those days, all large accounting firms relied heavily on temporary staffs, and large engagements were usually handled by a few experienced accountants assisted by a string of "floaters." As I have said earlier in this book, the whole emphasis in the accounting environment of forty years ago was on practical experience, with no thought of education as a continuing process.

Recruitment and training programs

Where did the experienced men of those days come from? Some of them came from the temporary staff, where occasionally a man with potential would develop gradually into a good practical accountant. Others came from Great Britain, where a modest and informal recruitment program was carried on by some of the larger U.S. firms.

The customary procedure in recruiting Britishers was to place an advertisement in an accountants' magazine in Scotland or England. Letters would be exchanged with applicants. Those applicants who appeared desirable would be interviewed the next time one of the U.S. firm's partners happened to be in Europe. Since the partners in Arthur Young & Company in the 1920s were all British, it was a fair assumption that at least one of them would soon be in Europe on vacation. Most of the Britishers thus recruited proved valuable additions to the staff. It could always be assumed that the prospective employee had a good fundamental education. It could also be assumed that he had a solid grounding in accounting theory, since only men with an accounting degree (either chartered accountants or incorporated accountants) were recruited.

Today, of course, the procedures used in hiring and developing accounting staffs are entirely different. Accounting firms in the United States no longer use temporary staffs, and they do not recruit abroad except in isolated instances. All of the large firms today invest an enormous amount of time, energy, and money in their recruitment and training programs and in the preparation of firm literature.

Good college graduates who are interested in careers in accounting are very much in demand today. It is not just accounting firms that want them; industry and government are also very keen on getting their share. To meet our U.S. firm's needs of about 250 men each year means visiting more than a hundred colleges and interviewing more than 2,500 graduates.

Training programs, seminars, and meetings of all kinds are now routine procedure for all the large accounting firms. In Arthur Young & Company, for example, we have as the heart of our training program what amounts to an integrated five-year curriculum of courses and seminars. This program is designed to help the staff man take the next step forward at each critical stage of his professional career. We have found that this formal training program enables the young accountant to absorb experience much more quickly and completely than he could through on-the-job training alone.

Some idea of the substantial scale of our training efforts can be gained by considering merely one element of our program, the audit seminars. In 1964, thirty-two such seminars were held, with a total attendance of more than seven hundred people. The faculty consisted of 22 permanent instructors, 132 guest lecturers, and 13 graders.

In addition to these audit seminars there were staff meetings, tax seminars, management services seminars, computer auditing seminars, and so on. Obviously, any such comprehensive training program requires a tremendous amount of concentrated effort and a great deal of advance planning. As the firm's director of personnel education, Fred Horn carries a substantial burden of responsibility, and I never cease to marvel at how well he handles it.

OVER THE YEARS there have, of course, been great changes in the nature of our firm's practice. This is not the place to describe these changes, except to say that management services and tax work represent an increasing proportion of the firm's practice. Actually, of course, management services work in today's sense was virtually nonexistent until after the Second World War. The firm had always done a certain amount of so-called cost and systems work, but most of this work was elementary in comparison with the kind of work our management services specialists do today.

Other changes

In the past thirty years we have seen in all areas of business life an ever-increasing emphasis on human relations and public relations, and this emphasis has also made itself felt in public accounting firms. I think of the great change in our own firm in the relationship between partners and employees. Forty years ago this relationship was in many ways like that of master and servant; certainly it bore very little resemblance to the kind of cooperative relationship that we know today. There were few lines of communication between partners and employees in the old days, and what communication did take place usually had to do with specific engagements.

I recall that in my first few months with Arthur Young & Company none of the staff seemed to know the answers to what seemed to me to be perfectly natural questions: When was the firm founded? How many partners were there? Was Arthur Young alive? If he was alive, where did he live? What age was he?

Today we go to great lengths to maintain good lines of communication at all levels, and we even have a communications department at Home Office to help us achieve good communications both internally and externally. Through our recruitment booklets and through personal interviews, the new employee of today knows a good deal about the firm and the way it operates before he reports for his first day at work.

Long-range planning

IN 1921 there was no such thing as long-range planning in firms such as ours. The need for attracting talented people was, of course, well recognized, but the idea of establishing goals to be attained at specified dates in the future was unheard of.

Now things are entirely different. Most progressive CPA firms today recognize the necessity of making definite plans for the future. There are always many unknowns about the future, and at present one of the greatest unknowns is the impact of automation. Nobody at this point can be entirely sure what automation will eventually do to our business society because it has not yet progressed far enough to give us much of a guide. One thing does seem clear, however: ultimately, automation will materially affect our whole historical approach to auditing.

It was partly the need for long-range planning on a day-to-day basis that led us in 1965 to create the new position of director of practice development, which Charles Gillette now fills. Charles is a member of the firm's Management Committee and, until he moved to New York a few months ago to assume his new role, was administrative partner of the Los Angeles office. While Charles will be concerned with a diversity of responsibilities at Home Office, long-range planning is to be his major activity.

AS I WRITE these final chapters of my story, I am particularly aware of change, for the very surroundings in which I work have changed in the past few months.

In March of this year (1965), the firm's New York office and Home Office were moved from 165 Broadway to 277 Park Avenue—one of the awesome new steel-and-glass skyscrapers that have been springing up like grass in recent years in the midtown area of New York. This move from the downtown financial district is further evidence, it seems to me, of the way in which clients' needs will continue to affect the growth and development of accounting firms in the years ahead, for a major consideration behind our move was the fact that many of our largest New York clients are headquartered in the uptown area.

Though the New York office has had many different addresses over the years, they have all been in the downtown financial district—actually within a few blocks of one another—since Arthur Young first opened the New York office in 1907. We had been at our most recent location, 165 Broadway, for fifteen years, since the spring of 1950.

As I sit here, in these very modern new quarters, my mind goes back to the old days, and I remember the simple set of books that I used to keep in the New York office in the early 1920s. Even that comparatively routine aspect of the firm's operations has changed radically over the years. Thus, about six months ago we signed an agreement with our client, Radio Corporation of America, for a new RCA Spectra 70 electronic computer system to be installed in Home Office. The system consists of a central processor, four high-speed magnetic-tape units for data storage, a paper-tape reader/punch, a card reader, and a printer. Scheduled to go into operation in April 1966, this new computer system will enable the firm to handle centrally most of the internal accounting and analysis work that is presently performed in our forty domestic offices around the United States.

I wonder what Arthur Young would say if he could see these and all the other changes that have taken place since his time. I do not think he would be too surprised, for he himself was always keenly sensitive to the changes that were going on about him in the business community and in the world in general, and he had unlimited confidence in the continuing ability of the firm to keep pace with such changes and to prosper accordingly. I think he would be very proud of his firm today.

I HAVE MENTIONED at several points in this story my growing concern, since my illness in the mid-1950s, about providing for an orderly succession in the firm's management. This transition was accomplished in the spring of this year, when the Management Committee acted officially to name Ralph Kent my successor on October 1, 1965, with the titles of chairman of the Management Committee and managing partner of the firm. By this action, Ralph became the firm's new leader and its fourth senior partner. The news of this action came as no surprise to our organization, for, as Jim Burton had said about me eleven years earlier, Ralph had been senior partner in everything but name for quite a few years.

Ralph Kent becomes senior partner

I suppose it is only natural that I should take great personal pride in our firm's succession. I believe that I know Ralph Kent better than anyone else in the firm knows him, and I have not the slightest doubt that he will prove to be a great leader, preserving and advancing the best traditions of our firm.

It is time to be old,
To take in sail:—
The god of bounds,
Who sets to seas a shore,
Came to me in his fatal rounds,
And said: "No more!
No farther shoot
Thy broad ambitious branches, and thy root.
Fancy departs: no more invent;
Contract thy firmament
To compass of a tent.
There's not enough for this and that,
Make thy option which of two;
Economize the failing river,
Not the less revere the Giver,
Leave the many and hold the few. . . ."

RALPH WALDO EMERSON: First part of "Terminus"

CHAPTER NINETEEN

TIME TO BE OLD

How does it feel to be just a few months away from retirement? It feels wonderful. It feels very much as though I were preparing for a long vacation, without a worry in the world. For the first time in my life I will have plenty of time at my disposal. No more appointments unless I want them; no more worrying over disagreeable tasks.

I still have energy and enthusiasm, and a terrific curiosity about life. What are my plans? I have none. Absolutely none. Nor do I propose to make any.

But, while I have no plans, I know in a general way some of the things I would like to do. I would like to set out with Madge on a long voyage (not a cruise) on an ocean liner. I would like to sit on the sun deck and let the wind blow about me. Maybe I would memorize poetry. I used to do that in my twenties—one verse a day. I would write down a verse each night and commit it to memory the following morning during my fifteen-minute walk to the Staten Island ferry. Over a period of just a few years

Some things I would like to do

I learned a good deal of poetry in this way: Byron, Shelley, Keats, etc.

Then I want to refresh my memories of Ireland and linger around the spots that meant so much to me in the old days. I don't have too much time to do this, for the scene in Ireland, as elsewhere, is changing rapidly. The Model School and the Academy have both moved to larger and better quarters. The building that used to house the Academy is still there, but the Model School was torn down some years ago. It stood for over a hundred years on the banks of the River Strule and had long since outgrown its usefulness when the decision was made to demolish it.

Sometimes the Strule would overflow its banks and the school would close. I recall that one time the water was about six feet deep on the road in front of the school, and an enterprising fellow with a rowboat did a lively business transporting people. My brother Hugh used to pray for the school to be flooded. How excited he was when he made a trip in a rowboat past the front doors of the school and along the road for the equivalent of about three blocks!

Long stretches of the railways in Ireland have also gone. Early this year the Great Northern closed down what used to be its very active line from Portadown to Londonderry, which ran past Orchard Terrace, where I watched trains as a boy. Just a few weeks ago I stood on the bridge beyond Orchard Terrace and looked along the railway tracks. It was a sorry sight. Only the four walls were left of the engine shed which used to house the mighty locomotives, and grass was already beginning to grow over the tracks. Then I walked to the railway station, and it too looked forlorn and desolate. Two or three of the windows of the signal box, which used to guide the trains in and out of the station, were broken, and debris was scattered all around.

High on my list of the things I would like to do is to get better acquainted with New York City. I love New York, and the thrill I experienced when I first arrived in the fabulous city has never really left me. There are all kinds of interesting things to see and do in New York. It is really inexcusable that I have never taken the time to wander through St. Paul's Chapel and Trinity Church, and the two graveyards which surround these grand old churches, though I have passed them hundreds and hundreds of times. St. Mark's-in-the-Bouwerie is not too far away from where the New York office used to be, in the financial district, yet I have been in the church only three times, and never in its graveyard.

Most people, I suspect, are unaware of how much history is attached to some of these old churches in downtown New York. I imagine many people know that Peter Stuyvesant and Commodore Perry are both buried in the churchyard of St. Mark's, but I doubt very much whether many Irishmen realize that the remains of Thomas Addis Emmet, a leader of the United Irishmen in the eighteenth century and subsequently a leader of the American bar, also rest there. Thomas Emmet was the elder brother of the Irish patriot and martyr, Robert Emmet.

Strangely enough, while the remains of Thomas Emmet are in the churchyard of St. Mark's, a monument to his memory is in St. Paul's churchyard, resting over the remains of his widow's second husband. It is the most conspicuous object there—a tall white obelisk rising just to the south of the facade facing Broadway. I have always felt somewhat frustrated about this monument, because I find it impossible to read all of the faded inscription. I believe I could read the inscription from a fairly high stepladder, but somehow I have never thought it would be quite proper for me to be seen on a stepladder in the graveyard of St. Paul's. On October 1, 1965, however, there is really no reason why I should not satisfy at least this small curiosity.

Time for our family

WE ARE A CLANNISH FAMILY, and Madge and I both look forward to seeing more of our relatives than was always possible in my busy years. We are naturally close to our two daughters, now Mrs. Roy G. Davis and Mrs. Kenneth P. Knowles, and their families. Already I think I know our grandchildren better than I knew our daughters when they were of comparable ages.

My brother Hugh died in 1957, but we see his widow Maudie frequently. We also see a good deal of my sister Beth, who retired from the Metropolitan Life Insurance Company just a few months ago.

As I have said earlier, three of my father's sisters are still alive and continue to live in the old family home in Dervock. Considering their ages—80, 83, and 86—they are in good health. For the past twenty years Aunt Etty, the youngest, and I have exchanged letters every week or two. She has been a wide reader all her life, and her letters continue to be both interesting and stimulating.

Madge's two sisters and brother are also alive and well. All of them are married and have children. Bobby and Winifred live in Belfast, and Fred is the rector of St. Michael's Episcopal Church in New York City. We are closely in touch with all of them.

But it's not only relatives that I'll have a chance to see. Maybe

312

in my retirement I'll look up some of the other people who have played a part in my life. Over the years I have met thousands and thousands of people. Every once in a while one of them comes out of oblivion, stays briefly, and then disappears into the shadows again.

One such individual, a truly astonishing man, was Alexander J. Baxter, who was in the New York office from 1912 to 1920, and who in the last few of those years was in effect the administrative partner of the New York office under Arthur Young. When he retired from the firm in 1920, Baxter cut his ties with everything and everyone. Not only did he resign from the American Institute and the New York State Society, but he never once came back to visit the New York office.

An unusual accountant

I had always regretted never having met Baxter. I felt that he could have added a good deal to what I knew about the beginnings of the firm in New York. My curiosity was particularly aroused because people used to talk a good deal about Baxter: how he had retired very early in life; how he had travelled all over the world and then, when he returned, discovered to his considerable surprise that his fortune had increased appreciably in his absence; and how, in the late 1920s, he had come back again during the depression to find that he was practically penniless.

The years went by and nobody talked about Baxter any more. Then, suddenly one day late in 1958, thirty-eight years after Baxter had left the firm, I learned quite by accident that he was still alive and residing in Santa Monica, California. I was quite excited about this news and immediately telephoned Alan Petch, who was then in charge of the Los Angeles office. I asked him to rush around to see Baxter and to try to get him to talk before he died.

Back came the word from Petch that not only had Baxter no intention of dying in the immediate future but he talked a blue streak and had all kinds of information about the firm at his fingertips.

I was in Los Angeles a month or two after that, so Petch and I arranged to have lunch with Baxter. I found a small, spry, sharp-eyed Englishman, very articulate and very interesting, who talked at a terrific rate. At my urging, he agreed to write a memorandum about his early days with the firm. I received the memorandum soon afterward, and it was perfectly amazing. He recalled the names of client companies, how much people were paid, all sorts of things.

Then I went back and urged Baxter to write some account of what exactly he did after he abandoned the accounting profession in 1920. Once again he went immediately to work and this time he produced some 300 pages of memoirs (typed single-space), which he appropriately titled "No Destination."

It continues to amaze me how a professional man who obviously was highly intelligent and ambitious (he had passed the examinations for chartered accountant and incorporated accountant in London and then, later on, the CPA exam in New York) could at the age of 37 close the door on professional accounting and apparently never give it another thought.

Baxter unfortunately died quite unexpectedly, a few years after I met him, at the age of 79. He was unmarried and lived alone.

For many years accountants have had the reputation of being a rather dull and dusty lot. The picture that Charles Lamb drew of an accountant in his essay, "The South-Sea House," written in 1820, is not too different, I suspect, from what many people, even today, think the average accountant is like:

Of quite another stamp was the then accountant, John Tipp....
With Tipp form was everything. His life was formal. His actions seemed
ruled with a ruler. His pen was not less erring than his heart.... With all
this there was about him a sort of timidity—(his few enemies used to
give it a worse name)—a something which in reverence to the dead, we
will place, if you please, a little on this side of the heroic.... Tipp never
mounted the box of a stagecoach in his life; or leaned against the rails of
a balcony; or walked upon the ridge of a parapet; or looked down a precipice; or let off a gun; or went upon a water-party; or would willingly
let *you* go, if he could have helped it....

And then, of course, there is the much-quoted description of the "typical auditor" attributed to Elbert Hubbard:

... a man past middle life; tall, spare, wrinkled, intelligent, cold, passive, noncommittal, with eyes like a codfish; polite in contact but at the same time unresponsive; cool, calm, and as damnably composed as a concrete post or a plaster-of-paris cat; a human petrifaction with a heart of feldspar and without charm or the friendly germ; minus bowels, passion, or a sense of humor. Happily they never reproduce, and all of them finally go to Hell.

Though it is something of a digression in this story of mine, we are close to the end, and I cannot resist the temptation here to balance the literary scales a bit by quoting at some length from the opening pages of "No Destination"—the (to me) remarkable story of a remarkable man who was, among other things, an accountant:

As requested by you, I am giving you a condensed account of more than twenty years of my wanderings over the earth's six continents, several of such years being spent in the tropics. My longest journeys were undertaken for no other reason than to satisfy my curiosity regarding the

"No Destination"

world's natural features, and to indulge a taste for amateur exploring in little-known places.

Past experience had shown me that the more I avoided officials of all kinds, the easier it was for me to go just where I liked and do just what I wanted, and as I traveled light and traveled alone, I found I was seldom noticed as I moved quietly in and out of an area. I had, as I say, no object or ambition to achieve, but I did have a deep desire to visit the earth's great mountains, forests, and rivers, and I wanted to see as many and as much of them as I could in one short lifetime. To do this I endured a certain amount of hardship and had a few narrow escapes, but I never had even a headache from first to last, though I have been cold, hot, hungry, and thirsty often enough, not to mention having been host to every known variety of bug that stings or bites as well as those that scorn locomotion of any kind.

I have had to eat anything that came in my way, as I refused to subsist on canned foods which soon put you under the weather, and I have been helped by my recognition of the fact that if you eat one dead animal, it is mere prejudice to refuse to eat any other dead animal. Thus it is I have consumed dogs, cats, horse, goats, beetles, locusts, snakes, lizards, crocodile, elephant, caterpillars, bees in the comb, porcupine, various forest rodents, both land and sea snails, macaws, raw fish, sea gulls, sea slugs, blood drawn straight from cattle, besides quantities of food, both animal and vegetable, that I could not identify but which I took care to see was well cooked.

I have lived in huts with natives of all kinds, including some in advanced stages of every known disease, including elephantiasis, tuberculosis, leprosy, syphilis, sleeping sickness, and yes, even smallpox. Among other things I discovered I could sleep on the bamboo floor of a Brazilian Indian's hut in wet and muddy clothes, with babies crying at the other end and dogs cuddling up to me for warmth, and wake feeling fine except for the stiff lines made on my body by the bamboos, which took an hour or two to wear off, and in daylight start off breakfastless through the dark forest. If you balk at discomforts, you are obviously not fitted for this sort of life, but I can assure you that such things are speedily forgotten when set off against the wonderful compensations you encounter along the way.

So if you want to penetrate beyond reach of the comforts of civilization, and enjoy doing it, see that you start out with a good rugged constitution, no fads regarding food, and no prejudices against any of the members of the human race, however lowly they may at first appear. As you will find, you have to depend upon them for your very existence before you have finished. And now, although such travels are things of the past for me, I find that when any country or continent comes up for discussion, it is not merely a place on the map to me, but a living, breathing reality as once again I recall its natural features, its human inhabitants, and see them as they really are; so, with these introductory remarks, let me come down to cases.

As you already know, I have lived two completely distinct lives: my business life which I call my second-class life, which however I regard with gratitude for having supplied me with the wherewithal to live my other life, that of wandering over the earth's surface, which I call my first-class or real life, the one that has brought me more than falls to the lot of any but a very few men.

Though I retired from business in the year 1920, I had already done what was in those days regarded as an exceptional amount of travel. Thus, while living in Great Britain, I was constantly going beyond its borders—so much so, in fact, that I had crossed to the continent of Europe by as many as twelve different routes, and had lived in France and had seen Norway, Sweden, Denmark, Holland, Belgium, Germany, Austria, Italy, Spain, and Portugal, and made trips to the Canaries and the Azores, Madeira, Morocco, and Algiers; and I had in 1904 made an extensive tour of the United States and Canada, and then when I moved across the Atlantic to live in America from the years 1911 on to and including 1920, I covered America and Canada pretty thoroughly, and also spent some time in the West Indies, and in 1913 had made a journey far up the Orinoco River in Venezuela in the opposite direction to that taken by Alexander Humboldt in 1799, and I had also stopped off in Colombia and Panama on the way back. In addition, I had visited Newfoundland, Nova

Scotia, Bermuda, Jamaica, Cuba, and the Bahamas. These journeys, you might say, kept my traveling tastes alive and reconciled me to a period of business life before I was ready for the final take-off, which, as I say, happened at the end of 1920.

So it was at the very outset of 1921 I boarded the *Aquitania* in New York, the best sea boat I was ever on (and I have been on more than any ship captain I have ever traveled with), and left to visit friends in Britain and renew acquaintance with my old Latin Quarter haunts in Paris and a few other favorite spots, before taking a steamer from London, bound for the opposite side of the world (New Zealand, to be precise), and then, except for a brief passage through California into Mexico on my way south after circumnavigating the globe, I was not to see America again for some six years.

The first two of these years I spent in the South Seas, traveling on about a dozen steamers and several schooners all the way from the Admiralty Islands to the Marquesas. I followed no plan or program. I went whenever and wherever I felt like going. As the great Pacific Ocean stretches over a third or more of the earth's surface, it takes time to cover it. I visited some forty islands in all, and traveled in both Australia and New Zealand from end to end. It was with great reluctance I left the Pacific, but I had a rendezvous to keep with Africa, so there it was I proceeded to encounter an entirely new and different set of experiences; but before launching into these, let me touch upon a few instances of my South Seas life.

As evidence of my haphazard journeys, let me give an example: As I was walking one day down Lower George Street in Sydney, New South Wales, I ran into an engaging individual I had formerly encountered in some of the northwest Pacific islands. Seeing the grip in my hand, he asked me where I was bound for, and I told him to join such-and-such a ship for such-and-such a place, whereupon he said, "Don't go on that ship today—come with me to a more interesting island tomorrow." Knowing him as an island expert, I instantly agreed, canceled my passage forthwith, and went off with him at sunrise the next day.

New Zealand has a number of things to offer the traveler who does not mind leaving the beaten track. There it was I climbed a good way up its highest mountain, Mount Cook, twelve-thousand-odd feet, before being driven back by the frightful weather. The next day in the nearby lowlands, my car was stopped by a shepherd who asked me to send a telegram for him to the owner of the sheep we were passing by, telling him that some 500 had been frozen to death during the preceding night. This was in the South Island of the two New Zealand Islands, far more rugged and mountainous territory than the North Island, and reaching down quite a ways toward the South Pole. Huge trout abound in the lakes and rivers there, and the fishing around the coast and the sailing, too, are unsurpassed anywhere in the world. A keen fisherman when I entered New Zealand, I caught so many so easily I lost most of my taste for fishing.

While camping out on an island at the northern end of North Island, a school of blackfish, a species of whale, invaded our bay. One or two were washed up right in front of our tents where I was living with a friend, Bill Moore. In the evenings, giant sharks invaded our bay, and I have spent hours firing at their triangular fins with a .22 Winchester, with no apparent effect. While we went swimming a huge barracuda necessitated one man being on guard with a spear while the other kept in only waist-deep water.

I might add a word or two about Bill Moore. He was an ex-trapper from the Canadian Rockies that I met in London through an ad he put in the *Times*, asking to meet another man to share expenses on a hunting and fishing trip. He wanted to go hunting in Africa with the Kikuyus, now called the Mau Maus, while I wanted first to visit Australasia, so we tossed a coin for it and I won, so we left for New Zealand. I might add that he never did get to Africa for he fell in love with one of the gay and lighthearted Tahitian girls, married her and settled down in a bamboo house on a beach under the coconut trees, and was still there some years back. I met with other Americans and Europeans who had also married these girls, and I never heard of one of them that was disappointed. So there must be something in the tales you hear about them.

Some others who came back

NOW LET ME MENTION another man who came back from oblivion quite briefly. His name was Jack O'Callaghan. He was with H. B. Brandon & Co. in Omagh when Madge and I were there. Jack's father, who was the manager of the gas company, wanted Jack to be an accountant, but Jack was bored with everything about accounting and had a wanderlust that eventually carried him thousands of miles from Omagh. He joined the British Army during the closing stages of the First World War. He was with the occupation forces in Germany, then he went to India, and then, when he was discharged from the Army, he emigrated to Argentina.

Thirty years later I ran into Jack one day with his wife in the streets of Omagh. I saw him three times after that: once when he dropped in to see us, unannounced, in Ridgewood (he was then a widower); once when he came to borrow money from me (which he later repaid); and finally when he was dead. Although we never corresponded, for some reason or other he had my address in his pocket and someone telephoned me when he died (in his sleep) to find out his next of kin. He had been living alone and apparently had no close friends.

As I stood in an undertaking parlor in Manhattan, all alone, looking at Jack O'Callaghan, my mind drifted back to Brandon's and to how hard Jack had tried to bring excitement into what for him was a dull, drab, meaningless life. He hated everything that had to do with accounting or financial statements or routine of any kind, and his restless capers were unpredictable.

One day a widow, Mrs. Pollock, came into Brandon's. She ran what for Omagh was a large, active grocery shop. Everywhere she went a small Pomeranian dog was at her heels. One day, by some means or other, the dog was still in Brandon's when she left.

When O'Callaghan spotted the dog he trapped it under a typewriter cover (in those days, typewriter covers were made of tin), and then he sat down and howled with delight as the cover ran back and forth all over the office. After that episode the dog would never again come into Brandon's.

Another time O'Callaghan started horseplay with me. He swung a large heavy ebony ruler at me, but he lost his balance and the ruler came down full force on the ink wells which, with the impact, hopped almost to the ceiling. Red ink spilled all over one of the "day books" of *The Tyrone Constitution*. I was scared to death. The proprietor of the *Constitution* was a highly respected figure in Omagh; not only was he a well-known businessman, but he was also a leader in the public life of the town and county; and he took great pride in his books, which were like copperplate. The accident did not faze O'Callaghan, however. He immediately got a pot of paste and pasted together all of the pages that were spattered with ink, so that they could not be opened. I did not think the problem was that easily solved, but O'Callaghan was confident. Four weeks later, however, all hell broke loose when it developed that there was a difference in the customers ledger trial balance and Jamison, then in charge of the office, started checking the postings. He let out a terrific roar when he found out that a great many original entries were lost forever. Strangely enough, however, we never heard a word from the proprietor of the *Constitution*.

Let me give one more example of people coming back from oblivion. When I was the firm's cashier in the early 1920s I had two assistants, Rhea Silverberg and Alice O'Donoghue. I went on the audit staff in 1925, and not very long afterwards Rhea left to become Mrs. Riffkin, and later Alice left to become Mrs. Penny. I never saw either of them after they left the firm, nor did we communicate in any way—not even a Christmas card. Like so many others, they simply passed out of my life.

I did not know it but apparently both girls kept in touch with each other spasmodically over the years. One day they decided to look me up. When they learned I was ill, they came up to Harkness Pavilion to see me. It was more than twenty-five years since the three of us had been together, and they, with the passing of the years, had both become grandmothers. We had a grand time for an hour or so, reliving the old days, and then we said goodbye. They went back into the shadows, and I have not seen them since.

I suspect that others will pop in and out of my life in the years ahead. Perhaps Isabelle O'Grady will drop in some day to find out how I liked *If Winter Comes*.

Looking forward

I HAVE SAID that I will have loads of free time in retirement. In a sense this is true, but I know full well that none of us ever has as much time as he thinks he will have. Time is very elusive, particularly as we get older. The fact is that we splinter our lives into hundreds of little pieces. We spend a disproportionate amount of time reading newspapers and magazines and looking at television, a great deal of this simply out of habit, or because other people do so. I know I'll continue to think that this is bad, and I also know that I'll continue to do it. Human beings are like that.

Will I continue to be interested in accounting? I think so. I am deeply interested in the future of the profession and, of course, in the future of Arthur Young & Company as well. How could it be otherwise? I am naturally very proud of my long association with the firm. I hope I have contributed my fair share to its growth and development. More importantly, I hope I have contributed to its character.

Would I like to live my life over again? No. No part of it. Not even last week. Not even this morning.

Would I do things differently if I were given another go at life? I somehow doubt it. I have made mistakes as everyone has. Perhaps I would avoid making the same mistakes on a second go-round, but I'm sure I would make others, maybe a lot worse.

Let me close this story of mine with a quotation from Lin Yutang's *The Importance of Living*. It struck a responsive chord in me when I first read it some twenty-five years ago, and I find that it does so still:

> No one can say that a life with childhood, manhood, and old age is not a beautiful arrangement; the day has its morning, noon, and sunset, and the year has its seasons, and it is good that it is so. There is no good or bad in life, except what is good according to its own season. And if we take this biological view of life and try to live according to the seasons, no one but a conceited fool or an impossible idealist can deny that human life can be lived like a poem. Shakespeare has expressed this idea more graphically in his passage about the seven stages of life, and a good many Chinese writers have said about the same thing. It is curious that Shakespeare was never very religious, or very much concerned with religion. I think this was his greatness; he took human life largely as it was, and intruded himself as little upon the general scheme of things as he did upon the characters of his plays. Shakespeare was like Nature herself, and that is the greatest compliment we can pay to a writer or thinker. He merely lived, observed life, and went away.

Some Photographs

My sister Beth, my brother Hugh, and I (in the middle) in Omagh in 1904.

I had this picture taken a few months after I arrived in America, and sent it to Madge Corker.

Madge and I in Staten Island in 1929.

Madge in 1920 when she and I both worked in Brandon's.

Madge and I and her parents at their home in Omagh in 1926.

At our home in Ridgewood, with Sheila and Eileen, in 1944.

Madge and I at Cape Cod in the summer of 1965.

Arthur Young at his home in Aiken, South Carolina in 1938— the year I became a partner.

Jim Burton and I in 1960 at the firm's annual meeting in Hot Springs, Virginia.

Ralph Kent and I in the spring of 1965, in the old office at 165 Broadway.

Partners of Arthur Young & Company
1921-1965

PARTNERS OF ARTHUR YOUNG & COMPANY
From January 1, 1921, the Effective Date
of the First National Partnership, to June 30, 1965

Years of Active Partnership

Atlanta			Mock, H. A.	1956 –
Brown, D. M.	1963 –		Vasen, G. B.	1956 –
Reddicks, Jr., W. E.	1959 –		Wofsey, R. A.	1964 –
Baltimore			*Buffalo*	
Black, R. W.	1964 –		Clair, R. C.	1957 –
Birmingham			Pallin, A. D.	1959 –
King, C. H.	1963 –		Payne, D. N.	1961 –
Regan, Jr., J.	1963 –		*Chicago*	
			Ahlforth, F.	1933 – 1958
Boston			Baldwin, R.	1950 –
Brown, E. F.	1959 –		Boyack, H.	1921 – 1941 D
Claus, A. J.	1961 –		Brooks, R. A.	1960 –
Mitchell, R. E.	1964 –		Carracio, G. V.	1956 –

NOTE: Active partners are listed under the city in which they now reside. Retired partners are listed under the city in which they resided at the date of their retirement.

D *Deceased.*

* *Director. (The position of "Director" was established for those individuals who, while not partners in the firm, have all the qualifications for partnership except that they are not eligible for the CPA certificate because of education or experience requirements.)*

334

Cavanagh, Jr., H. L.	1930 – 1947 D	Dallas	
Collinson, J. B.	1950 – 1955 & 1957 – 1959	Adam, P. J.	1947 –
		Harris, J. C.	1953 – 1957 D
Doherty, H. J.	1964 –	Pollock, R. L.	1961 –
Ettelson, R. G.	1960 –	Prince, W. D.	1953 – 1959
Goldsmith, D. M. *	1962 –	Schumacher, A. C.	1959 –
Goss, D. E.	1962 –	Tannery, F. F.	1956 – 1957
Groves, J. M.	1936 – 1956	Taylor, I. N.	1957 –
Hensold, Jr., H. H.	1962 –	Denver	
Jackson, B. A.	1960 – 1962	Bartsch, R. R.	1962 –
Kirchheimer, H. W.	1960 –	Bidwell, Jr., E. E.	1962 –
McGregor, J. P.	1921 – 1939 D	Diss, W. T.	1964 –
McLaughlin, L. B.	1945 – 1962	Mayo, Jr., R.	1957 –
McPhee, A. V.	1936 – 1960	Mayo, Sr., R. B.	1955 – 1961
Miller, C. R.	1945 –	Troutfetter, V. E.	1957 – 1957 D
Murnane, E. J.	1942 – 1952 D	Zarini, C. A.	1960 –
Owens, E. C.	1949 – 1962	Detroit	
Penny, J. L.	1960 –	Handren, L. E.	1963 – 1965 D
Schornack, J. J.	1964 –	Hodkinson, G. J.	1959 –
Sullivan, T. J.	1951 – 1960	Janes, S.	1950 – 1962
Sutherland, W.	1921 – 1945	Olsen, E. G.	1960 –
Swanson, A. E.	1942 – 1949 D	Shaw, W. R.	1960 –
Thompson, H. A.	1960 –	Smith, B. M.	1956 –
Tobin, M. E. *	1961 –	Fort Worth	
Traynor, W. K.	1960 – 1965 D	Jenness, Jr., T. N.	1961 –
Cincinnati		Morris, C. H.	1961 –
Graham, B. G.	1956 – 1957 D	Pickens, H. A.	1961 –
Klehfoth, A. H.	1956 – 1958	Salmon, T. C.	1961 –
Morrison, F. S.	1957 –	Wagner, W. J.	1961 –
Phillips, W. E.	1958 –	Houston	
Rutenschroer, M. W.	1959 – 1963	Adam, A.	1954 – 1959 D
Simlick, W. N.	1956 – 1959	Harbin, W. D.	1960 –
Cleveland		Moore, G. S.	1962 –
Gwilym, J. B.	1962 –	Rush, B.	1954 –
Uebel, C. E.	1956 – 1960	Street, C.	1954 – 1958

335

Kansas City
    Barnes, P.   1950 – 1950 D
    Bowen, Jr., A. H.   1950 –
    Dobson, J. J.   1950 – 1952
    Kerr, P. H.   1937 – 1947 D
    Lunsford, H. E.   1950 – 1953 D
    Meyer, C. R.   1958 –
    Stiller, H. M.   1951 –

Los Angeles
    Burns, D. T.   1955 –
    Cole, L. H.   1956 –
    Gamble, D. H.   1957 –
    Jones, R. P.   1960 –
    Lamb, E. M.   1964 –
    Lampe, E.   1949 – 1951
    Lohman, W. H.   1960 –
    Mayhugh, W. J.   1959 –
    Miller, H. R.   1960 –
    Miller, L. W.   1960 –
    MacTavish, D.   1940 – 1948 D
    Petch, A. H.   1949 – 1961
    Roggeveen, J. E.   1957 –
    Samuelson, M. A.   1960 –
    Ward, H. E.   1947 –

Milwaukee
    Cerny, J. F.   1964 –
    Gerdis, J. F.   1942 – 1957
    Vaughan, B. M.   1953 –

Minneapolis
    Diracles, J. M.   1960 –

New York (Home Office)
    Crumley, C. C.   1959 –
    Deering, J. J.   1945 –
    Flynn, T. D.   1949 –
    Gillette, C. G.   1953 –
    Grumpelt, H. C.   1941 –
    Hicks, E. L.   1963 –
    Higgins, T. G.   1938 –
    Horn, F. E.   1954 –
    Ings, W. C.   1956 –
    Irvine, J. J.   1958 –
    Kent, R. E.   1949 –
    Miles, J. M.   1963 –
    Shaw, T. T.   1941 –
    Weston, F. T.   1950 –

New York (New York Office)
    Barry, R. F.   1950 –
    Bender, L. C.   1950 – 1963
    Binshadler, E. W. *   1963 –
    Birkhold, R. H.   1953 –
    Blomqvist, E. J.   1930 – 1947
    Botte, S. A.   1959 –
    Burton, J. C.   1921 – 1956
    Chapin, D. H.   1963 –
    Clarke, T. H.   1921 – 1940 D
    Colley, F. G.   1921 – 1933 D
    Conklin, W. D.   1949 –
    Daly, W. M.   1960 –
    Dolan, T. J.   1950 – 1953
    Fennelly, D. J.   1953 –
    Galpin, R. H.   1940 –
    Gladstone, W. L.   1963 –
    Gough, J. R.   1961 –
    Gould, J. S.   1957 –
    Hawxhurst, E. F.   1963 –
    Hertenstein, P. L.   1961 –
    Kanaga, W. S.   1960 –
    Lewis, R. F.   1956 –
    Macaulay, H. L.   1950 – 1962 D
    Maiden, N. G.   1943 –
    McGregor, W. D.   1921 – 1948

Meighan, H. V.	1959 –	St. Louis	
Murdoch, R. G.	1944 – 1960	Brining, R. L.	1957 –
Nissley, W. W.	1929 – 1950 D	Pelot, Jr., F. L.	1960 –
Norton, G.	1932 – 1940	Smith, R. V.	1961 –
Pitney, T. C. *	1961 –	San Diego	
Romak, T.	1961 –	Scharff, Jr., E.	1963 –
Stella, J. S.	1950 – 1955 D		
Stewart, J. H.	1956 – 1963	San Francisco	
Summa, D. J.	1958 –	Alber, H. E.	1956 – 1962
Tilt, R. G.	1952 –	Brown, F. H.	1956 – 1957
Young, Arthur	1921 – 1948 D	Hefter, G. E.	1956 – 1959
		Herrick, A.	1956 – 1957
Newark		Kemmerle, A. F.	1959 – 1961
Foley, Jr., D. W.	1961 –	Lanigar, M. E.	1957 –
Formichella, M. J.	1958 –	Macrae, E. W.	1957 –
McGordy, J. H.	1963 –	Mahoney, F. J.	1960 –
		Nelson, F. C.	1956 – 1957
Oklahoma City		Page, D. F.	1959 –
Hurst, K. C.	1961 – 1965	Severns, E. E.	1956 – 1961
Petty, M. D.	1963 –	Sullivan, J. M.	1957 –
Williams, T. D.	1961 –	Wittman, Jr., C. W.	1953 – 1959
Philadelphia		San Jose	
Brombach, A. C.	1959 –	Fennell, J. F.	1964 –
Bryant, R. J.	1959 –	Frazer, Jr., R. R.	1962 –
Metz, Jr., A. G.	1959 –	Frazer, R. R.	1962 – 1963
Phoenix		Santa Ana	
Donohoe, M. J.	1962 –	James, D. L.	1963 –
Pittsburgh		Seattle	
Brown, J. P.	1940 – 1956	Wiles, E. H.	1956 –
Harvey, Jr., J. L.	1951 –	Toledo	
Weidert, W. F.	1957 –	Ehler, H. W.	1956 –
Wood, E. O.	1963 –	Floyd, R L.	1951 –
Portland		Jacoby, W. A.	1962 –
Holm, W. H.	1960 –	Kirk, R. J.	1954 –
Wood, I. D.	1960 – 1961		

Leitner, C. E.	1951 – 1962	Porter, S. P.	1955 –
Madden, J. E.	1950 – 1959	Savage, G. A.	1943 – 1962 [D]
Tanner, H. W.	1962 –	Warner, R. T.	1963 –
Villhauer, M. H.	1959 –		
Waterman, J. M.	1959 –	*Washington*	
Wideman, C. H.	1950 – 1957	Hamilton, L. W.	1962 –
		Moyer, E. C.	1960 –

Tulsa

Brown, D. W.	1963 –	*Westbury*	
Godfrey, R. F.	1963 –	Hogg, H. W.	1962 –
Groth, R. E.	1961 –		
Keene, P. R.	1962 –	*Wichita*	
McAfee, H. B.	1963 –	Smith, V. A.	1950 – 1954 [D]
Miller, K. G.	1954 –	Ward, W. E.	1954 –

INDEX

Abercorn, Duchess of, 18
Abernethy, William, 171
Adam, Paul J., 216, 217, 226, 267
Ahlforth, Frank, 159, 181, 206, 212-213, 219, 225, 226, 245
Ahoghill, 5
Alan Wood Steel Company, 125
Allen, Fred J., 34, 40
Altschul, Frank, 141
American Accounting Association, 294
American Association of Public Accountants, 118 (*see also* American Institute of CPAs)
American Institute of Accountants, *see* American Institute of CPAs
American Institute of CPAs, 114, 117, 118, 120, 150, 152-153, 160, 166, 167, 174, 181, 210-211, 245, 263, 313
  Accounting Principles Board, 153, 272-273, 285-295
  activities of T. G. Higgins, 272
  Bureau for Placements, 123, 210
  Committee on Accounting Procedure, 153, 166, 207, 211, 272, 292, 294
  Committee on Professional Ethics, 272-273, 279, 282, 285
  Committee on Selection of Personnel, 186, 211
  Council, 166, 169, 253, 272, 282, 288, 290-293
  Executive Committee, 167, 268, 272, 288, 290-291
  presidents of, 271-272, 291
  Research Division, 211, 295
  Rule 4.04 (on professional conduct), 277
  Rule 13 (on independence), 281, 284
  Special Committee on Auditing Procedure, 169
  Special Committee on the Development of Accounting Principles, 153
  Standing Committee on Accounting Procedure, 153
  testing program, 186, 210
American Stock Exchange, 160

American Telephone and Telegraph Company, 116
Andersen, Arthur, & Co., 255
Armour and Company, 115
Armstrong Cork Company, 294
Arthur Young & Company, see Young, Arthur, & Company
Asian and Pacific Accounting Convention of 1960, 273
Atlantic Monthly, The, 118
Aughnacloy, 4, 9, 12
Aurelius, Marcus, quoted, 204

Bacon, Francis, quoted, 270
Banking Act of 1933, 163
Barnes, P., 217
Barry, Richard F., 127
Baruch, Bernard, 135
Baxter, Alexander J., 98, 313-314; quoted, 315-319
Beaverbrook, Lord, quoted, 258
"Bishop of Wall Street," see Wilkinson, Rev. William
Blomqvist, Erik, 74-78, 202, 206
Bosworth, R. L., 142
Boyack, Harry, 60, 65, 158, 172, 179-181
Brandon, H. B., & Co., 33, 43, 45, 54-55, 104, 107, 320-321
Brandon, Jamison & Co., 40
Brisbane, Arthur, quoted, 128
Broads, Paterson & Co., 98, 99, 214, 221
Brookhart, Senator, 133-134
Brown, John P., 216
Buckeye Pipe Line Co., 201
Buffalo Bill, see Cody, William
Bureau of Yards and Docks, 199, 200

Burlingham, Charles Culp, 240-241
Burton, James C., 67, 80, 96, 99, 108, 143-144, 157-159, 164, 169, 172, 173-174, 179, 183, 190, 193, 198, 200, 201, 202-203, 205, 209, 211-213, 216-217, 219-220, 224-227, 253, 300; quoted, 56, 155-157, 170-171
Business History Review, 148
Buttrick, Dr. George A., 207
Byron, Lord, quoted, 7

Carey, John L., quoted, 298
Carpentier, Georges, 71
Carracio, George V., 267
Carson, Betty, 198
Carter, William, 173, 175-176, 201
Catterall, John J., 171
Cave, John and Mary, 8, 11-12, 107
Central Foundry Company, 199, 200
Churchill, Sir Winston, 135, 198, 258
Clarke, Thomas H., 66, 98-99, 100, 122, 179-180, 186
Clarkson, Gordon & Co., 214, 221
Cody, William ("Buffalo Bill"), 127-128
Colley, Frederick G., 54-55, 59, 64-65, 73-74, 76-78, 80, 81, 83, 86-89, 95-99, 108, 129-131, 144, 179
Columbia Baking Company, 126
Columbia Presbyterian Medical Center, 245, 248, 251, 252, 254-257
Community Church, 232-233
Confucius, quoted, 69
Consolidated Vultee Aircraft Corporation, 189
Continental Oil Company, 140-144

Coons, Bob, 129
Corker, Fred, 105, 312
Corker, Gertrude ("Bobbie"), 104-105, 312
Corker, Madge, *see* Higgins, Madge Corker
Corker, Winifred, *see* Taylor, Winifred Corker
Corker family, 104-106, 133, 312
Corporation Securities Company of Chicago, 149
Cosgrove, James J., 142
Curb Exchange, *see* New York Curb Exchange
Curragh, 30-31, 105

Daly, Walter M., 171
Darrow, Clarence, 133-135
Davis, Mrs. Roy G., 312
Deering, John J., 171, 201, 246, 253, 263, 264
Deloitte, Plender, Griffiths & Co., 64, 181
Dempsey, Jack, 71
Depression, Great, 137-153
Dervock, 4, 6-9, 14, 107, 110, 133
Detroit Guardian National Bank, 158
Dewey, John, 235; quoted, 229
Dietz Company, R. E., 72-74
Dimond, Nathan, 86-88
Dolan, Thomas J., 218-221
Dowd, Tom, 201
Dublin, 110, 133
Dunkirk, 174
Durando, Maurice, 173, 177

Easter Rebellion, 110

Edison, Thomas A., 147
Edward, Prince of Wales (King Edward VIII, Duke of Windsor), 173, 200
Eisenhower, Dwight D., 202; quoted, 280
Ellis Island, 47
Emerson, Ralph Waldo, quoted, 308
Emmet, Robert, 311
Emmet, Thomas Addis, 311
Exchange Buffet, 95

Federal Reserve Board, 114, 160
Federal Trade Commission, 114, 119
Flynn, Thomas D., 203, 215, 217, 223, 227, 253, 267, 271, 274-275
Fry, Dean, 97

Galbraith, John Kenneth, quoted, 136
Galpin, Ralph H., 123
General Electric Company, 148
George VI, King of England, 173
Gillette, Charles G., 305
Graham, A. J. & A., 62
Great Northern Railway Company, 21, 310
Groves, James M., 212
Grumpelt, Harry C., 123, 216

Hampton, Vernon B., quoted, 90
Hansmann, Joe, 94
Hansmann, Margaret, *see* Higgins, Margaret Hansmann
Hansmann family, 51, 71
Harkness Pavilion, 255-257, 322 (*see also* Columbia Presbyterian Medical Center)
Haskins & Sells, 81, 116
Hayward, Richard, quoted, 16

Heimbucher, Clifford V., 291
Henderson, Martha Jane, *see* Higgins, Martha Henderson
Henkel, Ralph, 129
Herdman, Elizabeth, *see* Higgins, Elizabeth Herdman
Herrick, Anson, 251-252
Herrick, Lester, and Herrick, 251
Herrick, Louy, 252
Herrick, Robert, quoted, 102
Higgins, Eileen (daughter), 173, 201, 312 (*see also* Knowles, Mrs. Kenneth P.)
Higgins, Elizabeth ("Beth"; sister), 4, 40, 92, 110-111, 312
Higgins, Elizabeth Herdman (grandmother), 6
Higgins, Hugh (brother), 4, 40, 44, 48-55, 92-94, 110, 199, 312
Higgins, Madge Corker, (wife), 43, 45, 103-111, 132, 173, 198, 201, 231, 234, 244-245, 312, 320
Higgins, Margaret Hansmann ("Maudie"; sister-in-law), 48-49, 93, 312
Higgins, Martha Henderson (mother), 8-12, 40, 44, 92, 111, 202
Higgins, Robert McQuiston (father), 4, 9, 10, 40, 91, 110-111, 202, 230
Higgins, Sheila (daughter), 173, 312 (*see also* Davis, Mrs. Roy G.)
Higgins, Thomas (grandfather), 5-8, 107, 133
Higgins, Thomas G.:
  family background, 3-15; born in Aughnacloy, 4
  boyhood in Omagh, 16-31; religious upbringing, 23-25; at school, 25-33; employed at H. B. Brandon & Co., 33-41
  emigrates to U.S., 43-46; arrival in New York, 46-50; on Staten Island, 49-51, 91-94
  hired by Arthur Young & Company, 55; first year with the firm, 69-89; becomes cashier of New York office, 89, 95-96
  engaged to Madge Corker, 104; marriage, 109
  joins audit staff of Arthur Young & Company, 108; life on the audit staff, 125-128; experience in the oil industry, 128, 140-143; home life in the 1930s, 131-132; the Great Depression, 137-153
  daughters Sheila and Eileen born, 173; visit to Europe in 1937, 173
  admitted to partnership of Arthur Young & Company, 174; increased responsibilities during war years, 190-203; extracts from diary (1942-1945), 198-203
  elected to Management Committee of Arthur Young & Company, 206; succeeds J. C. Burton as senior partner of the firm, 227
  views on religion, 229-241; work for local church, 249-251
  struggle with cancer, 243-259
  first professional activity, 207; active in American Institute of CPAs and New York State Society of CPAs, 271-297
  withdraws as active member of firm's Operating Committee, 275; succeeded by Ralph Kent: as managing partner, 276; as senior partner, 307
  thoughts on retirement, 309-323

Himmelblau, David, 115
Holmes, John Haynes, 232-233; quoted, 235-236
Home Rule, 30-32
Hoover Commission Task Force on Budget and Accounting, 264
Horn, Dr. Frederick E., 171, 215, 261, 303
Hostler, Dr. Amy, 296
Howe, Harry, 276
Hoxsey, J. M. B., 121, 141
Hubbard, Elbert, quoted, 315
Hull, Cordell, 200
Hunter, Finlay, 130
Huxley, Aldous, quoted, 258

Illinois Society of CPAs, 282
Indian & Central Refining Company, 76
Ings, William C., 171
Inniskilling Fusiliers, Royal, 17-22
Insull, Samuel, 147-149
International Minerals & Chemical Corporation, 182, 199, 200, 202
Investment Bankers Association, 119
Investment Company Act of 1940, 163

Jamison, J. P., 39, 44, 321
Jennings, Alvin, quoted, 292
Jones, Ralph, 294
Journal of Accountancy, The, 117, 154, 161-162, 167, 178, 210, 281, 292
Judson, Charles, 99-100, 122
Judson, Higson and Clarke, 66, 100

Kaufmann's Department Store, 67
Kennedy, Tod & Company, 61
Kent, Ralph E., 217, 223, 227, 245, 253, 267, 274-276, 307

Knight, Paul, 255
Knowles, Mrs. Kenneth P., 312
Kreuger, Ivar, 160-162
Kreuger & Toll, 154, 160

Lamb, Charles, quoted, 243, 314-315
Lamont, Thomas S., 142
Landis, James L., quoted, 166
Lend Lease Administration, 196-197
Lewis, Ralph F., 261-262, 267
Lin Yutang, quoted, 323
Lincoln Cathedral, 97
Lissanoure, 14
Lockheed Aircraft Corporation, 187-190
Logan, Gilbert (great-great-grandfather), 5
Lunsford, H. E., 217
Lunsford, Barnes & Co., 216-217
Lybrand, Ross Bros. & Montgomery, 116

Macartney family, 6, 12-15
MacDonald, Ramsay, 144
Maclean, Fitzroy D., 80
MacLysaght, Edward, quoted, 2
MacTavish, Donald, 188
Manhattan Oil Company, 76
Manning, Bishop William T., 231
Marwick, Mitchell & Co., *see* Peat, Marwick, Mitchell & Co.
Mason, Perry, 294
Matador Petroleum Company, 76
Mautz, R. K., quoted, 124
May, George O., 118-121, 141-142; quoted, 113, 150, 163
Mayo, Ralph B., & Co., 245
McCallum, James A., 61
McDonald, Forest, 149

McGregor, James P., 64, 158, 171-172, 179-180, 181
McGregor, William D., 66, 98, 109, 142, 144, 158, 179, 183-185, 205-206, 300
McKesson & Robbins, 167-169
McLaughlin, L. B., 216
McPhee, A. V., 181, 182-183, 206, 212-213, 219, 225-226
McQuiston, William John, 5
Mellis, Margery, 198
Metropolitan Life Insurance Company, 52-53, 92, 312
Middle West Utilities Company, 149
Midvale Company, 109, 125
Mills College of Education, 296-297
Montgomery, Robert H., quoted, 150
Moores, Carson & Watson, 66, 67
Moran, D. J., 143
Morgan, J. P., & Co., 83, 97, 142
Murison, A. B. L. (Tony), 169, 173
Murphy, Justice Frank, 200

National Association of Railroad and Utilities Commissioners, 153
Netherlands Purchasing Commission, 197, 198, 200
New Ice Company, 126
New York Curb Exchange, 138, 160
New York State Society of CPAs, 207, 253, 272-273, 276-279, 313
New York Stock Exchange, 119-121, 137-139, 141, 159-160, 162-163
New York Telephone Company, 294
New York *Times*, 137-139, 241, 319
New York Transit Company, 199

Newsom, Earl, & Company, 263, 267-269, 273
Nissley, Warren W., 121-123, 164-166, 171-172, 185-187, 201, 203, 206-207, 208-213, 216, 217, 219-220, 224-225, 264
North American Provision Company, 115

O'Callaghan, Jack, 320-321
O'Callaghan, P. J., 106-107
O'Donoghue, Alice, 321
O'Grady, Isabelle, 86, 88-89, 322
Omagh, 16-31, 104-107, 132-133, 310, 320-321
Omagh Academy, 25-30, 32-33, 310
Omagh Gas Company, 37-38, 106
Omagh Methodist Church, 23, 109, 132
Omagh Model School, 25, 310
Ovens, Ernest, 81-84, 96
Ozark Pipe Line Corporation, 76

Parkinson, Reggie, 107
Paton, William A., 182
Pearl Harbor, 185, 189, 192, 198
Peat, Marwick, Mitchell & Co., 66, 67, 99, 100
Penney, Louis H., 291
Perdue, Henry A., 26-29
Perry, Commodore, 311
Petch, Alan H., 313-314
Philadelphia Coke Company, 125
Pierce, Mr. & Mrs., 93-94
Pike, Bishop James A., 239-240
Potter, Charles Francis, 231
Prairie Oil & Gas Company, 128-129
Prairie Pipe Line Company, 128-129

Price Waterhouse & Co., 52, 115, 119, 121, 142
Printers' Ink, 294
Prohibition, 108, 133-135, 145
Public Service Company of Colorado, 126-127
Public Utility Holding Company Act of 1940, 163

Quillinan, Francis, 200

Radio Corporation of America, 306
Randall, Capt. Robert R., 92
Reece Corporation, 294
Reed, Lansing, 142
Reid, Robert L., 33-34, 39
Reiland, Dr. Karl, 231, 233
Reliance Manufacturing Company, 115
Revenue Act of 1962, 285
Revenue Act of 1964, 288
Ridgewood, 198, 199, 234, 246, 249, 253, 320
Riedell, Fred, 54, 78-80, 86-89, 96
Ripley, William Z., 118-119
Robinson, Bishop John A. T., 239-240
Robinson, Rev. F. Gault, 207
Rodger, Rev. Alexander M., 234
Roosevelt, Franklin D., 163, 202
Roxana Petroleum Corporation, 76
Ruggaber, Martin, 202
Ryan Aeronautical Co., 189

Sailors Snug Harbor, 91-92
St. Elizabeth's Church, 234, 249-251
St. George's Church, 231-233, 240
St. John the Divine, Cathedral of, 97

St. Mark's-in-the-Bouwerie, 311
St. Paul's Chapel, 311-312
Salary Stabilization Unit, 192-196, 199, 200-201
Sargent & Company, 294
Scopes, John Thomas, 231
Securities Act of 1933, 163, 164, 170
Securities and Exchange Commission, 166, 167, 169, 282, 287, 289
Securities Exchange Act of 1934, 163, 170
Shaplen, Robert, quoted, 160-162
Shaw, T. T., 192-194, 215
Shell Company of California, 76
Silverberg, Rhea, 321
Sinclair Oil Corporation, 53, 129
Smith, Father George L., 208
Smyth, Ralph, 6
Socony Mobil Oil Company, Inc., 131, 142, 193, 198-201, 246
Socony-Vacuum Oil Company, Incorporated, 131
Sousa, John Philip, 94
Standard Oil Company of New York, 130
Standard-Vacuum Oil Company, 200, 202, 246
Stans, Maurice H., 280
Staten Island, 46, 49-51, 90, 92-94, 111, 198, 202, 309
Steele, J. Gordon, 76
Stewart, J. Harold, 263-264, 267, 272
Stewart, Watts & Bollong, 263
Stokes, Archdeacon John Whitley, 9, 11-12
Stone, Amos, 201
Straton, John Roach, 231
Strong, Dr. Edward K., 186
Stuart, Charles Urquardt, 58-59, 61

Stuart & Young, 58, 61
Stuyvesant, Peter, 311
Sutherland, William, 63-64, 156, 157, 158, 172, 179-181, 300

Taylor, Andrew, 132-133
Taylor, Arthur, R., quoted, 148
Taylor, Winifred Corker, 105, 132-133, 312
Texas Company, 74
Tide Water Associated Oil Company, 130
Todd Shipyards Corporation, 185
Tourtellot, Arthur B., 268
Trinity Church, 200, 311
Trobridge, Charles, 101
Tyrone Constitution, The, 37, 321
Tyrrell, Charles, 173

Ulster Herald, The, 37
Ulster Plantation, 24
Union Oil Company, 75-77
United States Rubber Company, 116

Vacuum Oil Company, 130-131
Vega Aircraft Corporation, 188-190
Vultee Aircraft Company, 188

Waldschlagel, A. G., 53-55, 65
Wall Street Journal, The, 287
Ward, Herman E., 187-190, 216, 226, 251-252, 263, 267
Welldon, Sam, 208
Weston, Frank T., 199, 200, 261-262
White & Case, 201
Whitney, George, 142

Whitney, Richard, 141
Wideman, Cyril H., 218-221, 226
Wideman, Madden & Dolan, 216, 217-221
Wilkinson, Rev. William, 97-98
Williams, T. Dwight, 272
Winchester, James, 86-89
Wise, Rabbi Stephen S., 232
Wolfe, Thomas, quoted, 42
Wood, Dr. Ben D., 186, 210
World War II, 174-177, 179-203

Young, Arthur, 57-63, 155-157, 169, 172, 179, 183, 207
Young, Arthur, & Company, 55, 57-67, 69-89, 322
　Advisory Committee, 216, 222-223, 253, 267
　Annual meetings, 171, 174
　Auditors' certificate (1926), 115
　Boston office, 214, 262
　Caracas office, 214
　Chicago office, 57, 59, 63-65, 100, 115, 146-147, 157-159, 172, 174, 181, 187, 191-192, 212-213, 216, 225-226, 300
　communications, 262, 304
　Dallas office, 100, 146, 158, 174
　depression years, 146-147
　Detroit office, 146, 158, 216, 217-221
　Executive Committee, *see* Management Committee
　Handbooks, 217
　Home Office, 191, 198, 261, 304-306
　Houston office, 214
　international expansion, 262-264, 300

Kansas City office, 100, 129, 146, 174, 216, 217, 300
London office, 99-100, 173, 214
Long-Range Planning Committee, 263-267
Los Angeles office, 59, 100, 146, 158, 174, 187-189, 216, 300, 305, 313-314
Management Committee, 155, 157-159, 171-172, 174, 180-181, 187, 205-206, 213-214, 221-227, 253, 261, 263-267, 273-276, 278, 299, 305, 307
management services, 215, 261, 303
managers, 159, 195, 196
Milwaukee office, 59, 100, 129, 146, 174, 300
national partnership, first, 56, 333
New York office, 57, 59, 66-67, 69-89, 95, 100-101, 113-114, 125-126, 129, 146, 157-159, 169-171, 172, 174, 190-193, 202-203, 211, 212-213, 215-217, 223, 226, 275, 300, 305-306, 313
Operating Committee, 265-266, 275
Paris office, 173, 214

partners: administrative, 266; general, 159, 179; "local," 159; list of (1921-1965), 333; meetings, 169, 171, 174, 190; regional, 267
personnel recruitment and training, 171, 215, 261, 301-303
Philadelphia office, 214
Pittsburgh office, 59, 100, 146, 174, 216, 300
public relations, 262-263
regional plan of operation, 267
San Francisco office, 251-252
SEC and research activities, 261
seniors, 114, 195
Staff Manual, 113-114
staff school, first, 171
Standard Working Papers, 113-114
tax practice, 193, 215, 303
Toledo office, 129, 217-221
Tulsa office, 129, 146, 201
Wichita office, 216, 217
Young, Robert, 63
Young, Stanley, 58